D1334444

CAMILLA, DUCHESS OF CORNWALL

CAMILLA, DUCHESS OF CORNWALL

From Outcast to Future Queen Consort

ANGELA LEVIN

**SIMON &
SCHUSTER**

London · New York · Sydney · Toronto · New Delhi

First published in Great Britain by Simon & Schuster UK Ltd, 2022

Copyright © Angela Levin, 2022

The right of Angela Levin to be identified as the
author of this work has been asserted in accordance
with the Copyright, Designs and Patents Act, 1988.

1 3 5 7 9 10 8 6 4 2

Simon & Schuster UK Ltd
1st Floor
222 Gray's Inn Road
London WC1X 8HB

www.simonandschuster.co.uk
www.simonandschuster.com.au
www.simonandschuster.co.in

Simon & Schuster Australia, Sydney
Simon & Schuster India, New Delhi

The author and publishers have made all reasonable efforts to contact
copyright-holders for permission, and apologise for any omissions or errors in
the form of credits given. Corrections may be made to future printings.

A CIP catalogue record for this book is available from the British Library

Hardback ISBN: 978-1-3985-1306-8
eBook ISBN: 978-1-3985-1307-5

Typeset in Sabon MT Std by Palimpsest Book Production Ltd,
Falkirk, Stirlingshire

Printed in the UK by CPI Group (UK) Ltd, Croydon, CR0 4YY

MIX
Paper from
responsible sources
FSC® C171272
FSC
www.fsc.org

For Daren

Contents

Introduction

I have always been curious about people. As a journalist, I like to start without any preconceived opinions, dig deep, and then use whatever insight I have, together with what the person I'm writing about and the people around them say, to create a rounded portrait. I have written extensively about the Royal Family, and for some years have longed to write at length about Camilla, Duchess of Cornwall. I wanted to bridge the gulf between her public image and what she is really like. I was curious to know how she has dealt with the appalling abuse she received for decades because of her relationship with Prince Charles, and why some people still blame her for the death of Diana, Princess of Wales, when we know that Diana's marriage to Prince Charles was a disastrous misfit and her death the result of a drunken driver.

I was keen to understand her strengths and weaknesses: she has been strong and persevering in her love for Charles, but dislikes making public speeches, flying – especially by helicopter – using lifts, and can't bear needles. I also hoped to discover how she has survived the cold-heartedness within the royal ranks.

I spent a few months with her in 2015 to write a profile for *Newsweek* magazine and was surprised how good she was with people, how welcoming she seemed and how she dealt with unexpected nerves.

It wasn't enough in words or time for me to get a fully rounded picture of her, and I wanted to see and write more. My personal alarm was triggered while watching the third season of *The Crown* on Netflix and seeing how negative it was about Camilla. I was equally shocked by what Prince Harry, whose biography I wrote in 2018, said about his family when he and his wife Meghan were interviewed by Oprah Winfrey on American television in March 2021, and when he listened in silence to Meghan's grievances when he knew some were untrue. I was particularly surprised as he was seen as the most family-conscious royal and good at repairing feuds. Sadly, all that seems to have been washed away. I decided that the time was right to write Camilla's biography.

Camilla's life is comprised of two very different parts: before and after she and Prince Charles married in April 2005. For years I have been piecing together a wide variety of views from her friends and those who have worked with and for her. I have also spoken to key individuals who are connected to her in a variety of ways. Very few asked to be 'off the record'; they were only too pleased to present 'the real Camilla'.

What was unexpected was that most of them, who had no idea who else I would talk to, described her character and temperament in very similar ways. I couldn't keep repeating the same analysis in the biography, so halfway through my research I started telling my interviewees that I had heard their descriptions from other people. They weren't surprised. 'That's because she's authentic,' I was told, and 'she doesn't pretend to be what she's not.' Someone who has known her for a very long time said, 'She hasn't changed a bit.' To say such things about a woman who has been assailed by vile verbal attacks but has managed to retain her dignity, self-respect and mischievous sense of humour is extraordinary.

Camilla has got used to Charles being a workaholic and doing his best for Queen and country and his hundreds of charities, and she has developed her own strenuous work ethic. Her primary role is to be there for Charles, and she has made a huge positive difference. She is trustworthy and has good instincts, and he knows she is on his side. She has shown no sign of crossing any royal lines and attempting to job-share with her husband. Most of the time when they are on an official engagement together, she walks just behind him and sometimes hovers in the background. It is not because she feels inferior or diminished; she respects and loves Prince Charles and, on such occasions, defers to him.

When she undertakes solo engagements, she comes into her own and is daring and brave. She does a considerable amount of research beforehand, makes original suggestions that she will ensure come to fruition, and wants to help rather than be praised. In the same way, she encourages rather than lectures and usually tries to get ordinary people and children along to any suitable engagement. I was surprised to discover how much work she did for her various charities behind the scenes, quietly, effectively and without looking for applause.

Her inner strength has meant that she doesn't claim to be a victim and it has become very clear that the work she does is not chosen to boost her ego. She has used her experience of a positive childhood and a stable, loving family plus her own powerful instinct to find something positive in whatever she does or happens to her. She has taken on charities that other members of the Royal Family would prefer to sidestep, such as those dealing with rape and violence to women. It has made her a great asset to the Royal Family.

Nor does she seem to worry about her age. She accepts it,

wrinkles and all, and seems to have more energy the older she gets. She even jokes about it. She and Prince Charles returned from a four-day official visit to Jordan and Egypt in November 2021. On the flight back she stressed that their foreign tours were working trips and not holidays. 'I'm a lot older now,' she said, 'but to quote Richard Ingrams [former editor of *Private Eye* and the *Oldie*], I like to think we've still got a "snap in our celery". It's such a good expression!'

I think the Royal Family and the public are lucky to have her and hope that readers will put aside the weight of media bias over the past twenty-five to thirty years and take a fresh look at our future queen consort.

Chapter 1

A GLIMPSE AT CAMILLA

Even the most diehard royalist would have to concede that the British monarchy has begun to look a bit wobbly over the past few years. It is surviving largely thanks to the personal popularity of Queen Elizabeth II, who celebrated a record-breaking seventy years on the throne on 6 February 2022. Despite the harm done to the institution by the disgrace of Prince Andrew and the self-exile and departure from the Royal Family of Prince Harry, the Queen has laid out the road ahead by naming her heir Prince Charles's wife Camilla, Duchess of Cornwall, as the future queen consort, finally laying to rest the long debate as to whether she should receive that title or be merely known as princess consort.

Although Camilla's name and face are recognised around the world, what she is really like as a person has remained shrouded in mystery. Having immersed myself in Camilla's story, I see her as her own woman who is happy to learn from others but is comfortable in her own skin – a quietly determined female with a hint of vulnerability who enthusiastically supports women but not to the detriment of men.

The Queen is renowned for her belief in the stiff upper lip and has rarely revealed her feelings in public, with the exception maybe of when one of her horses wins a race. She has also encouraged senior members of the family not to show any emotion when they are on duty, even if it involves their children or something distressing. Camilla is not like that. Depending on what the distress is about, she can sometimes wait until she is home, where she will cry alone. Yet if what she sees or hears is extremely distressing, she doesn't feel self-conscious crying in public.

As a young adult Camilla didn't yearn to make an impact on the world. Her expectation of life was to marry, have children, ride, read and spend time in the countryside. An easy-going optimist, she saw the best in people, was fun to be with and had lots of friends. She wasn't insecure or envious of others. Many of Camilla's positive qualities have stayed with her during her mature years. At twenty-four she was the right woman for the then rather gauche 22-year-old Prince Charles, but the timing and mood of the country was wrong.

Their extraordinary love story began more than half a century ago when their mutual friend Lucia Santa Cruz acted as cupid as she was concerned about Camilla's relationship with Andrew Parker Bowles, and instinctively felt she and Charles would get on. They did, but their relationship was unable to be sanctioned due to the protocol of the times. Yet it has endured the kind of pressure in the public eye that few of us can imagine, during which time they have managed to overcome the many stumbling blocks that have affected their lives. Camilla has been relentlessly accused of destroying Prince Charles's first marriage to Lady Diana Spencer and she has had to cope with appalling verbal attacks. They have understandably left scars, but that in turn has helped her develop a protective skin. Camilla and Charles's relationship was eventually sealed by their marriage in 2005. Mark Bolland, Prince Charles's deputy private secretary in the 1990s, says of their closeness: 'There was never any sense that either of them had other people. It was just them.'

The moment they were married, Camilla moved from being an outcast to becoming the second highest-ranking woman in the British order of precedence next to the Queen and is now on the verge of being queen consort to Charles when he becomes king. What a journey it has been. How has she survived?

Her close friend Catherine Goodman, the Founding Artistic Director of the Royal Drawing School, an independent charitable art school in London's East End, is impressed with how she adapted to royal life in her mid-fifties. 'She is a countrywoman who was educated and cultured but nevertheless was an army wife and lived in Wiltshire. A lot goes with that. Her horses and dogs and a good walk can sort most things out for her. She wasn't somebody who was travelling the world or running to art fairs.'

Gyles Brandreth, broadcaster and former MP, who has known Camilla since her school days, has a slightly different take. 'She never complains in public and is very self-contained. Her family is key to her, especially her sister [Annabel], her former husband [Andrew Parker Bowles] and her children [Tom and Laura]. Andrew is now a friend and joined in celebrating her seventieth birthday party. She hasn't changed a lot over the decades, but she has adapted very skilfully to the situation she's in and blossomed into the role. She seems to be the same person, just doing different things and surprising herself by doing much more.'

He believes Prince Philip helped too. 'She has so much in common with the late Duke of Edinburgh and is never in competition with the Prince of Wales, just like the duke never was with the Queen. Instead, she is always Prince Charles's ally, being supportive and completely discreet. Prince Philip was also Camilla's role model, which is why she regards that it is her job to be one step behind Prince Charles when she is not on her own and be on show when she is on her own and not a support act. Nor does she stray into areas she knows nothing about. You don't find her talking about the environment or science. But she can talk endlessly about literacy.'

Other people I spoke to think Queen Elizabeth the Queen Mother had more effect on her. The historian Andrew Roberts comments: 'I think there is a very strong element in Prince Charles that sees his wife as giving him the same kind of good counsel as his grandmother gave him. If you have somebody who gives you good counsel and who you know is always on your side in your life, you don't want to let them go. He could have let Camilla Parker Bowles go several times in the last century and he was under the most enormous pressure to do that. He also wanted to stay as heir to the throne. How ridiculous it seems when one looks back . . . that the heir to the throne couldn't marry someone who was divorced, when today about forty per cent of marriages end in divorce.

'I think Camilla is much calmer and more contemplative and I wonder whether she holds him back sometimes. I wouldn't be surprised if she gives him the kind of counsel that the Queen Mother gave George VI, putting her hand on his sleeve occasionally and saying, "No, this is the right way to do it." I think he very much appreciates having that kind of wisdom by him because there are any number of advisers who are just yes men.'

Gavin Barker, who runs a talent agency and manages *Strictly Come Dancing* judge Craig Revel Horwood, is a great friend of Camilla and sees many similarities between the two women. 'Charles was so in awe of the Queen Mother and Camilla has the same lovely charm. Her great sense of humour is like his grandma's, and she puts people at ease like she did. I've come across the Royal Family a lot, and admire the Princess Royal, but find her terrifying, whereas Camilla is so warm, calm, natural and has a sort of naughtiness about her that makes you feel relaxed.'

Camilla's shyness can come to the surface when she goes to a crowded event. She likes someone to take her round, do the introductions and, after a few minutes, move her on. She doesn't enjoy being in the spotlight, which suits the sometimes sensitive Prince Charles very well. She is not in competition with him and her choice of charities, some of which deal with domestic violence, are not subjects he would get involved with. Above all, her number one priority is to back him. As the Clarence House website declares, 'The Duchess of Cornwall supports her husband, The Prince of Wales, in carrying out his work and duties as Heir to The Throne.'

She won't, however, be pushed where she doesn't want to go, especially when it comes to choosing her patronages. She chooses more artistic and humanitarian areas over science and technology and particularly enjoys meeting all sorts of people in person. Whatever she is involved in she wants to be useful, not just cut a ribbon, unveil a plaque or be merely a name on the charity's headed notepaper. She regularly asks the relevant person, 'What can I do to help?' Then she does it.

The charities she agrees to be patron of are not chosen for her own self-glorification. She is not a phoney and genuinely wants to help others. She has, for example, been determined to draw attention to SafeLives, a charity dedicated to ending domestic abuse, even though many of the stories she has been told have left her traumatised and given her nightmares. Chief Executive Suzanne Jacob finds Camilla 'phenomenally committed', adding: 'All the way through the pandemic she has been so proactive in asking "Tell me what I can be doing, I want to help." She has put our charity on the map, in a very big way. She is also really motivating, which makes a huge difference.'

She takes each patronage very seriously. Claire Horton, former

Chief Executive at the Battersea Dogs and Cats Home, says: 'The duchess always reads and understands the briefings she is given and has been very interested in the behind-the-scenes work, so she really understands what we are doing.'

Camilla's younger sister Annabel, who rarely talks openly about her, told the London *Evening Standard* in June 2015: 'Unless she's travelling or I'm travelling, we speak most days. She has stepped up to the mark wonderfully. I am so proud of her, my parents would have been so proud, Mark [their late brother] would have been so proud. We are a very close-knit family. We have families who have grown up together; our children are virtually brothers and sisters.' She also described Prince Charles as 'an extraordinary man'.

Camilla holds on to who she is through thick and thin, helped by her sense of humour and a mischievous glint in her eye. Broadcaster Clare Balding says: 'I am a big fan of hers. She and Sophie Wessex are my two top of the royal pops, as it were. They understand how they have to behave in certain situations but also maintain their real friendships and roots and have not lost track of the fact that you are a human being at the end of it all.'

As a journalist I have been to many of Camilla's engagements, and it has been clear that anyone who has spent time with her has usually become a fan. Journalists and photographers are used to being ignored by senior royals. Camilla understands that members of the press have a job to do, is co-operative and regularly stops for a brief chat when she is at an engagement. More surprisingly, she will remember and refer back to a previous conversation weeks or months later.

Ian Jones, a royal photographer since 1992, has regularly travelled with her and Prince Charles on overseas tours. 'She has always been a pleasure to work with,' he says. 'There is a genuine warmth about her, plus grace and elegance. She has never been a Diana, but she looks fabulous in everything she wears and has great style and poise.' He specifically remembers a tour to India in 2010. 'We visited a village where it was unbearably hot. I remember her remaining dignified and didn't once complain, which almost anyone else would have done. It was so hot at one point that she and Prince Charles sat down on a wooden plank, and he fanned her with an Indian fan.'

So why, after all this praise, hasn't she got the positive support she deserves from the public? There has been a slow but sure increase in the percentage of supporters since Diana's death in 1997, but she remains only the eighth most popular royal in the latest opinion polls. The support for her being queen consort has risen too, but despite the Queen's endorsement coming on the first day of her Platinum Jubilee year, it is still less than 50 per cent in a variety of polls. Hardline Diana fans, along with those who believe that Camilla should still be punished for adultery decades ago, both hold grievances without recognising that most people have baggage in their past.

Artist Catherine Goodman wonders whether Camilla doesn't always come across well in public because 'she herself is genuinely realistic and quite modest about the impact she can make. She also doesn't like wearing her heart on her sleeve and isn't someone who is going to stand up and say: "I am the Queen of Hearts." But she is really empathetic when someone talks to her about their own problem.'

Another explanation is her reluctance to be in the spotlight, which can make her come across as rather withdrawn, particularly when she walks behind Prince Charles. It is her way of being supportive and letting him take the limelight. Trying to avoid attention is one reason why for years she was too nervous to make a speech for the charities she supports. She eventually decided that her voice being heard on behalf of the charity was more important than her own feelings. She has now largely overcome her anxiety, although she keeps her speeches quite short. She is not, however, at all scared of the subject matter even when it's intimate. In October 2021 she shocked people by delivering a pointed and passionate speech for WOW Foundation's Shameless! Festival in London when she called on the world to come together to stop sexual violence against women. Few other royals would have done the same.

Camilla doesn't pretend to be someone she is not in the hope that people will like her. She prefers to meet them so they can make up their own mind about her. In a way this is what happened during the Covid pandemic. Until then, only a small number of people had seen her at royal engagements, and even fewer had heard her speak. Once the pandemic was under way, many people who were stuck at home watched more television and saw how genuinely sympathetic she was, how funny she could be when connecting to the old, young and vulnerable, and how caring and hard-working she is.

While being modest is partially responsible for holding her back from being a magnetic public figure, the same trait has been admired by others. One would have expected Camilla to have changed during her seventeen years as a senior royal, but time after time a wide cross section of people who had known her before she married Prince Charles all said that she hadn't changed at all, and it certainly hasn't gone to her head.

For example, Amanda MacManus, who was an aide to Camilla for over twenty years, says: 'I've watched how she has blossomed but believe that those who have known her for an even longer time think that although her work ethic may have changed, she hasn't at all as a person. Her character is just the same. She has adapted to her situation, which includes going to big dinners and traditional functions, and adjusted very well. One of the nice things is that her position hasn't gone to her head. There is a lack of vanity, and she doesn't look in mirrors all the time. Of course, she always likes to look as lovely as she can, but there is no real vanity there.'

Camilla's long-term friend Lucia Santa Cruz said, 'Camilla hasn't become at all imperious since her change of lifestyle. Sometimes when people have had a transformation into something grander and more important it goes to their head and they change, but Camilla hasn't, apart from having less time and dressing differently. Everything else is the same in our conversations. She is interested in my children; I am interested in hers. We talk about everything. There is nothing different and I think it is wonderful.'

In these days of cynicism, deceitfulness, disloyalty and hypocrisy, it is refreshing when money and titles haven't taken over from authenticity. It's hard to believe that any of the vicious online trolls, who have called her 'the most hated woman in Britain', 'ugly' and 'a wicked woman' have actually met her face to face or spoken to her. No one is perfect, but few individuals could have worked as hard as Camilla for citizens young and old, both in the UK and Commonwealth. It is certainly not up to the public to choose who anyone should marry or to refuse to accept that marriages can also go wrong.

Lord Carey of Clifton, the former Archbishop of Canterbury who knew Camilla, Charles and Princess Diana well in the mid-1990s, says he 'couldn't believe the press could say that she was a scarlet woman when she was so deeply loved by Charles. She just couldn't be like that because he is a very sensible man. At the time I thought I must give this some support.'

A couple of characteristics that she may not have needed very much when she was younger but have developed since she partnered Prince Charles are determination and resilience, which have proved to be vital to her survival. She had to wait decades for Charles to marry her and barely less time for her in-laws to soften a little and speak to her. There has also been the recent change in Prince Harry's attitude to his family, which must be a bit like waiting in a firing line and not being able, as a senior royal, to speak up for yourself. It is something that Harry's wife Meghan Markle found hurtful, and which contributed to her decision to step back from her royal status.

Camilla has shown what love and support can do. It's easy to see how at ease she and Charles are with each other. He is a transformed man who feels loved and accepted for himself, which will doubtless make him a better king.

Andrew Roberts points out: 'He fell in love with her when he was very young, and they've now been together for half a century. You can't be in love with somebody for that long without them having a huge effect on you, your personality and the way you look at the world and have the same sense of humour. You can't understand Prince Charles without appreciating the enormous influence for good that Camilla Parker Bowles has had on him.'

Chapter 2

WHAT'S IN A NAME?

The Queen, who had been totally against seeing or speaking to Camilla for decades, largely because she was extremely worried about the effect she could have on the monarchy, used her Platinum Jubilee written message to the nation to back the Duchess of Cornwall as queen consort and not princess consort. She said, 'I remain eternally grateful for, and humbled by, the loyalty and affection that you continue to give me. And when in the fullness of time my son Charles becomes king, I know you will give him and his wife Camilla the same support that you have given me; and it is my sincere wish that, when that time comes, Camilla will be known as queen consort as she continues her own loyal service.'

The personal endorsement followed a New Year's Eve announcement that the Queen was giving Camilla the highest honour possible by making her a Royal Lady of the Most Noble Order of the Garter. This royal seal of approval, that only the Queen can give, is recognition for the hard work, loyalty and tactfulness Camilla has shown since her marriage to Prince Charles in 2005 when she finally became a senior royal. It was an extraordinary change of heart.

The future queen consort expressed her gratitude to Her Majesty when she was out and about on royal duties. Her first visit, on 6 February 2022, was to Nourish Hub, a community kitchen in Notting Hill, west London, where she helped prepare a rice-based Iranian dish called *loobia polo*. From there she went to Paddington Haven, a sexual assault referral centre, and then on to the Thames Valley Partnership in Aylesbury, which is another charity helping survivors of abuse. It was typical Camilla to reply to the Queen's honour by being in an ordinary community kitchen in west London rather than through the normal official channels of Clarence House: 'I feel very honoured, very honoured and very touched,' she said.

It was the sort of comment expected, but her location gave the impression she had another point to make. This surely was that although she was 'honoured' and 'touched', the grandest of titles was not something she craved. She already had what she wanted – the opportunity to help a wide array of people who were suffering in one way or another; to be alongside Prince Charles, the man she loved so much, and to have the opportunity to do her absolute best for her immediate family.

Her title was sealed during the Garter Ceremony on 13 June 2022. This oldest honour in Britain was established nearly 700 years ago and has an estimated global audience of a billion watching the procession. Camilla wore a dress designed by Bruce Oldfield with a traditional floating blue velvet robe and black velvet hat with ostrich feather plumes. The Queen did not take part in the procession, due to her health, but did attend the lunch and the investiture ceremony. The question of whether Camilla should be called queen had hovered over the United Kingdom and the Commonwealth ever since she emerged as Prince Charles's partner after the death of Princess Diana. It hung on just one word: queen or princess, with princess being the lesser title.

The answer should have been easy. According to tradition, the title princess consort is given to the spouse of a sovereign prince, that is the prince who is closest to the throne, like Prince Charles, while the title queen consort is used for the wife of a reigning king. But the tradition was firmly disregarded by Clarence House, which announced at the time of the couple's wedding in 2005 that if and when Charles became monarch, Camilla would be princess consort rather than queen consort, largely because they were nervous about public reaction.

It was a curious backwards move for a monarchy that has wanted to embrace modernity. Prince Charles himself was not keen to talk about this break in tradition. In November 2010 he was interviewed by the American TV network NBC, ostensibly to mark the publication of his book *Harmony*, about sustainable living. All went well until the questioning became more personal and he was asked: 'Does the Duchess of Cornwall become Queen of England if and when you become the monarch?' He looked awkward, hesitated, and then mumbled: 'We'll see, and I don't know if I'll . . . if I'll still be alive, but that . . . that could be . . . it is better not to have to think too much about it, except, you know, obviously if it comes, then you have to deal with it.'

It's hard to believe that the long procrastination over something that seems so straightforward is, according to historians and constitutional experts, partly due to the fact that nearly thirty years ago the duchess divorced her first husband, Andrew Parker Bowles, a gregarious army officer, and that as a divorcee she remained unworthy of the proper royal title.

Yet the role of consort, whether male or female, has always been an important factor for the stability of the British monarchy. The consort is crucial for many reasons, not least the maintenance of the line of inheritance. The traditional role of the female consort is to provide 'an heir and a spare', which Queen Elizabeth the Queen Mother and Princess Diana, for instance, managed perfectly. The trouble caused when the queen consort could not provide an heir was exemplified by the reign of Henry VIII, who had his marriage to Catherine of Aragon annulled when she failed to supply a male heir, although their daughter eventually became Queen Mary I. We are still living with the historical fallout from the failure of Henry's first marriage. Indeed, he did not sire a legitimate male heir (the future Edward VI) until his fourth marriage, to Jane Seymour.

While there has been nothing to emulate the chaotic events of Henry's reign, the 'wrong kind' of consort, or would-be consort, as recently as the 1930s, still provided a potent threat to the very future existence of the monarchy. Mrs Wallis Simpson – already forty years old when she married Edward VIII and, in those days, unlikely to provide an heir – was also divorced. This proved unacceptable to the country, and that in turn proved unacceptable to King Edward VIII, who abdicated rather than give up the woman he loved. Many feared the monarchy would not survive the abdication crisis, but it did, thanks to King George VI's sensible handling of the succession and the support of his wife Queen Elizabeth (later the Queen Mother). This is the other vital role of the consort: to back the monarch while at the same time finding their own particular niche in the life of the country. Queen Elizabeth's place in the affection of the people was cemented by her conduct during the Second World War, when she and King George shared the dangers and deprivation that afflicted everyone.

It is never easy for the consort to find a role that combines staying in the background while finding something useful to do with their life. Prince Albert did his bit in the succession stakes by fathering nine children with Queen Victoria, and during his short life made an enormous contribution to the public life of his adopted country in the fields of the arts, sciences, technology and public welfare. Prince Philip found the role of consort at first constricting – he had to give up a highly promising career in the Royal Navy for an ill-defined role in the wings while the young Queen Elizabeth basked in the glow of public affection as Britain revived after the hardships of the war years. He eventually carved out a distinctive role for himself, founding the Duke of Edinburgh's Awards, which have transformed the lives of generations of British teenagers, helping to launch the World Wildlife Fund, which has done extraordinary work in animal and environmental protection, and involving himself in innumerable other good causes.

The historian Andrew Roberts, commenting before the Queen's granting of the title queen consort to Camilla, noted: 'Even considering that the Duchess of Cornwall should not be known as the Queen of England when that very sad day dawns, is wrong. It is axiomatic in British legal history that wives take the rank, title and status of their husband. The idea that over two millennia of the British monarchy would make an exception for the Duchess of Cornwall as if she was a uniquely evil and sinister figure would have been a disgrace. Also, if Her Majesty the Queen should die during the present premiership [that of Boris Johnson] it would have been extraordinary to have a situation whereby the prime minister could have any number of ex-lovers, wives and children but the new king could not have the one woman he's been in love with for half a century sit beside him on the throne of England in Westminster Abbey and be crowned queen. How could you have done that to someone?'

Others blamed the British Constitution, perhaps not realising that Britain, unlike nearly every other country in the world, does not have a proper written constitution, or even one legal document that sets out in one place the fundamental laws outlining how the state should work. Instead, there is an 'unwritten' constitution, which makes matters far more complicated.

Vernon Bogdanor, one of Britain's foremost constitutional experts, who has written extensively on political and constitutional issues, explains: 'Much of our constitution is based on common law and on convention not statute. By common law the wife of the king is queen, and she is normally crowned with the king in the coronation service, although she has no legal right to be crowned. But these rules do not apply to male consorts, which appears to modern eyes somewhat sexist. The Duke of Edinburgh was not crowned at the Coronation of Queen Elizabeth in June 1953 and was not known as king consort.

'The absence of a constitution provides a certain flexibility which, so it appears, the public like, and the various conventions depend in the last resort largely upon public feeling. Today of course, public feeling is very different from what it was in 1936 when Edward VIII abdicated the throne.'

At the time, the rules of the Church of England, of which the sovereign is the Supreme Governor, did not allow for marriage to a divorced person whose spouse was still living. Since then, the rules of the church have changed. So has public feeling. When Charles married the Duchess of Cornwall, his marriage was blessed by the Church afterwards, a sign of Church approval.

Bogdanor concludes: 'It is now clear that when the Prince of Wales becomes king, the Duchess of Cornwall will become queen consort and will be crowned alongside him. That seems very much in accord with public feeling.'

In a sign of how sensitive the issue was, in March 2018, a revamp of Prince Charles's Clarence House website removed anything to do with Camilla's future rank. Until then the title 'princess consort' had been included on the site's frequently asked questions section and in Camilla's biography. However, a rather jittery Clarence

House swiftly issued a clarification, saying: 'The intention is for the duchess to be known as princess consort when the prince accedes to the throne. This was announced at the time of the marriage and there has been absolutely no change at all.' It added that the changes were made to the website because the issue of Camilla being called Queen had not been raised 'recently'.

Camilla's friends say she is not too bothered about titles, despite Prince Charles longing to have her as his queen. She wouldn't have wanted any title she took to upset Prince Charles. It was more a sign that Clarence House didn't wish to tread on fragile ground, as public opinion was at the time paramount in the decision making, and it was felt it could go either way, particularly if a significant number of the public still nurtured the belief that she broke up the prince's marriage to Diana. In addition, it was taken for granted that the loss of Prince Philip and Queen Elizabeth would weaken the monarchy, and no one wanted the word 'queen' or 'princess' to tip the balance as to its survival. The Queen's firm statement in favour of Camilla has stopped a lot of future dithering.

However, an insider firmly believed that the prime minister should have been involved instead of just being 'informed'. 'I thought the best answer about the title was [to leave it] up to the prime minister, as ultimately, he is the most powerful person to make the decision. But he needs to be strong [with a balance of power], while letting the Palace have a say. They would also have needed to deal with the issue quickly and still might. If there was a massive debate and dither about the title, things could go wrong as people get nervous about change. Unfortunately, courtiers are not always the strongest of people, and triangulate to the lowest common denominator. Personally, I think it would have been awful if she was given the title of princess. The title has no constitutional powers, but it would be a very different situation if she is not crowned alongside of the Prince of Wales.'

Prince Philip was always aware of how the public mood and opinions about the monarchy ebbed and flowed and mentioned the subject in Canada in 1969. 'It is a complete misconception to imagine that the monarchy exists in the interests of the monarch,' he stated. 'It doesn't. It exists in the interests of the people. If at any time any nation decides that the system is unacceptable, then it is up to them to change it.'

He also understood that the Royal Family had to earn the public's respect and support. The Queen agreed and felt she and other working royals had to be seen by the public wherever and whenever they had royal engagements.

Opinion polls have shown that the popularity of the monarchy fluctuates considerably, and largely depends on the Royal Family's actions. They also show that an increasing number of 18–24-year-olds would prefer an elected head of state to the monarchy. So far, however, the older generations remain strongly supportive. One of the questions opinion polls also often ask is whether the public would prefer Prince Charles or Prince William to inherit the throne; William usually wins. Courtiers are particularly concerned about the monarchy in the gap between the death of the Queen and her son's coronation, fearing that republicans will try to take advantage and advance their cause.

Despite the Queen's clear wish for Camilla to be queen consort, which for many would appear to be the end of the matter, there are still some who question Camilla's right to take the title. There also remains a very small but hard core of persistent hostility from some older members of the Church of England towards Camilla and Charles because of their civil marriage, which they believe renders their wedding illegitimate. While younger people are not bothered about divorce, many have no interest in the monarchy either, in which case they couldn't care who is on the throne.

Andrew Roberts believes 'the institution works and keeps us

safe from dictatorship and over-mighty politicians and presidents. Camilla divorced nearly a quarter of a century ago, and the idea that, after all of the incredible work she has done, and all the water that has flowed under the bridge since then, that we are upset that two thousand years of constitutional and legal history could have prevented this very impressive and marvellous woman from becoming the Queen of England would have been a constitutional abomination.'

Lord Carey, former Archbishop of Canterbury, agrees. 'It is important to remember that sexual morality has changed and, as a society, we are much more open to how people live. I think people have accepted Camilla believing she will be a very good queen consort.' Camilla's supporters have argued that her growing importance within the family, particularly following the exit of the Duke and Duchess of Sussex, along with her increasing popularity means that the public would be happy for her to become queen consort.

Amanda MacManus, Camilla's recently retired aide, says: 'It will be a huge job to support Prince Charles when he is king and a lot more work. But she has the strength, and in the last year or two has been doing even more work and regularly acting on behalf of the Queen. She is in training and well prepared for it.'

Vernon Bogdanor agrees: 'The public work the duchess has done is very important to the monarchy and should be recognised. It is also hard rather than glamorous work. In addition, she has to remember not to express any political opinions, which isn't as easy as people think. Yet she hasn't put a foot wrong. She and Prince Charles make a very good team. When he gets tremendous responsibilities, it is important for him to have a supportive wife. It's very difficult to carry the heavy burdens of the monarchy without one.'

The author Dame Susan Hill thinks: 'Camilla should be whatever Prince Charles wants her to be and that is queen consort. Basically, it's down to whatever seems right. The one thing she should never be is Princess of Wales, which she hasn't taken up out of respect for Diana. There are still lots of diehard Diana fans out there who hate Camilla and would immediately kick off.'

By contrast, David Yelland, former editor of the *Sun*, who got to know Camilla very well when she and Prince Charles supported him during his late wife's cancer, says Camilla is 'a very nice person', but he believes 'she should have side-stepped being queen consort. Despite all the work that has been done, I think Queen Camilla will be quite a difficult concept for people to swallow, partly because we are way into the twenty-first century and the idea somebody should be called queen just because they are married to a king doesn't quite work anymore. I am also not sure that people will accept Kate [Middleton] being called queen when we get to that stage either. To have that particular title for their other halves is not quite in keeping with the times. Prince Philip wasn't king. People will accept she is effectively queen, but I don't think they [will] want to have to call her queen or [have] her appear on our stamps. Having a different title won't make any difference to anything, really.'

Gyles Brandreth, says: 'I don't think she wants to be queen, but she is ready to be queen and to serve in whatever way is appropriate at the time. We live in a world where there are many people who have second marriages, and people who have stepchildren.' Ben Elliot, Camilla's nephew, co-chairman of the Conservative Party and businessman, admires her hugely. He told me: 'She has no ambition to be queen. She just wants to support her husband. Camilla is a jolly good egg and a marvellous aunt, mother and grandmother. Her parents and grandparents were kind, welcoming, generous people and she has inherited these qualities. What you see is what you get.'

Mark Bolland, who helped change both Prince Charles's and Camilla's image before they married, said: 'When I was there, I never had any sense that she wanted to gain anything or do anything which would bring a cloud of controversy back into their lives and her life. Her sense of probity is immense.'

He knows he is not a constitutional expert but perhaps Craig Revel Horwood, best known as a judge on the popular BBC series *Strictly Come Dancing*, represents a widely held public view, and he is one hundred per cent for Camilla to be queen. 'I think Camilla should legally be queen consort and I think she would be wonderful and the most humane queen the world has ever seen. I think it's really important that whoever is king and queen understands life and understands people, and I'd rather have Camilla as the queen who has lived an ordinary life and is knowledgeable, and has been through despair and heartache – someone who has been loved and wants to be loved. People that have actually been through life like that learn from it. No one is perfect and I don't think she should be punished because she had an affair decades ago.'

Andrew Roberts concludes: 'The good thing about the monarchy is that it's made up of several chapters and you just turn over a page. The end of the Queen's reign will obviously be the end of a very long chapter. But the genius of the institution is that there is always another royal chapter waiting.'

Chapter 3

THE MAKING OF CAMILLA

When Camilla Shand was ten years old, she stated proudly in the classroom of Queen's Gate School, South Kensington, in London, 'My great-grandmother was the lover of the king. We're practically royalty.' She was not to know, of course, that she too would become the mistress of the Prince of Wales – although she went one better than her colourful ancestor by eventually marrying him.

Her great-grandmother Alice Keppel was born in 1868 in Duntreath Castle, Scotland, the youngest of nine children of Sir William Edmonstone, Bt, a retired admiral in the Royal Navy, and his wife Mary Elizabeth. Alice grew up to be beautiful – with blue eyes, chestnut hair and a large bust, highlighted by her slim waist. She had a kind nature, possessed unlimited energy and easily made people laugh. She turned down several proposals until June 1891 when she married the Hon. George Keppel, third son of the seventh Earl of Albermarle, who served in the Gordon Highlanders and rose to become a colonel. She was twenty-two, he was twenty-six. They moved to London and soon began mixing in high social circles. Within months of marrying, she is also said to have taken a wealthy lover. Her first daughter Violet (whose own love life as Violet Trefusis was to become as notorious as her mother's) was born in 1894, and the father was rumoured to be Ernest William Beckett, the future Lord Grimthorpe.

In 1898 she met Edward Albert, Prince of Wales, commonly known as Bertie, Queen Victoria's eldest son, who later became King Edward VII. She was by then twenty-nine with a reputation for having a voracious sexual appetite, and an even greater appetite for money. Bertie was fifty-six. Clearly smitten, he called her 'La Favorita', and within weeks she became the latest in his long line of mistresses. She was also the most public of all of them, and he regularly visited her at her home in Portman Square in London. She turned out to be the most highly regarded society hostess of the time, entertaining aristocrats and politicians from all around Europe.

In addition, she managed to juggle her husband and lover efficiently enough to have another daughter, Sonia Rosemary, in May 1900. Sonia was Camilla's grandmother. Although she was conceived while Alice was still Bertie's mistress, most people believe she was George's child. George was even tolerant when a grand duke is said to have insulted him by asking, 'Are you related to the king's mistress?' a question he is said to have ignored. If she had been an unacknowledged illegitimate child of Edward VII, then Prince Charles would be her half-second cousin once removed.

Alexandra of Denmark, whom Bertie married in 1863, is said to have preferred Alice to his previous mistress, Daisy, Countess of Warwick, because of her discretion. Queen Victoria died early in 1901 and Bertie ascended the throne as King Edward VII. Adept at keeping everyone happy, Alice partnered the king for yachting at Cowes and even helped him choose presents for his wife, while managing to preserve her own reputation and her marriage to acquiescent, tolerant George Keppel. George also had several affairs of his own and, when asked about his wife, reportedly said: 'I do not mind what she does as long as she comes back to me in the end.'

As well as becoming an important addition to the king's court, Alice was also his confidante and could be relied on to be very discreet (a quality inherited by Camilla), a combination that made her an ideal communicator between the king and his ministers. She knew how to present a topic to him so that he would listen, even if he occasionally disagreed. The only things she failed to change were his smoking and the vast amounts of food he ate.

Although Alice was the acceptable face of Edwardian adultery, she refused to tolerate her daughter Violet's passionate and rather tortuous love affair with the writer Vita Sackville-West, a relationship that was frowned upon at the time. To avoid inevitable scandal, Alice used all the force she could muster to suppress their affair. She insisted that Violet marry Denys Trefusis, which Violet initially refused to do but submitted in 1919 on the condition that she and Denys never had sex, to which he agreed. She continued to see Vita – who had married diplomat Harold Nicolson in 1913 – whenever possible and they ran away to France several times. Eventually Alice cut off her daughter's allowance, which brought an end to the affair.

In 1910, when Edward VII was on his deathbed, he asked for Alice to come to him. Queen Alexandra reluctantly agreed but only while he remained conscious. As soon as the king lost consciousness, she is believed to have murmured to the doctor, 'Get that woman away.' The new king and queen, George V and Queen Mary, were far more traditional, and Alice was not invited to be part of the court. Instead, in November 1910, she and her husband went travelling to the Far East, Ceylon (now Sri Lanka) and Italy, settling finally in Florence. They returned to the UK in

1940, due to the Second World War. Alice died aged seventy-eight of cirrhosis of the liver on 11 September 1947 – just two months after Camilla was born; she never saw her new great-granddaughter. Alice's marriage to George lasted fifty-six years and it was said that he couldn't live without her; he died only two and a half months later in his suite at the Ritz.

Alice eclipsed her daughters and Sonia, in particular, lived a quiet life. In November 1920, she married The Hon. Roland Calvert Cubitt, 3rd Baron Ashcombe at the Guards' Chapel at Wellington Barracks, London. They had three children of which Camilla's mother, Hon. Rosalind Maude Cubitt, was the eldest. There were two younger siblings – Henry, who succeeded his father as 4th Baron Ashcombe, and Jeremy, who died when he was thirty. The couple divorced in July 1947 and Roland married twice more. He was a hugely rich aristocrat and had developed large swathes of central London, including Belgravia and Pimlico.

On the other side of the family, Camilla's father, Major Bruce Middleton Hope Shand, had an unsettled and insecure childhood and was looked after in turns by his mother, stepfather and paternal grandparents. It gave him a template he was determined not to follow, and he instead grew up to be a devoted family man.

Camilla's paternal grandfather, Philip Morton Shand, was born in January 1888. He was educated at Eton and King's College, Cambridge, where he was renowned for wearing 'daring neckties'. He became a respected journalist and critic. Writing about architecture, he described London in the 1950s as 'a nightmare of hideous and shoddy Americanised buildings'. He also became an authority on food and wine and had a particular interest in writing about fruit.

In 1916 he married Edith Marguerite Harrington. It was an unhappy marriage. Philip was a serial womaniser, enjoyed his colourful life and had no interest in his only child, Bruce. He married three more times and had innumerable lovers, ranging from one-night stands to established mistresses. Edith detested his behaviour and divorced him four years after their marriage, when Bruce was only three. Divorce carried a huge stigma in the 1920s and Philip was so angry with Edith for divorcing him that he refused to have anything to do with his son, including providing for him. Bruce, an only child, did not see his father again until he was eighteen, when they both attended his grandmother's funeral. There was subsequently no further contact for twenty years, by which time Bruce was married and had fathered three children of his own.

Abandoned, Edith was desperate to remarry, not least to have someone to support her and provide for Bruce. At the time single men who were keen to marry were hard to find as so many young men had been killed in the First World War and many more had been crippled by their injuries. Edith was lucky enough to meet a survivor, Herbert Charles Coningsby Tippet, whom she married in 1921 in London. Tippet had been a brave officer: in November 1917, he was mentioned in dispatches for gallantry at the Battle of Passchendaele and he also took part in the first Battle of the Somme, during which he suffered a head wound from shrapnel. He was subsequently awarded the Military Cross for 'acts of exemplary gallantry during active operations against the enemy'.

Being a front-line infantry officer left him suffering from severe shell shock. He was invalided out of the army two years later but was unable to cope with sudden loud noises for the rest of his life. He had to find a new career and, being a keen golfer, decided to try his hand at golf course design and administration. His timing was just right as the sport had become extremely popular after the war, especially in America. He moved there with Edith and Bruce and successfully built several golf courses in Florida, but then work began to dry up and the family returned to the UK in

1927. They lived in London for ten years while Tippet found work at Royal Wimbledon Golf Club and designed a course in Ireland. He died aged fifty-six in 1947 without a will, leaving only £666 in cash for Edith. It left her in much reduced circumstances and she moved to a small cottage in Kent. She died in January 1981 aged ninety-two.

Bruce's wealthy Shand grandparents, Augusta and Alexander, took Bruce under their wing after Philip Shand and Edith divorced. His grandmother, whom he adored, sorted out his education while his grandfather paid for it. Neither of them bore a grudge against Edith for divorcing their son; their offer was purely for Bruce's benefit. His grandmother did however blame Eton, the school both her husband and son Philip went to, for Philip's womanising and multiple marriages. She refused to let Bruce go there and instead chose Rugby School in Warwickshire. Bruce's opinion was not asked for. He found the school oppressive, and he disliked being a boarder. Its saving grace was that he developed a huge enthusiasm for horses and riding. The Shands subsequently paid for him to go to the Royal Military Academy, Sandhurst, and in 1937 he was commissioned as a second lieutenant in the 12th Lancers.

Two years later war was declared, and Bruce was to distinguish himself. In 1939 he was sent to northern France and won his first Military Cross in 1940 in the retreat to Dunkirk before the fast-advancing Germans. The citation spoke of his 'skill and great daring' and how by 'the fearless manoeuvring of his troop, he covered the withdrawal of a column in the face of fire from four enemy tanks'. In 1941 Shand, promoted to the temporary rank of captain, was sent to North Africa. In January 1942, in a confrontation with the Afrika Corps, and under heavy fire, he managed to organise the evacuation of twenty armoured cars, which would otherwise have fallen into enemy hands. As a result, he was awarded a second Military Cross, a rare honour. This citation said he had constantly proved himself a cavalry leader of 'the first order'.

Soon afterwards his squadron was ambushed. A bullet went through his cheek, hitting and killing his radio operator. He managed to get out of the armoured car through the top of the vehicle before sinking into unconsciousness. The car then exploded in flames. His driver was killed and Shand was taken prisoner. He spent a month in hospital in Athens and was then moved to a prisoner-of-war camp near Kassel in northern Germany, where he was held for two years. He may have been physically unfit, but his courage never deserted him. He decoded messages in BBC broadcasts so that other prisoners could listen to them on a hidden radio receiver. He was liberated in 1945 and returned to England. The army had been his life, but his wounds had made him unfit for active service and he was retired two years later.

Like many military men of his generation who had experienced horrifying incidents at war, Shand was reluctant to speak about his experiences. His daughter, Camilla, has tried to keep the memory of his bravery alive, and confirmed his reticence in 2020 in a public telephone conversation during the coronavirus pandemic. She said: 'My father was a soldier in the war and we could never get him to talk about it. But when the grandchildren came along, he started talking about it and we got him to write a small book. I think it was a huge load off his mind to be able to tell people about it.' His self-deprecating memoir, *Previous Engagements*, which modestly doesn't mention that he won the MC twice, was published in 1990 and dedicated to his grandsons. Shand had also written letters, kept a diary, and written two accounts of his life while a prisoner-of-war, which were sent to England via the Red Cross, and were kept in the Historical Section of the War Office.

Bruce Shand's wounds were significant enough to impact on his post-war life. He was also handicapped by a lack of money and was almost penniless for a short while. Luckily, he was helped financially to get on his feet by his paternal grandfather and friends. Soon after the war he then met and fell in love with Rosalind.

In 1939, as was customary for a young woman who came from a wealthy and privileged background, Rosalind was a debutante and had the expected coming out party to mark her formal entrance into society. The debutantes' ball was also intended to let eligible bachelors and their families know a young lady was ready for marriage to someone within her 'suitable circle'. Her party in 1939 took place just before the start of the war and was attended by King George VI and his wife Queen Elizabeth. The press subsequently awarded her the much sought-after title of 'Deb of the Year'.

Rosalind was twenty-four and Bruce nearly twenty-nine when they had a quiet wedding ceremony on 2 January 1946 at St Paul's Church, Knightsbridge. Thanks to the generosity of the Cubitts, the newly-weds acquired a five-bedroom former rectory near Plumpton, East Sussex, conveniently just opposite Plumpton race-course. Their second home was a three-storey Victorian house in South Kensington, which Bruce would often use during the week when he was working in town. Having wealthy and generous in-laws meant that, compared to the standards of post-war austerity, they were comfortably off but not rich. Bruce didn't have to worry too much about money but, as a married man, he had to be financially responsible for the couple's rather grand lifestyle.

Early in the 1950s he became a partner in the Mayfair wine merchants Block, Grey and Block. He did well, turning into a traditional English country gentleman with time to fulfil the duties of a Vice Lord Lieutenant of East Sussex (1974–92), Deputy Lieutenant of the former county of Sussex, and Joint Master of the Southdown Foxhounds (1956–75). He also served the Queen as an officer of the Queen's Bodyguard of the Yeomen of the

Guard, a ceremonial role but one he was hugely proud of. He was equally proud that, unlike his wayward father, he had maintained a good marriage for forty-eight years until Rosalind's death in July 1994 from osteoporosis. Bruce Shand passed away from cancer in June 2006, aged eighty-nine, at home in Dorset. Thankfully, he lived long enough see his adored daughter marry the man she loved, the Prince of Wales.

Chapter 4

CHILDHOOD

Camilla Rosemary Shand was born on 17 July 1947, a week after Christian Dior launched his 'New Look' in London – a milestone in women's fashion that helped brighten what had been a pretty grim year. The winter of 1946–7 had been one of the coldest on record: in January the snow reached seven metres deep in some places and did not thaw until March. Rivers froze, power cuts came into effect and factories closed. Food supplies were already a problem because so many merchant ships had been sunk during the Second World War. Vegetables froze in the ground. Almost everything was still rationed. In fact, there was more rationing in the late 1940s than there had been during the war. This was the time of Austerity Britain. Despite all this hardship, live births in the United Kingdom were more than one million, a record surpassed neither before nor since. Camilla Shand was one of the famous post-war baby boom births. Just a week before her birth, the nation was absorbed by the news that Princess Elizabeth, the elder daughter of King George VI, who was to become Queen Elizabeth II, announced her engagement to Lieutenant Philip

Mountbatten, the future Duke of Edinburgh. They married that November.

Camilla, Bruce and Rosalind Shand's first child, was born safely at King's College Hospital in South London. The obstetrician was Sir William Gilliatt who, by extraordinary coincidence in light of later events, delivered Princess Elizabeth's first baby, Prince Charles, at Buckingham Palace sixteen months later. This fascinating fact was only revealed when Prince Charles and Camilla visited the hospital in January 2014 and Charles surprised the staff by telling them: 'My darling wife was born here, but amazingly we had the same gynaecologist and nurse.'

The Shands had two more children: Camilla's sister Annabel was born in February 1949 and her brother Mark in June 1951. He tragically died in April 2014 from a serious head injury caused by a fall. Camilla, who is said to have inherited many of her qualities from her father, has said her childhood was 'perfect in every way'. Unlike Prince Charles, who was a lonely, rather tense child and had only minimum contact with his parents, her family life was rich, happy and stable. She loved both her parents, but from early childhood her father was the favourite of the two. Bruce was a warm-hearted, upbeat father, the epitome of stability, and always there to encourage and protect Camilla. (He was to get angry with Prince Charles at one point in his relationship with Camilla as he felt the prince was taking advantage of her.)

The Shand home was usually full of people, flowers and books, and one of Bruce's priorities was to encourage his children to read. During the 2020 coronavirus pandemic, Camilla mentioned her gratitude in a video. She said: 'I think [my love of reading] certainly came from my father; he was probably the best-read man I've come across, anywhere. He devoured books. He read to us as children . . . the love of books was ingrained in us, because it was there from such an early age.' When times have been difficult, Camilla often takes a book to help her escape from reality.

Camilla benefited enormously from her parents' happy marriage and their easy-going ways. This included not minding in the least how untidy she left her bedroom. They also believed in encouraging their children rather than telling them off. Her mother liked to look smart and conventional. She wore suits or skirts, chose bright-red lipstick and regularly smoked small cigars. She did not mind if her children's friends called her by her first name, which was very unusual in high society in the 1950s. Rosalind loved giving dinner parties but didn't cook herself. Instead, she employed an Italian couple, where the woman would cook and the man serve the meal. Other staff were employed, but the Shands chose not to have a nanny as Rosalind wanted to be a full-on mother. Family and the three children's friends were always welcome, and whenever possible they swam in the garden pool. There were many regulars, not only because they enjoyed Camilla's company, but they also liked her parents. Pet dogs and cats abounded.

She was not, however, casual about mealtimes. Instead, they adhered to the gradually fading tradition that everyone had to dress smartly for dinner. Women would also leave the dining room after the meal so the men could smoke cigars, drink port and enjoy male-orientated discussions.

Rosalind was strict about manners and self-discipline, insisting that her children behaved well and were socially adept. Camilla was forced from a young age to join her parents for their dinner parties, despite telling her mother that she found them boring. Rosalind stood firm and insisted it was a good opportunity for her to practise making conversation. Camilla said her mother told her: 'The minute there is silence, talk! I don't care what you talk about, [whether it's] about your budgie or your pony but keep the conversation going.' Camilla has admitted that what she learnt from her mother has been a valuable asset as a royal: 'I've never been able not to talk. It's in the psyche not to leave a silence.' She was also brought up 'to believe you stuck at things and didn't give up'. Something she must have relied on during her long-term relationship with Prince Charles.

Author and historian Andrew Roberts adds: 'Half a century ago someone from the upper class had the capacity of talking with and to people and not down to people. Camilla is brilliant at that. She engages immediately and in a way that makes you forget she is a royal . . . it might sound like a snobbish thing now, but in those days the entire class were taught leadership. And part of leadership is to . . . engage in a meaningful way. That I think is why she has turned out to be such a good royal.'

Her sister Annabel said: 'We had an enchanted childhood. Unlike a lot of our generation, we had this incredibly warm, easy relationship with our parents . . . All our friends growing up would immediately be drawn to my mother. She was completely straightforward and one of the warmest, kindest people.'

Both Bruce and Rosalind were humanitarians. Rosalind regularly went to Chailey Heritage, a school for disabled children outside Lewes, to help thalidomide children. The couple also held fundraising events, including letting the public visit their lush garden with its more than five acres of land, meticulously kept wide lawns, a secret garden, an orangery, vegetables, fruit trees and archways full of roses and paddocks. One distinctive highlight was a fig tree grown from fruit that the Shands had brought back from the Garden of Gethsemane in Jerusalem. Another was an oak sapling bought on the 900th anniversary of the Battle of Hastings.

One of the joys of young Camilla's childhood was learning how to ride. She has described herself as being 'pony mad' and joined Pony Club camps and won lots of rosettes at various gymkhanas. She fastidiously looked after her favourite pony, Bambina, who was kept in a field at the bottom of the garden that had been rented from the next-door farm. Her parents encouraged her to be adventurous and she was allowed to ride on the local Downs with friends or even by herself, which meant she had more than two thousand miles of tracks to choose from. Neither parent minded if she was away all day, and she even slept out in the open with her friends. Mobile telephones had not been invented, nor was she expected to search for a phone box to call home and tell her parents all was well.

When Camilla was nine, Bruce introduced her to fox hunting. It became another activity they enjoyed sharing. Like him, Camilla loved the thrill of the chase and was a capable and courageous rider. As Joint Master of Southdown Foxhounds from 1956 to 1975, her father had to be impeccably dressed in the correct hunting clothing and insisted Camilla was too. Although she has always felt most comfortable in casual clothes, she looked immaculate when hunting.

Camilla was an extroverted child, and at the age of five was sent to Dumbrells, a co-educational school in nearby Ditchling village. It believed in discipline and that a tidy girl had a tidy mind. Camilla remained an exception. Morning prayers were held every day before lessons started and learning French was an important part of the curriculum. Pupils could not start their lunch until all the children had been given their meal. Knives and forks had to be used correctly and everything on the plate had to be eaten, if not at mealtime, then later in the day, ignominiously in front of other pupils and a teacher. Teachers were strict, and if a child misbehaved during a lesson, they risked having a pencil or book thrown at them. Alternatively, they had to sit still and quietly under the headmistress's chair.

Afternoons were slightly more relaxed, and a teacher would often read the pupils one of the classics by Charles Dickens or

Robert Louis Stevenson. There would also be nature walks. Pupils would set off holding hands in a two-by-two crocodile. They were encouraged to pick wildflowers and then paste them into a book. Camilla had a happy time at the school, and during her first marriage to Andrew Parker Bowles regularly went back to visit her teacher when she visited her parents.

In 1958, when Camilla was ten, she changed schools and became a weekly boarder in London at Queen's Gate School, where she was known by the nickname 'Milla'. Here she developed what her classmates called her 'inner strength, magnetism and confidence'. She was very popular because she had 'bright and lively' qualities that would in future help her cope during difficult times with her first husband Andrew Parker Bowles, her relationship with Prince Charles and her troubles with the Royal Family.

Camilla likes to stay in touch with Queen's Gate as well as her primary school. She visited the school in 2016 when she officially opened a new science laboratory. She said, 'I wish I could say I was a head girl, or even a prefect or captain of games – I was none of those, but I might have been in the swimming team.' She was, however, admired for being able to 'talk to boys about things that interested them', and although she wasn't a rebel, she enjoyed taking risks. It's alleged she once climbed onto the school roof to have a sneaky cigarette.

Camilla only boarded for the first two years. Her mother then bought a nearby apartment for her and her sister Annabel, who also went to Queen's Gate, so that they could become day pupils. Wisely, she asked one of her friends to be a chaperone and keep an eye on both girls.

Queen's Gate wasn't a school that expected or pushed its students to get places at university. Higher education, particularly for girls, was still unusual. Instead, they were imbued with the idea that being good at sewing and cooking would please a future husband. It's perhaps one reason why Camilla, who had been left a £500,000 inheritance from the Cubitt family, quit school in 1964 with just one O-level. She commented on the school's aims when she unveiled a plaque to mark her 2016 visit. 'I did leave when I was sixteen. I didn't go on to the sixth form. I think in those days we weren't encouraged to go to university. I think the very, very clever girls went on, but nobody seemed to give us much inspiration to go on. So we went off and explored the university of life, and Paris and Florence and London.' Not that her parents were in the least disappointed. A good marriage with children, dogs and horses was their dream for their daughters, and originally Camilla's dream too.

Camilla spent the summer after she left school learning to drive, riding her horses and lazing around the swimming pool – usually with girls and a selection of boyfriends to keep her company. She and her friends also enjoyed going to nearby Brighton, hanging out in coffee bars or pubs or going to the cinema and the theatre.

At the end of the summer, her parents sent her to the Mon Fertile finishing school near Geneva for an eight-month course to give her the skills that would help her best present herself to the outside world. In the 1950s and early 1960s the world's wealthy thought it vital to send their daughters to Switzerland to be 'finished' after the rough and tumble of ordinary school. It was believed to be a crucial step in completing a girl's social education in the hope she would come home 'a lady' and net the 'right type' of husband. Camilla was taught the finer points of etiquette – how to improve her deportment, how to cook and choose wine, how to dress a table for a formal dinner party and how to arrange flowers, sew and type, plus a sprinkling more of French. The girls were also watched carefully so they didn't get into trouble.

A few years after Camilla left, finishing schools began to be seen as out of date due to the rise of gender equality, women's liberation and higher education for females. Changes were made to appeal to young women of all ages, rather than those who had just left school. This included professional women. The schools changed to focus on international etiquette, protocol and diplomacy.

Forty-five years after Camilla left her finishing school, she met up with one of her friends, Charlotte Ericson. It was 2009 and Camilla, by now HRH The Duchess of Cornwall, was on a royal tour of Canada with the Prince of Wales. Charlotte was waiting in the crowds outside the Parliament building in Victoria, British Columbia. She held up a bright yellow placard with basic details of their friendship, which to her delight caught Camilla's eye.

Camilla was very pleased to see her friend after such a long time and they had a chat. Mrs Ericson said afterwards, 'We were just typical crazy teenage girls, into the Beatles, hair, make-up and clothes. We would stay up late talking about the boys we fancied and eating Swiss chocolate and giggling.' She added, 'I'm sure her time at the school helped her deal with being the Duchess of Cornwall.'

After Camilla's eight months in Switzerland, she chose to go to the Institut Britannique in Paris for six months to improve her spoken French and knowledge of French literature. She had a great time socially, apart from getting stuck in a lift for seven hours, which has left her with a lifelong fear of lifts.

A glamorous and sexy Camilla, who had strong views that she rarely let herself be persuaded to change, returned to London in 1965 – right in the middle of the Swinging Sixties. Not that it influenced her. She was more likely to be seen dressed in knee-length skirts, twin-sets and pearls than Mary Quant's mod look or a mini skirt. Although she smoked almost non-stop, drank copiously and loved going to parties, she wasn't a rebel. Nor did she have any interest in taking drugs, joining demonstrations to ban the bomb or constantly challenging her parents. She was grateful for her upbringing and felt she had nothing to rebel against.

Although Camilla's untidiness didn't bother her parents, it left a mark on her friend Virginia Carrington, daughter of Lord Carrington, a senior figure in the Conservative Party during the 1970s and '80s, who became Foreign Secretary under Mrs Thatcher. The pair rented a large apartment in Belgravia, one of London's smartest areas, when Camilla was seventeen. In her book, *The Duchess of Cornwall: Camilla's Story and Secrets*, Jessica Jayne quotes Virginia describing Camilla as a 'total slob' who left her clothes everywhere. She said: 'Upon coming home, she would just drop her clothes on the floor on her way to her bedroom.' Another friend is quoted as saying, 'Camilla's bedroom always looked like a bomb had hit it . . . You should have seen the state of the bathroom after she'd been in it.' Nonetheless, Virginia admitted she wasn't cross as she found Camilla such fun to share a flat with.

All in all, Camilla's upbringing – a combination of structured freedom plus lots of love – had given her confidence and charm, a sense of loyalty and independence. With no money worries, she was free to enjoy herself and under no pressure to earn a living, choose a career or make a mark in her life. Fate would decide otherwise.

Chapter 5

MEETING CHARLES

Like many women of her class and generation, Camilla originally had no interest in pursuing a career. She just wanted to be kept occupied, so, after she got back from France, she got a job as a receptionist at the design and decorating company Colefax and Fowler. She lasted only a week as she arrived late one morning after a party the previous night and her boss sacked her on the spot despite her apologies. Camilla was not particularly perturbed by this unfortunate start to her working life. There were more exciting options around, one of which was to be a debutante and officially come out into society. In March 1965, Camilla joined 310 other young women between seventeen and eighteen years old for a year of balls and parties. Its aims had not changed since her mother's time and stayed restricted to those who had aristocratic or upper-class family backgrounds. It was also still seen as an ideal opportunity to be shown off in the hope that an eligible bachelor from a similarly select circle would want to marry her.

It was traditional for debutantes to wear white, but Camilla chose a black silk and chiffon dress for the cocktail party for 150 guests that her parents hosted in Knightsbridge. During her year of parties, she met Andrew Parker Bowles, a highly regarded officer in the Royal Horse Guards who played polo with Prince Charles. His younger brother, Simon, who worked in the same wine business as Camilla's father, made the introduction. Camilla and Andrew were an on-and-off item for the next six years. Andrew was not faithful and had a succession of relationships with other women, some of whom were Camilla's friends.

The arrival of Lucia Santa Cruz in Camilla's life helped to save her from a broken heart and put her on an unexpected path that enabled the real love story of her life to emerge. One that has gone down in history.

The two young women had met at various dinner parties and began a genuine friendship in 1970. Lucia had already made friends with Prince Charles soon after he became an undergraduate at Trinity College, Cambridge. She was the daughter of the long-time Chilean ambassador to the UK, Victor Santa Cruz Serrano, and five years older than Charles. She was also glamorous, spoke four languages, had degrees from King's College, London, and St Antony's College, Oxford, and was working as a research assistant to Lord (Rab) Butler, the distinguished former Tory politician who was then Master of Trinity and writing his memoirs.

In the spring of 1969, Butler invited Lucia along with her parents to a dinner party at the Master's Lodge. He also invited Prince Charles so there would be someone else around Lucia's age. She and the prince got on so well they became lifelong friends. It was said at the time, and for a long period afterwards, that she was his first proper girlfriend, but it wasn't the case. She told me she already had a steady boyfriend, Juan Luis Ossa Bulnes, whom she later married.

Lucia's father was replaced as ambassador in 1970, when Salvador Allende became president, and he and his wife returned to Chile. Lucia decided to stay in London and took a first-floor flat in Stack House, an apartment building in Westminster. Camilla was living in the flat below. Lucia explains: 'I was travelling a bit at the time and, whenever I arrived back, I'd go and see Camilla. We would have a glass of wine together, talk and then go our separate ways. I got to really like her. She made any story terribly entertaining and was incredibly kind and generous to me when I went through a very difficult time. Chile by then had a Marxist government and, once my father went back, I was on my own and it wasn't easy.

'Camilla was so incredibly generous. She not only let me borrow her clothes, she provided a sort of home for me. When I was going to be on my own for Christmas for the first time, she invited me to her join her family in the country. It was the best Christmas I ever had when it could have been the saddest. I'd never had a Christmas stocking before, and I also had a pillowcase full of wonderful presents. Our friendship has lasted ever since. She wasn't a hard-working person by any means. She just read all the time, and, if not, she was usually at a party. It makes it the more amazing the amount of work she now does.' Lucia, who now lives in Chile, is a director of Santander bank and has children and grandchildren. Whenever she and the duchess meet, she says, 'It feels like yesterday.'

Lucia introduced Camilla to Prince Charles after she had got to know him quite well. She is hazy about the actual date but thinks it was some time in 1970. Andrew had paused his relationship with Camilla that year and began dating Prince Charles's sister, Princess Anne, with whom he shared a love of equestrian sport. Their relationship was believed to have been intense but couldn't go anywhere. Andrew was a Catholic, so a long-term commitment or marriage was out of the question as, at the time, as it was unacceptable for a royal to marry a Catholic.

'The prince was coming for a drink before we went out and I

asked Camilla to come upstairs and meet him. I don't know why I put Charles and Camilla together,' she says with a smile. 'It wasn't rational, but it is a marvellous thing to do if it works and it really has done. At the same time, I said: "You two be very careful, you've got genetic antecedents."

'It was just a little joke and they both laughed. I'm very proud if I have done anything to make them happy.' Charles was twenty-two and Camilla twenty-four. They hit it off immediately and Camilla was temporarily diverted away from Andrew.

'I was also very close to Andrew,' says Lucia. 'He was charming but he had an infidelity syndrome. I knew Camilla had a difficult time before she married him because he was a tremendous flirt, so she was always sort of insecure. I think [the wedding] just happened because Andrew became a challenge because he was so naughty. I hoped when he married it would get better, but it didn't.'

Prince Charles meanwhile liked Camilla's naturalness and sense of humour and that she wasn't at all obsequious. They also shared very similar interests including a love of horses, the countryside, polo matches, long walks, horticulture, ballet and roaring with laughter at the classic radio comedy series *The Goon Show*. Their friendship blossomed into a love affair, and they spent eighteen happy months together. Being with her was comfortable and easy. She listened to what he had to say, something his parents were not the best at doing.

His great uncle 'Dickie' Mountbatten was the only royal Charles confided in, and Mountbatten had no compunction about offering Charles Broadlands, the Mountbatten family home in Hampshire, so that he and Camilla could be alone together. He didn't for a second think she would make a suitable wife because she had 'history', but he felt she could be a useful experience along the way. He made this point by writing to Prince Charles about the kind of woman he should marry. 'In a case like yours, the man should sow his wild oats and have as many affairs as he can before settling down. But I think for a wife he should choose a suitable, attractive and sweet-character girl before she has met anyone else [that] she might fall for.'

There are several different opinions on why the couple split after their close eighteen months. Charles felt unsure about marrying so young. He didn't want to go against the advice of his much-respected great-uncle or face his parents knowing full well that a female who married the heir to the throne was expected to be a virgin, and they were bound to find Camilla unsuitable. Another rumour was that Lord Mountbatten, Admiral of the Fleet and former First Sea Lord and Chief of the Defence Staff, deliberately set up a Royal Navy mission that would take Charles far away and make it nearly impossible for the couple to meet, hoping the relationship would doubtless fall apart. Queen Elizabeth the Queen Mother also disapproved of the possible match as she wanted Charles to marry one of the Spencer family granddaughters of her close friend Lady Fermoy. They were in cahoots to make it happen, despite Lady Fermoy's awareness of Diana's emotional instability.

Charles was set to sail on the HMS *Minerva* in mid-January 1973 for a seven-month voyage in the Caribbean. A month earlier, he took Camilla to Portsmouth to see the ship he would be sailing on. The couple spent the next weekend at Broadlands. Charles wrote in a sad note to Lord Mountbatten that it was 'the last time I shall see her for eight months'. Years later Charles admitted he knew that last weekend as 'the moment when he first realised for sure' that he wanted to marry Camilla – that she was his life's 'soulmate'. He just didn't have the courage to tell her.

Camilla was not the sort to hang around. After all, her younger sister, Annabel, an interior designer, had already got married in 1972. Annabel's husband Simon Elliot, a Dorset landowner, was the son of Air Chief Marshal Sir William Elliot and Rosemary Chancellor.

She and Andrew Parker Bowles were soon back together, and just a couple of months after Charles sailed away their engagement was announced in *The Times* on 15 March 1973. Charles was in the West Indies when he received the news and wrote again to his great-uncle how disappointed he was that 'such a blissful, peaceful and mutually happy relationship' had come to an end.

Camilla and Andrew married four months later at the Guards' Chapel in London, and it was one of the society weddings of the year, eclipsed only by that of Princess Anne and Captain Mark Phillips. Queen Elizabeth, Queen Elizabeth the Queen Mother, Princess Margaret and Princess Anne were among the eight hundred guests. Charles sent his regrets from the *Minerva*. If he had wanted to go, he could have been flown back to London, but it might have been too painful for him. Lucia, however, went to the wedding, as she did to Charles and Diana's wedding, and finally the marriage of Charles and Camilla when fate at last got it right.

Prince Charles was devastated when, in August 1979, Lord Mountbatten was assassinated in Ireland by the IRA. He turned immediately to Camilla Parker Bowles, who was still his soulmate and the only person he felt he could really talk to about his grief and anything else he felt was important.

Years passed, girlfriends came and went, and by the time Charles was twenty-nine, he felt tired of being browbeaten to get married and produce an heir as well as being anxious that none of his relationships had worked out. He had known Lady Diana Spencer since she was a small child. Her family lived in Park House, almost on the edge of the Sandringham estate, and when the Queen and family were resident over Christmas and the New Year, Diana and her two sisters Sarah and Jane, and later, younger Charles, were invited to tea parties. Prince

Charles didn't take much notice of her as he was twelve years older, an age gap that was to shape their future. Yet he found her 'very jolly and amusing' when he saw her at Althorp House, close to Northampton, where the family had moved when Diana was sixteen.

In theory she had all that was required: she was the daughter of an earl, had royal connections and did not have 'a past'. They started dating when she was eighteen despite his early doubts for the future. Diana and Charles visited Camilla and Andrew socially. Charles asked Camilla to be an older companion to Diana, as she seemed so shy, but didn't tell Diana that she had been much more than just a friend.

After six months, he misread a letter his father sent him advising him it was time to propose to Diana or let her go. Charles assumed he was being told to marry her, and in his eagerness to do the right thing for 'country and for my family', proposed to Diana at Windsor Castle on 6 February 1981. She accepted without hesitation, even though she had begun to suspect that Camilla Parker Bowles was more than Charles's best friend. They married in St Paul's Cathedral on 29 July 1981. Camilla came to the wedding, which didn't please Diana.

American royal biographer Sally Bedell Smith felt it was widely believed Charles and Camilla stopped being lovers between 1981 and 1986. Years later, Charles confirmed that Mrs Parker Bowles was a good friend but insisted he had been faithful to Diana until their marriage had 'irretrievably broken down'.

Diana was an aristocrat and at heart enjoyed tradition. She loved the monarchy and the fact that her own husband was going to be the future king. She made errors sometimes, for example, she refused security protection after her divorce though not because the royal family didn't offer her some, but was never systemically hostile to the institution or the people. She was also naive, instinctive, spontaneous, insecure, needy and suffered from eating disorders.

By comparison Charles seemed middle-aged. He had an established routine and, like his mother, put duty before family. He read non-fiction books and liked classical music and gardening, none of which interested Diana. She was bitterly disappointed and wanted her prince to be like one of the literary heroes she read about in romantic novels by Barbara Cartland, mother of Raine McCorquodale, who became her stepmother. Unsurprisingly their friends were incompatible, and the existence of Camilla Parker Bowles hovered over her like a ghostly shadow, even though Camilla and Charles were not yet seeing each other secretly.

By 1986, as is widely known, the marriage was in tatters. Charles lived mainly at Highgrove, his country house in Gloucestershire, tormented that he couldn't connect with his wife and had let her down. Diana stayed in Kensington Palace. Whatever the rights and wrongs, the background and upbringing of both of them had significantly reduced the chance that they would have a positive relationship together.

A despairing Charles wrote to a friend: 'How awful incompatibility is. How dreadfully destructive it can be for the players in this extraordinary drama.' Some friends believed he was on the verge of a nervous breakdown, and two of them so were so worried about him that they independently got in touch with Camilla and urged her to contact him. She picked up the phone to Charles and their friendship restarted from there. Charles felt she was the only one able to comfort him and share his woes.

Nobody knew much about Camilla until Andrew Morton's book, *Diana: Her True Story*, was published on 7 June 1992, when she talked about her unhappy marriage. The public heard that Diana had called her 'the Rottweiler'. Two subsequent intimate royal conversations became public sensations. The first was Diana talking to James Gilbey (heir to Gilbey's Gin) on New Year's Eve

1989. During their conversation, Gilbey called Diana 'darling' fifty-three times and 'Squidgy' thirteen times. Diana gave the impression she longed for every compliment she could get. Their conversation was illegally taped, labelled 'Squidgygate' and published by the *Sun* early in the new year.

The second was a very intimate bedtime telephone conversation between Camilla and Charles in 1989, when they were both still married. It was secretly recorded from several phone calls and no one has yet worked out how. Labelled 'the Camillagate tapes', the recordings were leaked to the press and published in 1993, a year after Charles and Diana's official separation. The conversation showed that the couple were obviously in love, longed to be together and found it hard to say 'goodnight'. Something neither of them felt was in their respective marriages. The transcript was reprinted in newspapers all over the world and left no doubt that Camilla was sleeping with the Prince of Wales. It was at the time one of the most embarrassing scandals the British Royal Family has ever had to cope with.

Meanwhile, the serially unfaithful Andrew Parker Bowles found himself in the bizarre position of being the maltreated husband. Morton's book and the conversations badly damaged Charles's public image and the media pilloried Camilla as if she were the wicked witch out to destroy Charles and Diana's fairy-tale marriage. She was branded a whore, a marriage wrecker and adulterer.

In 1994, Charles agreed to be interviewed on television by Jonathan Dimbleby. He admitted he had been unfaithful and spoke about his relationship with Camilla. He said: 'Mrs Parker Bowles is a great friend of mine . . . a friend for a very long time. She will continue to be a friend for a very long time.' Camilla hadn't wanted Charles to talk about their affair, but he wanted to correct the misunderstanding that he was unfaithful as soon as he and

Diana married. His personal confession was watched by fourteen million people

More was to follow and, on 20 November 1995, three years after the couple separated, BBC *Panorama* journalist Martin Bashir spoke to Diana in her first solo tell-all interview since her marriage to Prince Charles. Describing her marriage to Charles, she said: 'There were three of us in this marriage, so it was a bit crowded.'

The insinuation that Camilla was the third person involved has been a sentence that Camilla has had to live with ever since. (Bashir and his global scoop have since been discredited following an accusation that he used deceitful methods to gain Diana's trust.) Afterwards, Prince Charles's popularity rating plummeted to 20 per cent and many people felt he didn't deserve to be king.

There was no doubt that Diana won the popularity battle. She was a beautiful young princess who had been stifled by a stuffy royal family and felt she was up against an older woman with more experience of life. Little was known about Camilla until then when she became a household name. The public turned against her, but this only served to bring Charles and Camilla closer together.

Chapter 6

ANTI-CAMILLA

Andrew Morton's book on Diana's 'true story' exposed in breathtaking detail how her marriage had made her extremely unhappy. It contained such personal detail that a member of the Queen's staff asked Diana if she was involved with helping the author in any way. She said she wasn't and was believed until the truth was revealed years later. It showed that it was quite the opposite and she had in fact made audio tapes for Morton. After eleven unhappy years of marriage, in 1992 she went to the Queen and Prince Philip to ask for a separation. They granted her request; meanwhile, the couple continued with their royal duties.

It was a painful decision for the Queen, who is a deeply religious woman and believes that marriage is for life. But in one way it was also a relief as she was concerned that Charles and Diana's behaviour was damaging the monarchy. Serious discussions took place behind closed doors, some involving Dr George (now Lord) Carey, the Archbishop of Canterbury from 1991 to 2002.

'What I could do was very limited,' he told me. 'I didn't have any power. I was just a friendly outsider. I spoke to the Queen, whom I love, but she was always on her guard so I could only talk in general terms about Charles and Camilla. I was in a difficult situation because as archbishop I couldn't and wouldn't condone adultery, neither could I tolerate any relationship that did not have marriage as a goal.'

The Queen feared that Charles would reject Diana and strengthen his relationship with Camilla, which would be history repeating itself, and risked following in the footsteps of the Duke and Duchess of Windsor.

A major preoccupation during the Queen's long reign has always been to ensure that the monarchy survives and thrives. Anything that threatened to break the smooth succession of monarchy was bound to be a threat to the Queen, who had worked tirelessly for decades to maintain a successful reign and marriage. She felt relief and delight when Charles fathered not just one son, Prince William, born in 1982, but then a second, with the birth of Prince Harry in 1984. It gave her own son an 'heir and a spare'. Charles's rekindled relationship with Camilla wouldn't make any difference to the succession, but the Queen naturally disapproved, as Camilla was at this time married to someone else and would, in 1995, be divorced. She felt it made her unsuitable to be Charles's second wife and that it would damage his image as a future king. She blamed Camilla entirely for the marital infidelity and chose to have nothing to do with her, despite the fact that she had happily socialised with her early in her marriage to Andrew Parker Bowles.

As well as talking to the Queen, Archbishop Carey also reached out to Charles, 'who was pleased I was very positive about Camilla'. He also contacted Diana and Camilla to see if he could help. He had been made Bishop of Bath and Wells in 1987, so knew and liked the Shand family, who lived close to Bath. 'I contacted Camilla via Charles's office,' he continued. 'I hadn't seen her for a while and was so impressed when we met. Here was a very sensible, nice-looking woman, well presented, charming and highly intelligent. We had a good hour of chatting about her and Prince Charles and she traced the history of their relationship, which began when he was a young man. They had met quite often over the years, liked one another, developed a very strong relationship, and were totally committed to each other. But their relationship was not going anywhere and a deep relationship like that can only be fulfilled by marriage.'

Archbishop Carey also had various meetings with Diana. 'She was a lovely person, and I grew to like her very much. She was a caring person and deeply compassionate to those in need. The darker side, and we all have weakness, was that she was manipulative, especially where men were concerned. Many were charmed by her apparent naivety when, in fact, she was a calculating woman who became quite bitter as her relationship with Prince Charles fell apart. It was important to help but it was an extremely sad situation as, in other circumstances, Diana's life could have been wonderfully fulfilling.

'I believe the press was responsible for creating an image of both Diana and Camilla as scarlet women. Nothing could be further from the truth. Diana was a vulnerable and hurt young woman. Camilla was a deeply devoted lady, sensible and approachable. Following my first meeting with Camilla, it became my intention when I met the Queen and other members of the Royal Family to be totally positive about Mrs Parker Bowles and to be constructive. It was my spiritual duty.'

Once he let his views be known, the archbishop found himself deluged with hate mail. 'Sadly, I received a huge number of letters from the general public disgusted with me for putting up with adultery when they asserted I ought to be condemning it. How could I remain a member of the Church and Archbishop of Canterbury? It was sad to receive such well-meaning but ignorant letters. To some more sensible people I was able to write and explain that the role of a priest is not to condemn but to get alongside those seeking spiritual guidance and to do all we can to help.

'Diana was also better at dealing with the press than Prince Charles. She kept turning on him and manipulating the press, who were under her spell and went the way she wanted. But actually, it was Diana self-damaging her own reputation and other people gradually seeing through it.'

Camilla had never set out to capture a prince. She and Charles started out as friends with a lot in common and an understanding of each other. Charles felt he could trust her, and was comfortable in her company, and although they married different people, they remained friends. He said she was 'the only woman who really understands me'.

Charles had genuinely thought he could grow to love Diana. But in 1981, not long into their honeymoon, he found it very difficult to understand her emotional outbursts and swinging moods. Throughout the 1980s he despaired that the only things they had in common were their children. The press commented on how sulky and dour he looked while his courtiers found it hard to deal with his bleak moods. Diana, however, could put on a good front during engagements, but admitted she suffered from bulimia, self-mutilation, depression, acute anxiety and a fear of being abandoned.

Sally Bedell Smith wrote in her biography of Prince Charles that he told his cousin Pamela Hicks that Diana would resurrect a row with him even when he was saying his prayers. As he knelt by his bed, said Hicks, the princess 'would hit him over the head and keep on with the row while he was praying'.

Although the press was largely negative about Camilla, David Yelland, former editor of the *Sun*, which broke a succession of steamy royal stories at the time, felt differently: 'Camilla has the image of an old-fashioned person from a distant era. Having met her, I knew she was not. She's bright, switched on and tuned in to the modern world. She's also a great mother. She is exactly what the monarchy needs. She's probably the most sensible person who's been to the Palace for twenty years.

'As editor I watched the mailbag very closely to see what the readers were saying about her. These days we'd all be on the internet but in those days we weren't. About twenty-five per cent of readers hated Camilla and seventy-five per cent didn't. They wanted Charles to be happy and the boys to be happy and that was why I never bought into the anti-Camilla thing as I could see that it was positive.'

In September 1992, the news that Diana and Charles were separating was confirmed by Prime Minister John Major who, in the House of Commons, read a statement from Buckingham Palace. It stated that 'with regret' the Prince and Princess of Wales had decided to separate but had no plans to divorce, that the succession to the throne was unaffected and there were 'no constitutional implications'. Members of Parliament were told the decision had been reached 'amicably', and although the Queen and Duke of Edinburgh felt saddened, they hoped the couple would now be given privacy. The former Prime Minister Edward Heath, then Father of the House, described the news as 'one of the saddest announcements in modern times'.

The real surprise was the comment from Geoffrey Dickens, a Conservative MP, that: 'There is no reason why the Princess of Wales should not be crowned queen in due course.' At the time, the idea of the princess becoming queen while she was separated from her husband was 'out of the question'. Peter Butler, another Tory, warned that such an arrangement would amount to a 'constitutional travesty. The marriage in legal terms may still be alive, but in reality it is over, and just because she was a wife to the future king does not give her the right to be queen.'

After the release of Morton's book, Camilla escaped first to Wales to stay with an old friend and then to the Hotel Cipriani in Venice with her sister Annabel. The press found her and described her as 'tired and pale'.

On 17 January 1993, a few months after the separation announcement, the 'Camillagate' tapes were published in the *Sunday People* and *Sunday Mirror*. The embarrassment was acute, and Camilla said it was one of the worst days of her life. Prince Charles was abroad, and she was unable to get through and talk to him. His public image was badly damaged and for some time he wasn't taken seriously. Camilla became a prisoner in her own home, which was surrounded by reporters and photographers. She couldn't go out without her picture being taken. Nonetheless she kept a dignified silence despite the torrent of unpleasant comments and crude cartoons.

She also received anonymous heavy-breathing telephone calls day and night. Some of the late-night calls were from Diana, who didn't give her name but threatened Camilla with comments like, 'I've sent someone to kill you. They're outside in the garden. Look out of the window, can you see them?' which sadly showed how unstable she could be. It must have been terrifying as, at the time, Camilla had no security and was often alone in her country home. It showed she had remarkable inner strength, both physical and psychological, and if she felt overwhelmed and downtrodden she didn't show it in public. To add to the stress, she was also very anxious about her mother Rosalind, who was in a wheelchair due to the osteoporosis that was gradually killing her.

Presenter Clare Balding says: 'I know a little about when the press is for or against you. I think Camilla is very resilient and feel for anyone who the press decides is number one hate target.

She managed to live through it with huge grace and dignity. I am so glad that people are now getting to know what she is really like, and the support of the Queen is fundamental in that – the understanding that [she and Prince Charles] are a partnership and a relationship. That it really works and is based on true love.'

At the time Camilla, who doesn't like to be the centre of attention, found that her name and relationship with Charles was suddenly on everyone's lips. She was called the most vilified woman in the UK and was a hate figure for Diana worshippers around the world. It helped that she could rely on her father for support. His response on hearing about her affair with Prince Charles was: 'The best policy is to keep our traps shut.' Two years afterwards, when he was asked about the publication of their explicit intimate phone conversation, he said: 'Let's just say highly intrusive.' Subsequently he praised Prince Charles for his honesty in admitting he had committed adultery with Camilla. 'I believe he came across as very fair-minded and sincere,' Shand said. 'I am in no doubt he will make a perfect king.' Camilla's sister Annabel and her husband were very supportive and invited Charles and Camilla to take refuge at weekends at their Dorset home. She also had loyal friends whose presence enabled her to survive the hurtful allegations hurled at her.

Camilla also had the additional pressure of worrying about her children – Tom, then at Oxford, and Laura, then seventeen. Tom eventually talked about his feelings when he was thirty-one and agreed to be interviewed by Cassandra Jardine from the *Daily Telegraph*. He made it crystal clear he was totally behind his mother. 'When it first started we thought it was entirely normal growing up to have five or six paparazzi hanging around. We would [take] binoculars and say, "Oh look, Mummy, there's five today." It was entirely normal to be chased at high speed by those people on motorbikes or cars. They are bullies . . . and they made you very angry. When you were fifteen or sixteen and you're coming out of an airport and they were really winding you up, all I wanted to do was smack them in the face and beat the hell out of them, but you couldn't do that.

'Friends and family were everything. At home there wasn't a newspaper. At school [Eton] I've been lucky in having two or three friends, including my cousin Ben Elliot, who have been with me all the way through. By the time you are in your final year at Eton, when the gossip really started, no little bugger is going to talk and, if they do, friends would jump in. That gives you a security that runs deeper than anything.'

When asked specifically about the 'Camillagate' tape, he said, 'I sort of remember not looking at the paper because, you know, Jesus, the things that we've all said to people that we love . . . that you wouldn't want the world reading. I just felt pissed off. I wasn't going to read that sort of stuff about my mother just as much as she wouldn't want to read it about me.'

The interview also gave Tom an opportunity to correct other allegations that Camilla couldn't and wouldn't cook, and said his mother's cooking skills inspired him to become a food writer. Nor did he ever feel sorry for himself. Instead, he showed tremendous loyalty to his mother and was furious about how she was criticised. 'What pisses me off most of all is when someone who doesn't know her says she's been a bad mother. A couple of times I've read how she's put her children through this hell. She's been an exemplary mother. She never judges, she's very funny, she cooks the food I like and coming home is a joy. When I go back to Wiltshire for the weekend with my mother, I feel cocooned, totally happy and safe.'

He talked more broadly about growing up and not expecting parents to be perfect. 'People blame their upbringing for everything, but my childhood – and my sister's – was absolutely idyllic. My parents are still great friends, they go to each other's houses.'

The decision to keep Camilla away from the limelight in the hope that out of sight she would be out of the public's mind backfired and instead gave the impression that she and Charles were leading a clandestine life. Public disapproval slightly eased off after Charles and Diana's official separation, but Camilla stayed undercover and at home for weeks on end. It resulted in few members of the public being able to make up their minds about what sort of person she was; instead, they made judgements based on the stream of critical comments and gossip in the media.

Diana, however, believed she knew exactly what she thought of Camilla and recorded her thoughts on tapes that two years later were used in Andrew Morton's biography of her. Despite the fact that she and Charles lived very separate lives and she was having affairs of her own, in 1989 she brashly tackled Camilla at a fortieth birthday party for her sister Annabel that was thrown by Lady Annabel Goldsmith at her home in Richmond, an event Prince Charles tried to persuade her not to come to. Instead, she went up to Camilla and said, 'I would like you to know that I know exactly what is going on between you and Charles. I wasn't born yesterday.' It was a hugely embarrassing public scene.

In December 1995, after Camilla had divorced her husband Andrew, the press reported that Prime Minister John Major had told the Queen that marriage between Charles and Camilla was out of the question. He warned her at a Christmas audience at Buckingham Palace that neither the public nor Parliament would accept such a marriage.

Fortunately, there were sunnier moments when Charles and Camilla were together. When she wasn't by his side, his disheartened manner and irritability made it difficult for his aides to plan future engagements and go through the details of his commitments. It was a great relief when Camilla quietly arrived. She didn't get involved, but her presence put Charles in a better mood and made him easier to deal with. She also instinctively knew how to get Charles to do things that others couldn't. Once, when they were spending a weekend at Highgrove in the summer of 1998, Charles was expected to go to a sports event in the afternoon to collect a £1m cheque for The Prince's Trust, a charity founded by him in 1976 that aims to support vulnerable young people so they get into education, training and jobs. He didn't want to go, but Camilla asked him how many people could take a helicopter, collect £1m and come back in time for tea. He went.

Andrew Roberts comments: 'One of the things that I think is most interesting about Camilla is that she is sort of grand in the correct way and is able to be herself. I think the public have got that now, because they didn't know her at all during all the crises of the 1980s and 1990s. She was, as far as they were concerned, the Mrs Simpson woman who was coming in and destroying the fairy tale between Charles and Diana. Once they got to actually know how quiet, honest, down to earth and empathetic she was, and how accessible she was, and totally different from the monster she'd been made out to be, the tide turned.'

Despite it all, she had a reputation with her close friends for being good company and reliable. One of them said: 'If you wanted to be with someone who could go through the jungle and then scrub up in time for dinner, you couldn't find anyone better. This is not a wicked witch: the average Englishwoman has far more in common with Camilla Parker Bowles than the "fairy-tale princess". She will be just as touchy-feely; she will chat away to Aids victims – just give her a chance. She also doesn't covet titles.'

She would need all of those attributes in the years ahead, as the challenges she and Charles would face would only increase after John Major's comments.

Chapter 7

THE OUTCAST

The Queen was deeply shocked when three of her four children's marriages fell apart in 1992. In that one year, Prince Andrew's marriage to Sarah Ferguson collapsed in March, her only daughter Princess Anne's marriage to Captain Mark Phillips, an Olympic gold medal-winning equestrian, broke down in April, and, to her utter dismay, Prince Charles and Princess Diana told her and Prince Philip they were separating in December. The combination demolished for good the belief that the Royal Family was a wholesome role model of domestic bliss. A devasting fire at Windsor Castle, her much-loved home, that same year made matters even worse. It cost £35 million to restore. The Queen famously and evocatively described the year as her 'annus horribilis'.

For Prince Charles there was a ray of hope for the future. Camilla Parker Bowles's divorce from her husband Andrew went through in 1995, and Charles gradually began introducing her to the public, something that was done with the utmost care. Many people felt Camilla couldn't be compared to their adored Diana. More significantly it took a long time to find an opportunity to introduce her to his sons. Unlike Princess Diana, who brought various lovers back to Kensington Palace, sometimes in the boot of her car, and involved her sons in her romances, Charles made sure that Camilla was never at Highgrove when the princes came to stay. He tried suggesting the boys meet her a couple of months before Diana's unexpected death, but both went very quiet, and he immediately dropped the subject. Diana and Prince Charles's divorce went through in 1996. The same year, Prince Charles employed thirty-year-old Mark Bolland, initially as Assistant Private Secretary, and promoted him the following year to Deputy Private Secretary.

The tragedy of Diana's sudden death in August 1997 made Mark indispensable to Charles. He was handed what seemed at the time to be a near impossible task of changing Charles's negative public image, plus smoothing the way for the public acceptance of Camilla and remarriage. Bolland adopted a fearless if-you-want-me-to-put-things-right-you-must-listen approach. He told Charles he had to get out and let people see him rather than hide away or choose engagements where the public barely got a glimpse of him. Nor did he go along with the Queen's slogan 'don't complain and don't explain' extending to aides and members of the royal household. He insisted that palace staff had to speak out positively.

What Charles particularly liked about Bolland was that his opinion about Camilla was the opposite of that of both the public and the royals. 'From the beginning I felt she was terrific, and I liked her a lot,' said Bolland. 'She was loyal, straightforward, fun and quick-thinking and had a very good instinct.

'My mission was to bring honesty with the media and the public to their relationship and to give them freedom to live. Not in the full glare of the public eye but, if he went to the theatre with friends, she could too. Or stay with him in Birkhall, on the edge of the Balmoral Estate, for a holiday. And after the divorce to start to be a normal couple and so have space to work out the future of their own relationship. You can't fashion a normal life if you have to hide all the time.

'Camilla and I spoke a lot in those days. She could see and feel that there were forces against her, showed some anxiety about that, and needed help to manage it. Because of the job I was doing I needed someone to talk to as well and she was a great therapist for me! I thought she had been very, very unfairly treated. There were stories I heard about later, like bread rolls being thrown at her in a car park, that were completely untrue. Whenever she went to a supermarket in Wiltshire people were curious but kind, and she had never had that sort of hostility. But these things were written about and became real. Camilla and I are still in touch from time to time and at one level she hasn't changed a bit.'

In the years both before and after his divorce, Prince Charles was thought of as old-fashioned, out-of-touch and a father who had distant, rather formal relationships with sons he barely saw. Bolland believes that the timing of his arrival was 'framed by the breakdown of the prince's marriage. It was the time of the so-called 'War of the Waleses', and Camilla was one of the people on the battlefield. There was no real understanding of who she was, what she was and why she was around. And their whole relationship was framed as a secret, which clearly needed to change if it had a future.'

On 31 August 1997, shortly before midnight, a Mercedes carrying Princess Diana and her playboy boyfriend Dodi Fayed en route to Fayed's Paris flat tragically crashed at speed into a pillar in the Pont de l'Alma tunnel in Paris. Diana, Fayed and their intoxicated driver Henri Paul died of their injuries. The investigations that followed showed that if they had been wearing seatbelts such a tragic outcome might have been avoided.

Prince Charles, Harry and William were with the Queen at

Balmoral. Charles was devastated and didn't know whether to wake the boys in the middle of the night to tell them. He talked it through with his mother, who suggested that they should be left to sleep. He then rang Camilla. He couldn't go back to bed and instead went for a solitary walk on the moors. His feeling of loss and personal failure overwhelmed him, and he anguished over how to break such devastating news to his children.

Diana was only thirty-six years old and had become the most famous woman in the world. She was beautiful, charismatic, brave, unpredictable and flawed, an irresistible combination that made so many love her. She was also seen as an icon who could bridge the gap between royals and ordinary people.

After church on Sunday, Prince Charles flew in an RAF plane with Diana's sisters Sarah and Jane to Paris to collect her body. Mark Bolland went with him. He recalls: 'He was extremely upset and distressed. I also spoke to Camilla. Her first and principal reaction was to ask how the boys were and she was obviously very, very upset for William and Harry. At this stage she hadn't even met them. She was, of course, worried about Prince Charles but her reaction first and foremost was that of a mother.'

Not only did Prince Charles feel distraught, he also felt guilty and realised that the impact on William and Harry of losing a much-loved mother would prevent any further attempts to try to introduce Camilla to his sons for the foreseeable future. He also knew it wouldn't be appropriate to be seen in public with her.

Soon after Charles and Diana's separation, Camilla, who had wanted to feel secure for some time, bought herself a Georgian mansion, Ray Mill House, near Laycock, Wiltshire, for £850,000, which was largely paid for by her divorce settlement. It has a swimming pool, stables, a vast garden and was only a fifteen-minute drive from Prince Charles's country home, Highgrove House, in Gloucestershire. Ray Mill House became her 'bolthole'. At

Highgrove, Charles can be fussy about where things are placed, how clean and tidy everything is and the exact time for meals. Taking short breaks in her own home gives her a chance to get away from such a meticulously ordered life. She still enjoys relaxing at Ray Mill with her family and is not put out by clutter. It was a place for her to be a loving mother to Laura and Tom, and later a doting grandmother to her five grandchildren, who she lets run around and make as much noise as they like as they won't disturb Prince Charles.

Laura loves the mansion so much that when she married chartered accountant Harry Lopes in May 2006, she held her wedding reception there. She and Harry have a daughter, Eliza, born in 2008, and twin boys, Gus and Louis, born in 2009. Eliza was a bridesmaid at the wedding of Prince William and Catherine Middleton in 2011. Tom Parker Bowles married Sarah Buys in 2005, but the marriage ended in divorce in 2018. The couple had a daughter, Lola, in 2007, and a son, Frederick, in 2010.

Camilla, who is a long-time fan of the BBC Radio 4 rural drama series *The Archers*, also enjoys being able to cook at any time she chooses. Her close friend Lucia Santa Cruz reveals: 'She likes to cook for her family when she is at Ray Mill. The food is simple but wonderfully cooked. I absolutely believe she makes the best roast chicken. Tom has said so too. Her love of food has passed down to him in a multiplied way. She also cooks a wonderful leg of lamb and the best Dover sole, which I am treated with when I visit.'

Relationships can change when a mistress becomes a wife and Camilla never wanted Prince Charles to take her for granted. Escaping now and then to her own home gave her some independence and perhaps kept Charles on his toes. The late billionaire financier and politician Sir James Goldsmith was notorious for speaking from his own experience of this issue: 'When you marry your mistress you create a job vacancy.'

Mark Bolland explains that at the time Camilla 'wasn't a constant presence in [Charles's] life at Highgrove. She would usually stay one night a week. She had a real life of her own. She worried about money, bringing her children up on her own, going to the super-market herself, hiring her own staff and getting parking tickets like everyone else. She didn't have motorcycle outriders; instead, she had a normality about her life that he never had. He had none of the awareness, knowledge or experience which she brought.'

Lucia Santa Cruz admits that at times she was worried about Camilla's safety. 'I once took her to the theatre and afterwards for dinner in Soho. We expected to be able to get a taxi but there weren't any and we stood for quite a long time at Piccadilly Circus waiting for one. A car full of young people recognised Camilla, stopped where we were and started chatting to us. They weren't hostile in any way, but it made me think what could happen if it had been a car with hostile passengers. I thought she couldn't be so vulnerable to be exposed in this way. I remember telling her she couldn't go on like this. Luckily it didn't last very long and soon afterwards she had a driver.'

Mark Bolland explains: 'Prince Charles's household couldn't provide the help Camilla needed, which was someone who could be an assistant, PA, secretary and organiser, because she wasn't married to Prince Charles at the time. We were willing to help but it would obviously be more straightforward if the prince found someone to help her.' The task was handed over to Amanda MacManus, a charming force to be reckoned with.

Although Camilla left Ray Mill House in 2003 – and, despite the Queen's continued disapproval, moved to live with Prince Charles at their main London residence, Clarence House – she retained the property as a base of her own.

One of the friends Camilla made during this difficult time was Catherine Goodman, artist and co-founder of Prince Charles's

Royal Drawing School, launched in 2000. 'Just before I started the school, I met Her Royal Highness as Prince Charles had asked me to do a portrait of her just because he wanted to have her painted,' she said. 'I went to see her at Ray Mill and we got on really well. I knew that she had been quite traumatised by press intrusion and Princess Diana dying, which must have been very difficult. At that time in her life, she kept away from the public eye and those years were very much about bringing her out of purdah. I am not a quick portrait painter. It takes me quite a long time as I like to work with the relationship of whoever I am painting. That way I see people in different moods.

'She had just one dramatic change of mood in the summer of 2001, when Prince Charles fell off his polo pony and was knocked unconscious. It was awful. I could feel her tension. She was really upset and terribly worried.' The prince was taken first to Cirencester Memorial Hospital and then to Cheltenham General. He left hospital the following morning smiling and waving and telling reporters, 'I'm all right, thank you very much. I'm still alive,' before being driven to London for his grandmother, Queen Elizabeth the Queen Mother's 101st birthday celebrations.

Catherine continues: 'We had long sittings for hours when she'd chat non-stop, and we got to know each other well over the two years it took me to finish. She didn't seem to be anything like the person who was portrayed in the press. I thought she was great, modest, incredibly well-grounded with a wonderful sense of humour. She is also quite straightforward. What you see is what you get. There are no layers of undisclosed unconscious behaviour going on. Her father Bruce, who I was very fond of, stayed with her a lot. I got to know him and her children well too.' The painting, showing Camilla dressed very informally in a blue polo shirt, now hangs in Clarence House. Catherine smiled. 'She loves it and so does [Charles].'

Catherine also introduced Camilla to Lady Sarah Chatto. She is the only daughter of Princess Margaret, much-loved niece of the Queen and godmother to Prince Harry. A shy but talented painter, she keeps well away from the royal spotlight. She and Catherine Goodman studied at the same art school and shared a flat. 'Camilla is very fond of Sarah, her husband Daniel and their two sons,' said Catherine. The family were at Prince Philip's thanksgiving service at Westminster Abbey on 29 March 2022 and at the Platinum Jubilee celebrations three months later.

Guided by Mark Bolland, Prince Charles's public image slowly improved, and he began to be seen as a single parent anxiously trying to protect and nurture his sons, rather than an uncaring father who didn't have time for them. Photographers were encouraged to take numerous pictures of the brothers and their father, which not only got public sympathy but encouraged Charles to immerse himself more in their lives. It was hoped that in time the impression he gave would help the public accept his relationship with Camilla.

In order for this to happen, it became a high priority to build a strong rapport between Camilla and William and Harry – something Camilla's close friend Gyles Brandreth had no concerns about. 'I remember going to a fund-raising charity event at Highgrove in the late 1990s a few years before she and Prince Charles got married. I was so impressed by how at ease she was with Harry and William and how relaxed Prince Charles was too. The boys had taken a table with their friends for the event and, just before Charles and Camilla were going off to bed, she squatted down by their table and chatted to them. I watched the body language and thought, *This is no wicked stepmother or trying to be what she isn't*. She was perfectly normal and so were they, and I thought this is clearly going to work for the family.'

The actual role of a stepmother is difficult to define, apart from knowing it requires emotional and mental strength and a lot of patience. Making headway with the princes was a huge challenge. Diana had given the impression to both of her boys that Camilla was her bitter enemy, and as a result Camilla had been unjustly blamed for her death. If they found themselves liking her, they were also bound to feel guilty that they were not being faithful to a mother they both adored, despite the toxic troubled atmosphere they grew up with.

Trying to make any progress through the complexities of their lives and build a positive relationship would be difficult for Camilla partly due to their unique and damaging childhood experiences. It is common for parents to pass on their destructive behaviour to the next generation, and it was feared the brothers would stumble if not crash once they were older. Fighting the pitfalls they faced took a lot of hard work and soul-searching for both of them, and was particularly difficult for Harry.

Diana had already worried about Harry before she and Charles separated and spoke to a psychiatrist about her concerns over his possible reactions to the separation and his behaviour when she invited male friends to Kensington Palace.

There was no doubt Diana loved William, but as her marriage deteriorated, she leant too heavily on him emotionally. William was only ten when Diana and Charles separated. She admitted he became the man of the house and called him her 'closest confidant' and 'soulmate'. Leaning heavily on a child is unhealthy and damaging and a harsh burden to place on young shoulders, as his perception and experience were limited to those of a young boy. A mother's duty is to care for her son, not the other way round, and a son needs to be a child and not his mother's best friend. Diana even talked to him about her lovers and took him through the complexities of her divorce terms before she agreed to sign them. She told a TV interviewer that she wept behind a locked bathroom door after an argument with Charles. Apparently, William, who was only ten years old, bent down outside saying: 'I hate to see you sad,' and stuffed paper tissues under the door. An anecdote which must have caused William considerable anguish, but which Diana spoke about with pride rather than guilt.

In the early 1990s, divorce carried greater stigma than it does today, so although William and Harry were unlikely to have been the only children at school whose parents had a failed marriage, none of them would have had the excruciating experience of having their parents' mutual antagonism played out in front of the whole world. They had, however, been brought up to have the best manners and could put on a good front when needed, and especially in public, even when their hearts felt torn apart because their parents obviously didn't like each other.

Wisely Charles waited a year after Diana's death before once again approaching his objective of getting Camilla accepted by his sons. This time he invited Camilla's children, Tom and Laura, to stay at Birkhall, the Queen Mother's 53,000-acre estate at Balmoral, which Charles would inherit after she died in 2002. There were also other guests to lighten the atmosphere. Charles was enormously relieved that, despite Tom and Laura being older than William and Harry, all four offspring seemed to have got on well.

It was around this time that William and Harry showed some warmth towards their father when they decided to throw a surprise party for his fiftieth birthday. His actual birthday is in November, but they chose to have the party at the end of July as the school holidays had begun but it wasn't yet time for the family to decamp to Balmoral. They knew their father would want Camilla to be invited and that it would be best all round for them to meet her privately first. They knew how negative their mother had been about her but wanted to make up their own minds.

William told his father he would be coming to London and asked him to arrange a meeting at 7pm on Friday 12 June 1998. William, who had a self-contained flat at the top of St James's Palace, turned up unexpectedly early. Camilla offered to disappear, but her aide Amanda MacManus suggested it would be a good idea if they met earlier. William agreed. They talked for about half an hour and their meeting apparently went as well as could be hoped for. William was friendly and Camilla was sensitive enough to let the relationship progress at his pace and not ask difficult questions. When it was over Camilla announced: 'I need a gin and tonic!' She and William met again for lunch soon afterwards. She had tea with Harry a few weeks later, which also seemed to go well.

William and Harry went full steam ahead for the party to be held in the Orchard Room at Highgrove. They enlisted the help of Tiggy Legge-Bourke, a nanny/companion to the boys, and Prince Charles's former valet, Michael Fawcett, but the ideas, energy and enthusiasm came from them. Both brothers made enormous efforts to ensure that the party was kept secret. They sent handwritten invitations to the Queen, who at the time turned down going anywhere Camilla might be present. This extended to this particular birthday party that her much-loved grandsons were painstakingly organising for their father. Prince Philip also declined. Other invitations went to Princess Anne, Prince Andrew, Prince Edward, and about a hundred of Charles's friends.

All guests were charged £25 each because the brothers didn't want their father to have to pay for his own party. They arranged for the outside of Highgrove House to be decorated with wild-flowers while Greek statues were placed in the walled garden. Entertainment was a Blackadder-style comedy starring Rowan Atkinson, Emma Thompson and Stephen Fry. Unfortunately, one of the guests tipped off the *Daily Mirror* about the event and published details of the party. Both princes were angry and upset as, yet again, they felt press intrusion had destroyed something that was important to them. In an unprecedented move, St James's Palace issued a statement condemning the paper for publishing details of their treat and 'spoiling' the surprise.

The birthday party itself was a success, apart from one embarrassing incident involving Prince Harry. Charles was enormously touched by the trouble his sons had taken and particularly that they had invited Camilla and sat her in a prominent place. The one embarrassment was that Harry and William staged a mock *Full Monty* strip. Harry, then fourteen, was said to have been so drunk that he didn't just remove a few items of clothing, as was arranged, but stripped off entirely and ran around naked in front of the guests. One of the guests said: 'Charles was visibly shocked and turned crimson but told a group of us later that it was just teenage high spirits and he himself had done much the same. It was the only time in my life that I didn't believe him.'

Despite Charles's gradually improving image it remained a complex task to rehabilitate both him and Camilla in the public's eye. Many people continued to believe that if Charles hadn't had his on/off affair with Camilla, or made more effort, his and Diana's marriage would not have broken down.

An insider said: 'At times during those early days it was a lonely battle to try to normalise the situation and bring Camilla into an area that wasn't controversial. The Palace institution was against it and a lot of people would have been very happy if she had just disappeared. The fact that the Prince of Wales made it very clear that she was non-negotiable sometimes brought them into conflict with other members of the Royal Family. It was a time when there was a lot of division.'

Charles needed to get away from the image that he was a selfish and unworthy heir to the throne to being someone the public could relate to and admire. He had, after all, been preparing to follow his mother as monarch since childhood; now he needed both the court of public opinion and the rest of the Royal Family to be positive about him and change their minds about him marrying Camilla.

Lord Carey feels it took 'a very long time even after Diana's death' in 1997 before they married in 2005. 'The courtiers were probably by nature very cautious, whereas I would have tried to push it through. Probably their judgement was right. I found with Charles and other members of the Royal Family that being surrounded by courtiers who are probably even more cautious than they are themselves, although Charles and Camilla wanted to move on, the advice given all the time was "slow down", when I thought she needed to be seen out doing things, and then the public would eventually take her to its heart, which of course came true.'

Meanwhile, Camilla wanted to be seen as a grounded, loyal and stable person who made Charles happy rather than the brazen, manipulative hanger-on many thought her to be at the time. Some discounted her merely because of her looks. One particularly offensive female commentator said: 'I cannot understand why Charles loved a woman who looks like a horse more than one of the most beautiful women in the world.'

The author and diarist James Lees-Milne frequently met royalty and wrote in December 1996 that he met Prince Charles and Camilla when they were all guests of the Duke and Duchess of Devonshire. 'Camilla is also at Chatsworth, and the prince blossoms in her company. It was there that they first met, twenty-four years ago.'

Working out a relationship with William and Harry that didn't show any attempt to take over from Diana was inevitably going to be difficult, but not nearly as challenging as getting the Queen to accept her both as a member of the Royal Family and her daughter-in-law. Her Majesty had found Charles rather irritating as a child and his refusal to move on and abandon Camilla meant he was still not doing as he was told. The Queen was also influenced by her mother, Elizabeth the Queen Mother, who had wanted Prince Charles to marry Diana and enjoyed a warm relationship with Andrew Parker Bowles. She wanted nothing to do with Camilla. According to royal author Robert Jobson, in his 2006 book *William's Princess*, she bore an icy disdain for Camilla. Jobson wrote: 'It was a fact that Camilla's name was not allowed to be spoken in the presence of Queen Elizabeth the Queen Mother.'

Prince Charles's fiftieth birthday could have been a dignified opportunity for the Queen to lift her long-term snub of Camilla and instead begin to appreciate how devoted Camilla was to Charles and how much he in turn loved her. Lucia Santa Cruz believes that the Queen's strong rebuff was less about Camilla as a person and more about her concern that her son and heir wanted to marry an 'experienced' woman who was below his rank: 'When Camilla was married to Andrew Parker Bowles, she used to go to Balmoral with him and join the Royal Family. They got on marvellously well with her. In fact, she was considered to be perfect, but when the marriage failed and she was with Prince Charles, she was rejected and got all the blame, which was so unfair.'

The Queen had obeyed her mother from childhood but insisted on getting her own way only when it came to marrying Philip. She also knew how much her mother had wanted Diana to become queen, and was never going to argue with her over Camilla.

Chapter 8

SLOW PROGRESS

It was obvious that the Queen and other senior royals, notably Prince Andrew, did not want Camilla around, and Diana continued to be the highest-ranking royal in opinion polls even after her death. Prince Charles and Andrew have rarely got on well together, except for a short time while they were both married. This is partly because there is usually contention between the first and second in line of the succession; he is, after all, the 'spare' while Charles is the heir. Up until the birth of Prince William, Prince Andrew was the second in line to the throne. Though Princess Anne is nine years older than him, he was given precedence as a male, a rule that didn't change until the Succession to the Crown Act 2013. Most of all Charles and Andrew have very different personalities, values and approaches to life.

Mark Bolland decided the best opportunity for Camilla and Charles to make their first public appearance, and hopefully win the public round, would be the fiftieth birthday party for Camilla's sister, Annabel Elliot, in January 1999 at the Ritz Hotel in London. Media outlets were quietly informed and photographer Ian Jones was in the front line and positioned behind the crash barriers two days in advance to get the best view. 'There were 199 photographers there,' he claims. 'The duchess was having such a hard time; it was lovely to see them together at last. She might not be Diana, but she has always had grace, elegance and statesmanship.' Camilla, who wore a black cocktail dress with a pearl choker, arrived at 8.45pm with her children.

Prince Charles had a long-term obligation to host a charity dinner at St James's Palace and arrived just before 11pm. He stayed until nearly midnight when the couple suddenly appeared at the door. Charles walked ahead of Camilla but turned round to check that she was managing the stairs. Once she was down, he gently touched her arm before she climbed into their waiting car. He then walked round to the other side and sat next to her. The photographers' flashbulbs were so numerous and bright that the British Epilepsy Association issued a public warning that the television images could cause seizures. Photographs of them were in demand from around the world and their appearance, although brief, was the start of a new beginning for them both.

Despite the feeling that the public might at last be softening towards her, Camilla continued to be ostracised by the Royal Family. She wasn't invited to the wedding of Prince Charles's youngest brother Prince Edward, thirty-five, to Sophie Rhys-Jones, thirty-four, which took place on 19 June 1999. Sophie belonged to a middle-class family. Her father, Christopher, was a businessman, her mother Mary a secretary and charity worker. She was thought to resemble Princess Diana but her upbringing – a four-bedroom seventeenth-century farmhouse in Brenchley, Kent – was far more modest. She was working as a PR when she met Edward. On the morning of their wedding the Queen awarded them the titles Earl and Countess of Wessex.

Prince Charles and Prince Andrew were Edward's best men at

the ceremony at St George's Chapel, Windsor Castle. The wedding was less extravagant than that of Edward's older siblings, with only a few titled Europeans and no politicians in attendance. He is the only one of the Queen's four children whose first marriage has endured.

In September 1999 Mark Bolland took Camilla to New York, by Concorde, at Prince Charles's expense, to see how Americans reacted to her. 'I don't know if it was the right thing to do but we did it,' he admits. 'It was fun, and we got some good coverage.' It was obviously seen as very important as they flew out only three days after Hurricane Floyd blew in. The trip involved four flights, two by plane and two by helicopter, that must have been a nightmare for Camilla, who is terrified of flying even when there is no turbulence. In New York alone Hurricane Floyd had brought winds of up to 60 mph and up to 13.5 inches of rain. It caused fifty-seven deaths across the country and damage of nearly $6.5 billion.

It was Camilla's first visit to the United States for twenty-five years. She and Bolland were guests for two nights at the East Hampton home of financier Scott Bessent, who had generously given money to The Prince's Foundation, and she chose to spend the first day at the beach. She enjoys swimming in the sea as much as she dislikes flying. Joy Camm, her assistant private secretary at the time, recalls: 'There was never any question when the sea was near that she would go in, however cold it was.' Undaunted by the weather and regardless of a rough ocean, Camilla dived in and swam so vigorously that she frightened one of her hosts when at one point she couldn't be seen above the water. No one apart from Camilla herself relaxed until she swam against the tide back to the shore. Her courage of both flying in such atrocious weather and swimming in such a cold sea are indicative of her determination and bravery, characteristics sorely needed during this period of her life.

She and Bolland then had a very bumpy ride in a helicopter that had to fly low to Manhattan due to strong winds and poor visibility. Camilla apparently looked frightened throughout. The highlights of the trip were two lunches hosted by Brooke Astor, the doyenne of New York society, at her Park Avenue apartment. Among the guests were power players, A-listers and several millionaires, such as broadcaster Barbara Walters of ABC News, media tycoon Michael Bloomberg and United Nations General Secretary Kofi Annan.

Overall, the choreographed rehabilitation of Mrs Parker Bowles was going smoothly, but sometimes Camilla refused to budge. Bolland said: 'Camilla was a strong person but nonetheless went along with what we were doing most of the time. I am not a hunting or country person, and the press don't like hunting, so I occasionally suggested she dropped hunting. I got absolutely nowhere. We would normally speak in the morning, and I remember calling her one morning and there was no answer. She rang me back a couple of hours later and said she was out doing something I disapproved of even more – "cubbing" she called it, which is also known as early hunting. I thought, *Oh no*, but she was her own person.'

Camilla was out of step with most of the country over fox hunting. Cubbing, which involves training young foxhounds to chase and kill fox cubs, was particularly loathed. She and Charles wanted to carry on in defiance of the Commons vote but gave it up when they were given a warning by the police. The ban on fox hunting came into force in 2005, despite Charles writing to Tony Blair in defence of the pastime in 2002.

In May 2000 Prince Charles attended the week-long General Assembly of the Church of Scotland at the Palace of Holyrood House in Edinburgh. As Lord High Commissioner, Charles was the Queen's representative at the annual meeting that made laws governing the Church's operation. To the surprise of many, Camilla came too but she appeared only for the dinners. 'It was a big deal,' Bolland remembers. 'Camilla wasn't at the public events with Prince Charles because she wasn't his wife and it wouldn't have been right, but she appeared at the start of the evening meal, two of which had eighty to one hundred guests.'

Bolland felt Camilla's presence was 'an honest thing' to do as they were together. He also believes 'the Scots like honesty'. Yet to be on the safe side, guidance was taken beforehand when trusted Scots were asked what they felt about Mrs Parker Bowles coming to such a religious gathering. Prince Charles was very relieved when he sensed that the consensus was that Camilla would be welcome. Bolland adds: 'No doubt the people in Buckingham Palace thought, *What the hell is going on?* and didn't like it, but it was an important part of the campaign to bring her out into the open. It was a big move forward.' In his journal, the royal biographer Kenneth Rose tartly commented: 'Lord Reith [the founder of the BBC] must be turning in his grave. I suppose it is to prepare us for Queen Camilla.'

There was no official comment from the Church of Scotland on Camilla's presence, but insiders believed it was because the Church was divided over the matter. Some thought Prince Charles should formalise his relationship with Camilla by marriage. One member of the Assembly said it was 'their own business'. Others felt he was paving the way for a Scottish wedding: Princess Anne had married her second husband, Commander Tim Laurence, in a ceremony at Crathie Kirk on Deeside in December 1992. At the time the Church of England did not permit remarriage in church for people whose former spouses were still alive. The Church of Scotland had no such barrier.

Camilla's presence unleashed a torrent of media speculation

about an imminent marriage. The *Glasgow Herald* commented: 'While the official stance from St James's Palace is that the prince has no plans to marry, speculation over the union has been fuelled by the fact that Mrs Parker Bowles is increasingly seen at his side.' the *Sunday Times* went further, reporting that the prince was in negotiations with the Church of Scotland about remarrying in Scotland.

This prompted a furious reaction from Prince Charles. His office filed an official denial with the Press Complaints Commission, the first time he had resorted to the press watchdog. The letter was written by his private secretary, Stephen Lamport, and was said by *The Times* to have the full support of the prince and Camilla. 'A courtier' was quoted by the newspaper as saying: 'We have got to the end of our tether. There is no intention of remarrying. We keep saying it, but it is ignored, or dismissed as dissembling. This is not just about the Prince of Wales. He is concerned for the feelings of his children, the children of Mrs Parker Bowles, the memory of his late wife. By making this complaint, we hope it will formally lay down, on St James's Palace headed notepaper, that there is to be no wedding and so it is pointless speculation otherwise.'

The *Sunday Times* climbed down, printing a correction and an apology. 'The story was based on information from a source close to the Church of Scotland,' it read. 'Following assurances from St James's Palace that there was no foundation to the story, we acknowledge that the story was inaccurate and are happy to set the record straight. We apologise for the error.'

Pointless or not, the speculation continued unabated. Kenneth Rose wrote acidly in his diary: 'The Prince of Wales's office has just announced again that he will never marry Camilla. So why did he take her to Holyrood for the General Assembly?' Over the next few years nothing changed. Camilla seemed to have quietly accepted the status quo for a variety of reasons: concern for the young princes, realising that the country was not yet ready to accept her as Charles's wife, and the knowledge that the Queen was still dead set against the marriage.

Ironically, shortly afterwards, the Queen finally agreed to follow the recommendations of her advisers and end her long-running personal boycott of Camilla. An historic meeting between the two women finally took place on 6 June 2000. It was at the celebration of the sixtieth birthday of Prince Philip's first cousin once removed, the exiled King Constantine of Greece. As Camilla was no longer hiding away and the venue was Highgrove, the Queen knew Camilla would be there and it seemed to be a dignified opportunity for her to acknowledge Charles's companion.

It was a highly significant public moment. Although the two women did not sit at the same table, it was recognition that Charles, by then a grown-up 51-year-old, was determined, against all the odds, not to give up either the woman he loved or the succession to the throne. To avoid any doubts a Palace spokesman's announcement made sure the public were aware that the Queen knew exactly what she was doing. It said: 'The Queen attended a birthday party for King Constantine given by the Prince of Wales at Highgrove this lunchtime, and Mrs Parker Bowles was among the guests.' In his journal Kenneth Rose noted: 'It appears to be part of the prince's plan to accustom the nation to accepting Camilla as part of the family.' The next day, he added: 'Torrents of gush about the meeting between the Queen and Camilla. It changes nothing. If the prince marries Camilla, she will be Queen. If not, she will remain his mistress, though scarcely with the present Queen's encouragement.'

This gesture, however, didn't mean that a wedding would take place sooner rather than later. Constitutional expert Lord St John of Fawsley said at the time: 'It is a long step from [repairing the rift] to concluding that a marriage will take place between Mrs Parker Bowles and the prince.' Reading between the lines, it meant that Camilla still couldn't be involved in any official royal engagements but could attend certain of the Royal Family's private celebrations.

It would have been a welcoming gesture to invite Camilla who, after all, was not only Charles's soulmate, lover and closest friend, but also an enthusiastic partygoer with impeccable manners, to the Royal Family's Dance of the Decades on 21 June, just two weeks after Constantine's birthday party. But no invitation was proffered. The party was held at Windsor Castle and celebrated five millennial royal milestones: The Queen Mother's hundredth birthday, a forerunner of her own party the following month, Princess Margaret's seventieth, on 21 August, Princess Anne's fiftieth, on 15 August, the Duke of York's fortieth, and Prince William's eighteenth. William was the only one whose birthday was on the day itself. He wasn't even there, as he was revising at Eton for his History of Art A-level exam the following Thursday. He was, however, toasted by the guests and would have his own party with friends after his exams.

The party began with a dinner for about eighty close friends and selected royalty from Spain, Belgium and Norway, plus ex-King Constantine, who at the time lived in Hampstead, north-west London. Dinner guests were later joined by about seven hundred others for a drinks party in the castle's Saint George's Hall and adjoining rooms. It was reported that the Queen was in 'great form' at the royal ball and danced with several of her guests. Dame Darcey Bussell, the prima ballerina who would later become a judge on *Strictly Come Dancing*, was one of the guests. 'It was amazing to see all the royals on the dance floor enjoying themselves,' she told me. 'It was so nice to see them up and moving instead of just observing everyone else.'

Another guest whose appearance at the party surprised some was the Duchess of York. It marked the first time she had joined a Royal Family get-together since her divorce from Prince Andrew in May 1996. A souvenir booklet from the party also listed Prince Andrew's 'special guests'. Included were Ghislaine Maxwell, socialite daughter of the disgraced former press baron Robert Maxwell, and the New York financier Jeffrey Epstein. At the time Epstein was simply known as a man who enjoyed the company of beautiful women. It took several more years before he was finally arrested and charged with sex trafficking. He committed suicide in prison in August 2019 while awaiting trial in New York. Royal protocol dictated that only couples who were married or engaged could be named together, so Maxwell and Epstein's names appeared separately on the list. The Queen didn't block Andrew's 'special guests' but felt Camilla shouldn't be seen at the family gathering. Camilla's ex-husband, Andrew Parker Bowles, was invited as a guest of Princess Anne.

This public humiliation was demeaning enough that it wouldn't have been a surprise if Camilla had walked away, leaving her prince behind. But she is made of sterner stuff, with an ability to both self-protect and preserve. It helped nonetheless that she could lean on her rock-solid father Bruce Shand who was always openly on her side. Close friends also rallied round, with one of them volunteering to do her supermarket shopping and thus avoid potential unpleasantness from other customers. And as always, she could escape from the world by immersing herself in a good book. There was small compensation when she accompanied Prince Charles to semi-official functions the night before the party and the day afterwards, when he hosted a private dinner at Buckingham Palace for American supporters of his charitable work.

Charles and Camilla's next major joint appearance was when they hosted a black-tie dinner to celebrate the £6 million development of

The Prince's Foundation Shoreditch headquarters in east London, hoping once again it would boost public approval of their relationship. Unfortunately, as they arrived, they were subjected to a torrent of abuse from a vociferous group of anti-monarchists. They seemed momentarily taken aback when they heard cries of 'royal scum'. Although Camilla, who was wearing a pink chiffon Versace gown with a pink tulle stole, looked anxious, she managed to smile as they walked inside. Prince Charles remained stony-faced as he quickly walked the five yards from the car to the front door of the new headquarters.

A BBC camera crew and one reporter were permitted inside. There were about three hundred guests, but no members of the Royal Family to witness the culmination of the prince's long-held dream to bring all his architectural and environmental causes, aimed at helping to revive town and city life, under one roof. The couple left shortly before midnight to find that in contrast to their arrival they were cheered by bystanders as they walked to the waiting Bentley. The hundred or so photographers who were still there were reminiscent of their appearance at the Ritz eighteen months earlier.

The couple suffered another public snub when Charles was informed by Lord Powis that he could not stay in his flat in Powis Castle, near Welshpool, while he attended the Royal Welsh Show, if he brought Camilla. Plans were made so they could stay elsewhere. In his journal Kenneth Rose was by now exasperated with the prince: 'It is surely unusual for a member of the Royal Family to be accompanied by his *maitresse-en-titre*, except on private travels. He seems to want her to be recognised as his mistress.'

Although Prince William had met and talked to Camilla, a couple of face-to-face meetings could never have been enough to build any sort of relationship. William and Camilla had met a couple of times for tea, and also for lunch. But it wasn't until February 2001 that they were seen in public together. The occasion was a London party to mark the tenth anniversary of Britain's Press Complaints Commission. The *Sun* newspaper called it 'the star-studded party of the year' and guests, apart from Prince Charles, Prince William and Camilla, included George Michael, former Spice Girl Geri Halliwell and supermodel Claudia Schiffer, plus a sprinkling of soap stars, senior politicians and most of the national newspaper editors.

A senior royal would usually arrive after all the other guests, but on this occasion Prince Charles and William arrived ten minutes before Camilla, who bought her son Tom and her sister Annabel along with her. Although they were in the same place, Charles and William stayed on one side of the room while Camilla stayed on the other side.

Alexander Chancellor wrote a piece in *The Guardian* on 17 February about anticipated challenges at the event: 'This "party of the year" was an acutely embarrassing event, and I regard it as a privilege not to have been included. I wouldn't have recognised a single actor there from a television soap opera, and I would have found it no fun to gawp at the Prince of Wales and his son William as they pirouetted nervously through the throng at a safe photo-graphic distance from the royal mistress, Camilla Parker Bowles, so would not have enjoyed it anyway.'

Early in 2002, the Queen had to face the loss of two much-loved members of her family. On 9 February her younger sister, Princess Margaret, died aged seventy-one. She had had a high profile among the royals but an uneasy life. A heavy drinker and smoker, towards the end of her life she suffered a period of poor health, including an accident with scalding bathwater and three strokes that left her partially paralysed. The fourth stroke during the afternoon before her death proved to be too much. Her heart began to fail and she was taken from her home in Kensington Palace to nearby King

Edward VII's Hospital where she died the following day with her children Lord Linley and Lady Sarah Chatto by her side. The Queen loved her rebellious sister. The day was also a sad memory of her father's death fifty years and three days previously.

Queen Elizabeth the Queen Mother passed away just a month later at the age of 101. She was adored by the Queen and was a key figure in Prince Charles's life. He was her favourite grandson and the two shared a close bond from the prince's early years. Nonetheless she refused to give him her 'seal of approval' to marry Camilla that he longed for and couldn't understand why he didn't just find 'space' in his marriage to Diana for Camilla and that way avoid a distasteful divorce. While it was thought that the Queen had by then resigned herself to an eventual marriage between Charles and Camilla, she reportedly pledged not to sanction it so long as her mother was alive.

Despite depriving him of what he wanted most, Charles put that aside and delivered an emotional eulogy at the funeral: 'For me, she meant everything, and I had dreaded, dreaded this moment along with, I know, countless others. Somehow, I never thought it would come. She seemed gloriously unstoppable and, since I was a child, I adored her. Her houses were always filled with an atmosphere of fun, laughter and affection, and I learnt so much from her of immense value to my life. Apart from anything else, she wrote such sparklingly wonderful letters, and her turn of phrase could be utterly memorable. Above all, she saw the funny side of life and we laughed until we cried – oh, how I shall miss her laugh and wonderful wisdom born of so much experience and an innate sensitivity to life. She was quite simply the most magical grandmother you could possibly have, and I was utterly devoted to her. Her departure has left an irreplaceable chasm in countless lives but, thank God, we are all the richer for the sheer joy of her presence and everything she stood for.'

Not long after the Queen Mother passed away, the Church of England lifted its ban on second marriages for divorced spouses subject to a priest's discretion. Moreover, the newly installed Archbishop of Canterbury, Dr Rowan Williams, announced that Charles and Camilla should be 'treated as any other couple' and that he would 'happily preside over their union'. The lifted ban was very significant, as Prince Charles knew that the public would not accept him marrying with just a civil ceremony.

Chapter 9

OPINIONS CAN DIFFER

Although many of Prince Charles's friends were supportive of his relationship with Camilla Parker Bowles, others were not and saw her as a mistress rather than a life partner and definitely not as a wife. One of these friends was Hugh van Cutsem. He and Charles became close friends in the 1960s when they were both at Cambridge University. Van Cutsem became a successful banker, landowner and horse breeder. He and his wife Emilie had four sons between 1973 and 1979, and Charles became godfather to Edward, the eldest, who was a pageboy when he married Diana in 1981. Charles had encouraged both Tom Parker Bowles and Edward van Cutsem to act as unofficial older brothers to William and Harry during their adolescence, and more so after they lost their mother. Charles was therefore naturally delighted when he heard that Edward was going to get married in November 2004. His bride was 24-year-old Lady Tamara Grosvenor, daughter of the 6th Duke of Westminster, the wealthy landowner and philanthropist. It was expected to be the society wedding of the year, with the Queen, Prince Philip, Prince William and Prince Harry among the 650 guests.

Hugh and Emilie had happily offered privacy in safe houses after the break-up of Charles's marriage, so he and Camilla could be together, but felt it would be inappropriate for Camilla and Charles to sit together during the wedding ceremony at Chester Cathedral. It underlined their view that a mere 'mistress' could not sit with a member of the Royal Family in public. At the time, Charles and Camilla were living like a married couple at Clarence House and Highgrove, but both the van Cutsems, who are committed Roman Catholics, and the Grosvenors insisted that the separation of Charles and Camilla was a matter of royal protocol.

It is believed that Prince William, whom Edward had asked to be best man, shocked his father when he told him that the seating arrangements were that Camilla would sit several rows behind him during the ceremony, that each of them had to arrive and leave separately (using different entrances) and take separate cars to go to the lavish celebrations afterwards. It was obvious that the seating arrangements alone would have been a demeaning embarrassment to Camilla, but Charles was in the difficult position of deciding whether he would support the woman he had loved for decades or one of his oldest and closest friends. After much anguish he pulled out of the wedding, saying he had to visit the families of Black Watch troops stationed in Iraq, an excuse that made it easier for Camilla to decline her invitation too.

The incident also reignited an old feud with the van Cutsems. Hugh had warned Prince Charles about Tom Parker Bowles's drug-taking habits that he felt could affect Charles's sons. Camilla was furious over the van Cutsem's allegations, although Tom later admitted to taking cocaine. The van Cutsems were subsequently removed from the prince's guest lists. They no longer received Christmas cards, nor were they included in the prince's shooting parties. Despite the embarrassment, Edward and his brothers remained on close terms with William and Harry, and a couple of years later there was a rapprochement when Charles invited the family to a choral concert in Norfolk. Hugh van Cutsem died on 2 September 2013, aged seventy-two. His funeral took place in Brentwood Cathedral, Essex. William and Harry attended, as did Prince Charles and Camilla. Times had changed.

Meanwhile, the then 87-year-old Major Shand had grown increasingly concerned that, having waited so long to marry his daughter, Charles's relationship with Camilla might be becoming stale and he might move on, leaving her in the lurch. He took Charles aside and was said to have told him: 'I want to meet my maker knowing my daughter's all right.' In other words, it was about time he proposed.

Major Shand's wish wasn't powerful enough on its own to prompt Charles to ask Camilla to marry him. But the death of the Queen Mother on 30 March 2002 had liberated the Queen to acknowledge the reality of Camilla and Charles's relationship without feeling she was going against her wishes. As the couple were bound together it then made sense for it to be formalised as soon as possible.

Even Prince Philip disapproved of the procrastination and wanted the marriage to happen, but his manner was rather hard-nosed and very unromantic. Instead, he reportedly kept telling Charles to stop dithering as his failure to marry again could become a constitutional crisis. There had also been growing pressure from MPs regarding the prince's spending on his unofficial partner. Camilla, however, was largely content just to be with her prince.

There were also snubs from other members of the Royal Family. As well as talking to the former Archbishop of Canterbury, Dr George Carey, who was positive about Charles marrying the woman he loved, the Queen also discussed the matter with Prince Andrew. She has always had a soft spot for Andrew, who seems to have a way of persuading her to do what he wants. This time, a senior insider told me, he had a treacherous request. 'He tried to persuade the Queen to block Charles marrying Camilla by being quite poisonous, mean, unhelpful and very nasty about Camilla.' His claims included that she was insufficiently aristocratic and that she was not to be trusted.

The same individual went on to say that 'when Diana was alive, through her friendship with Andrew's wife Sarah, she plotted with Andrew to try to push Prince Charles aside so Prince Andrew could become Regent to Prince William, who was then a teenager.

'They were dark and strange times, where paranoia became reality, and this was a worry. Andrew lobbied very hard with the hope that Charles would not become king when his mother died, and that William would wear the crown. His behaviour was very, very negative and extremely unpleasant to the Queen, who disagreed. I was told it was one of the rare occasions he didn't get his way. Nonetheless, he was apparently very angry he couldn't rule the country in some way. He remained so hostile to Camilla's emergence and acceptance that it's doubtful it has ever been forgiven.'

Decades later, it was a surprise for many when it was announced in 2022 that Charles would lend Andrew £7 million to help reach a settlement over accusations by Virginia Giuffre, formerly Roberts, that he sexually assaulted her when she was seventeen, something he has consistently denied. It was noted that the loan would be paid back when Andrew had received the money from the sale of his £17 million ski chalet in Verbier, Switzerland. Andrew was in desperate need of financial help as, at the time, he had only ten days in which to pay the estimated £10 million agreed compensation to Mrs Giuffre, otherwise he would not be able to avoid the case going to trial in New York with all the attendant undesirable publicity. In June 2022 Charles, along with Prince William, 'blocked' Andrew from taking part in the Queen's Platinum Jubilee and

Garter Day. Meanwhile, as time went by, the anti-Charles-and-Camilla mood softened. Sir Roy Strong noted in his diary for 2 March 2005, at the memorial service for Princess Alexandra's husband Sir Angus Ogilvy in St George's Chapel:

> Down the line came Camilla Parker Bowles, shorter than me with the usual Household black kit and wearing a huge sloping hat. She had a warmth and a twinkle in her eye and didn't give me the Diana seduction glance, which had once made me blush . . . I rather warmed to her but, poor thing, what a burden is about to come her way . . . it was a relief to see someone not attempting to be anything other than her own age and unashamed of her smile wrinkles. Also, there's no sign of entering the fashion stakes. Who knows but that she might be just the thing?

In retrospect Sir Roy was right, but it would still take a long time for the Royal Family to agree. Princess Anne, for example, reportedly gave Camilla the cold shoulder. It was little consolation that Anne had also had a frosty relationship with Princess Diana, who she had no time for before she married Charles nor for Sarah, the Duchess of York. Her relationship with Camilla was particularly awkward as they had both been involved with the same man, Andrew Parker Bowles. Like many people who didn't know Anne well, Camilla found her frosty demeanour difficult and somewhat unnerving to cope with for several years.

Although only three years in age separated the two women, their experience of being a member of what is sometimes called 'The Firm', a term that originated with King George VI, was very different. Anne started her life as a working royal at eighteen and her sense of duty and work ethic are an intrinsic part of her character. Camilla didn't formally join the Royal Family until she was fifty-seven. Anne was for many years opposed to the idea of Camilla being granted the title of queen consort when Charles succeeded to the throne. She once claimed: 'Camilla will never be a true queen.' It's curious, however, that the two strong-minded women have maintained a warm friendship with Andrew Parker Bowles, despite his unfaithfulness. He is godfather to Anne's daughter, Zara Phillips, and Camilla asked Prince Charles to be godfather to Tom, her son with Andrew.

Time has proven to be a healer and Anne has seen for herself how hard Camilla has worked for the monarchy and her sense of duty. She has appreciated this and, as one of the hardest-working royals herself, gradually became more amenable. Horses were a common interest. The warmth has increased since Prince Philip died, as the priority to be there for the Queen and try to keep the monarchy stable and respected took precedence compared to small differences in the past.

By chance, Anne's decision to divorce her husband Mark Phillips and subsequently marry Commander Timothy Lawrence, with whom she had been having an affair in Scotland, created a precedent for Prince Charles. It made royal divorce seem not so shocking.

Prince Charles knew there would be no encouragement from Andrew or Anne to marry Camilla. Nor are Charles and Prince Edward particularly close, and for a time his wife Sophie was believed to be unhappy about the wedding because she didn't want to curtsy to Camilla. This was later denied. The key issue that really held Prince Charles back was that he was deeply damaged by the last few years of his marriage to Diana and, as a result, was in no hurry to get married again. He was also aware of the public affection towards Diana coupled with its hostility towards Camilla, whom they held responsible for breaking a marriage they wrongly believed was a fairy tale.

A quick marriage to Camilla could therefore be counter-productive and he felt he should wait until the mood began to change. Another priority was that he wanted to give his sons plenty of time to get to know Camilla and feel relaxed in her company. Added to this he is a naturally cautious man not given to making impulsive decisions. In the end he waited a full eight years after Diana's death. In retrospect, he was surely right to take the long view and wait until the public had warmed, however slowly, to Camilla and opinion polls began to show that a majority of the British people now approved of the marriage – which it did as long as Camilla did not become queen. As for Camilla, she stayed content with the status quo. Gradually the changing circumstances and her continued impeccable conduct helped create a sense that the world might not end if Charles and Camilla were to marry.

Chapter 10

A LASTING MARRIAGE

A rather nervous Prince Charles told his sons early in 2005 that he wanted to marry Camilla. It wasn't a surprise, but nor was it going to be easy for the princes to accept the woman their much-loved mother, Princess Diana, had blamed for the break-up of her marriage. You could tell William was glad his father was happy just by looking at his face while Harry was more effusive. At the time, he was able to see things from other people's point of view and was quoted as saying: 'To be honest, [Camilla] has always been very close to me and William. She's not a wicked stepmother. Look at the position she's coming into. Don't feel sorry for me and William, feel sorry for her. She's a wonderful woman and she's made our father very, very happy, which is the most important thing. William and I love her to bits.'

Unlike any other 56-year-old man, as the heir to the throne, Charles first needed to get the Queen's blessing to marry Camilla. He finally proposed during his and Camilla's New Year break at Birkhall, the hunting lodge near Balmoral Castle, where the Queen spends her summer holidays and which Charles inherited from the Queen Mother.

The lodge was built in 1715 and acquired by Prince Albert in 1852 when he bought the Balmoral estate for his wife, Queen Victoria. It was subsequently handed down the royal line and used by the Queen's parents, the Duke and Duchess of York, later King George VI and his wife Queen Elizabeth, for family holidays with their children Princess Elizabeth and Princess Margaret. Princess Elizabeth and Prince Philip spent some of their honeymoon there. The lodge has always been somewhere Charles retreats to and is important to him both historically and personally. It is also a place Camilla has grown to love and where they chose to spend their honeymoon. They also self-isolated there in March 2020 when the prince tested positive for Covid-19.

The news of the engagement was leaked by royal author and commentator Robert Jobson in the London *Evening Standard* on 10 February 2005, but nothing was spoilt. Although a target date had been arranged, everyone involved knew the secret was unlikely to hold. It triggered differing reactions. Some thought it was about time Prince Charles did the honourable thing; others, largely fans of Diana, were outraged and showed it any way they could. The traditionalists believed that the marriage would destroy the monarchy and Charles would never become king.

Camilla had accepted Prince Charles's proposal and, after a 35-year relationship, the formal announcement that Prince Charles and Camilla were engaged to marry was at last confirmed by Clarence House that same day. Whatever they felt inside, William and Harry behaved with dignity and responded quickly and positively with a joint statement: 'We are both very happy for our father and Camilla and we wish them all the luck in the future.'

Mark Bolland explains: 'It was an extraordinary thing to wait so long for someone. I think they both waited because it was real love.' Back in 1981, Prince Charles had been ambiguous about declaring his love for Diana. He had famously retorted 'whatever in love means' when the couple faced the media for their post-engagement interview. Mark Bolland was confident that this time the prince had no such qualms: 'We all define love in different ways and clearly with Camilla he had found somebody who understood him, loves him and accepts him as he is, including his inevitable emotional baggage (which we all have) and he clearly loves her.'

It was one thing for the brothers to accept Camilla because she made their father happy, but it would be quite another should she try to replace their mother. The marriage of his father to Camilla would make it awkward for Harry to open his heart in the future about his grief at losing his mother. Years later, it was revealed that he still desperately grieved for her and was filled with resentment over her premature death. It painted a rather different picture. Harry told me when I was writing his biography in 2017 that, instead, he 'buried his head in the sand' and tried to forget what had happened.

Although at the time Prince Harry managed to put on a good front, inside he was falling apart. It wasn't until 2016 that he confessed that the previous few years had been a real struggle, that he'd bottled up his emotions for two decades, but following William's advice he sought professional help when he was twenty-eight.

At the time he felt trapped by his royal life as well as grief-stricken, and he badly needed someone to talk to, but it was hard to find anyone emotionally available he felt he could lean on. It was not a subject he felt able to raise with his father, who was very happy with Camilla, and had made a new, more contented life for himself. Harry was pleased for him, but how could he pour his heart out about how much he missed his mother, longing to feel at peace in her arms, when he knew full well how devastated she had been by Camilla's presence. Nor could he open his heart to the Queen and the Duke of Edinburgh, who had mixed feelings about the charismatic but troubled princess, and also firmly believed in maintaining a stiff upper lip no matter what. Harry, like his mother, does not.

The engagement announcement itself was carefully timed to coincide with the couple attending a glitzy gala dinner at Windsor Castle that evening. Camilla looked stunning in a fiery red V-necked dress enhanced by three rows of pearls, but the main interest focused on her new platinum and diamond engagement ring. It was a 1930s art deco design with a five-carat central square-cut diamond and three smaller ones on either side, worth about £100,000. It had belonged to the Queen Mother and was passed down to the Queen, who in turn gave it to Camilla.

When asked by the assembled reporters how she felt, Camilla said jovially that she was just coming down to earth. The inevitable next question was: did Prince Charles go down on one knee? She replied, 'Of course,' but it was one of her wily replies that wasn't totally accepted as an answer. The Queen's generous gift proved that she had finally accepted Charles's determination to marry Camilla. One wonders if her new-born sympathy reminded her of her own insistence on marrying Philip, with whom she fell in love when she was only thirteen. Her mother, then queen consort, felt her daughter could do much better than a poverty-stricken, homeless young man with a dysfunctional background, but gave up trying when Princess Elizabeth instantly dismissed every wealthy aristocrat or royal suggested to her as an alternative.

Camilla's friend Gyles Brandreth felt the decision was more pragmatic. 'I had lunch with Prince Philip in the week when Prince Charles and Camilla were married, and it was clear to me that he was very happy that it was all going to be regularised. The Queen and Prince Philip are from a different generation and for people of that generation you have to get married.'

Journalists and photographers rushed to Windsor to get words and pictures to write the beginning of a happy ending and congratulations came pouring in from around the world. The Queen and the Duke of Edinburgh made sure the public knew they were now supporting the couple's decision in a statement from Buckingham Palace: 'The Duke of Edinburgh and I are very happy that the Prince of Wales and Mrs Parker Bowles are to marry.' Tony Blair, then prime minister, sent a goodwill message on behalf of the government. The then Archbishop of Canterbury, Dr Rowan Williams, congratulated them on taking 'this important step'.

Prince Charles spoke about his engagement in glowing terms: 'Mrs Parker Bowles and I are absolutely delighted. It will be a very special day for us and our families.' One of the most important phone calls for him to make was to Lord Carey, who had been the previous Archbishop of Canterbury and had tried to encourage the Queen to support Charles's wish to marry Camilla. 'I was in retirement and visiting New Zealand at the time giving speeches when I received a late-night call from Prince Charles,' he said. 'He sounded very excited as he said the wedding was going ahead and thanked me for my support. He also asked if I would do the first reading and I said I would be delighted to.'

A whirlwind of rumours swept the country after the announcement was made about what kind of marriage service they would have and what Camilla would be called. It was soon made clear that as a sign of respect Camilla wouldn't take the same title as Diana, Princess of Wales, and would instead be Duchess of Cornwall. The other question was whether or not she would become Her Royal Highness. On 12 February 2005 Kenneth Rose wrote in his diary: 'The Camilla engagement rumbles on. Press comment extends from the mildly approving to the vindictively hostile.'

Having waited an exceptionally long time before they got engaged, they wanted to marry as soon as possible and the date was quickly set for 8 April 2005, just two months later. The announcement that they would have a civil marriage ceremony at Windsor Castle followed by a service of blessing at St George's Chapel proved it was going to be a royal wedding unlike any other. There were glitches almost immediately: shortly after announcing where the ceremony would be, they rather embarrassingly had to move the civil marriage out of the castle and hold it instead at Windsor Guildhall, a modest register office on Windsor High Road that was licensed for civil ceremonies. Apparently, no one realised that Windsor Castle didn't have a licence to hold wedding ceremonies; if it did, it would have to be available for anyone to tie the knot there.

Gyles Brandreth confessed that Prince Philip said firmly to him, 'It was all your fault.' When Brandreth was Conservative MP for Chester, he successfully piloted a private member's bill through Parliament that became the Marriage Act 1994 and allowed marriages to be solemnised in certain 'approved premises'. 'Prince Philip said I had caused all this trouble and Prince Charles's original choice of venue had to be changed because of my legislation.'

The civil ceremony also avoided any controversy over Charles – who will when he becomes king also be the Supreme Governor of the Church of England – marrying a divorcée in a religious ceremony. It had taken more than twenty years of debate for the Church of England to finally give its blessing in 2002 to the remarriage of divorced people in church, subject to a priest's discretion. Dr Rowan Williams stated: 'These arrangements have my strong support and are consistent with Church of England guidelines concerning remarriage, which the Prince of Wales fully accepts as a committed Anglican and as prospective Supreme Governor of the Church of England.'

The result was that Prince Charles had to pay £285 to hire the Ascot Room within the Guildhall. It was hardly fit for a future king, although the name might have fleetingly reminded Camilla of happy times at Royal Ascot. The Ascot Room had black stains on the brown carpet, various electrical junction boxes on the walls and a sticker left above the light switch that read: 'Help conserve energy. Please turn off the lights.' A single brass chandelier hung in the centre of the room and fourteen rather antique paintings hung on the beige-coloured walls. The only picture of a monarch was one of Queen Victoria. A spokeswoman for the Royal Borough of Windsor and Maidenhead said: 'The prince and Camilla have asked that there be no extra cost to council tax-payers for their marriage. There will be no flowers from us or anything else on the day.' A spokesman from Clarence House stated that there would not even be an official photograph of the ceremony released to the public. Instead, they declared, 'It will be a completely private event.'

Although some people disapproved of a divorced Prince Charles marrying a divorced woman, it also created a precedent. One result was that there was very little reaction when Prince Harry, then sixth in line to the throne, married divorcée Meghan Markle, whose first husband was Trevor Engelson, an American film and TV producer. They had a full ceremony in St George's Chapel at Windsor Castle while Prince Charles only had a blessing.

Another obstacle occurred just five days before the due date, forcing the wedding to be postponed for twenty-four hours, showing that even Charles's wedding day came second to his royal responsibilities. Pope John Paul II died on 2 April and Prince Charles's duty was to fly to Italy on the original date of his wedding to represent the Queen at the funeral in the Vatican. There was no way of getting out of it. Camilla understood and accepted the change without a fuss. As a result, the 720 guests had to be contacted individually, giving them five days' notice to turn up on Saturday, rather than Friday. Almost no one dropped out. As fate had it, Friday turned out to be a cold, windy day with hailstones. Saturday, although still windy, was bright and sunny.

The change of date gave the royal florist Simon Lycett a nail-biting day. He subsequently told *Hello* magazine: 'We always try to have our flowers on point for the actual day and time of the event. There was a bit of a white-knuckle ride to try and make sure that everybody was keeping everything fresh and perfect . . . [as] the flowers all had to last another day.'

Camilla is usually a calm, easy-going and capable woman, but understandably she became increasingly stressed as the wedding day approached. An insider told me that one of her worries was whether the eight years she and Charles had waited between Diana's death and their engagement was enough to calm the unstable, precarious relationship between Charles and his sons and those members of the public who were still grieving for Diana.

Another anxiety was how the press might gloat if no one turned up to cheer them. Camilla had waited so long for this special day that the final build-up made her increasingly nervous and emotional. She hated, but to some extent had become used to, individuals shouting obscenities at her when she was on a royal engagement, but she dreaded the thought of people turning up outside the register office just to heckle. It would be too distressing on her wedding day.

Prince Charles adhered to the tradition of spending the night apart from his bride-to-be and stayed at Highgrove in Gloucestershire with Princes William and Harry. Camilla's close friend Lucia Santa Cruz stayed with her at Ray Mill House for a few days before the wedding. Camilla had been ill for a week and feeling so unwell made it harder for her to cope with the stress. Lucia recalls: 'She was so ill with an appalling cold and sinusitis that had given her a very croaky voice. I made her some chicken soup and told her that everyone gets well if they have chicken soup.'

For the last night before the wedding Camilla moved to Clarence House. Her sister Annabel and daughter Laura stayed there with her. Lucia was extremely worried about her health: 'She was still so ill we didn't know if she could make the wedding.' On the wedding day morning Camilla, who in a few hours would no longer be Mrs Parker Bowles, refused to get out of bed. A friend said it was 'a case of internal panic' and it took a lot of gentle coaxing from her sister and daughter, Lucia and her dresser to finally persuade her to get up with only just enough time to spare.

Charles and Camilla had given a tremendous amount of thought to their wedding and, as it was the second marriage for both of them, they wanted it to be low-key. Camilla chose not to wear a tiara as she had done when she married Major Andrew Parker-Bowles in July 1973.

Barriers were put up on both sides of the road close to the register office the night before the wedding in the hope that there would be enough onlookers for them to be needed. Very few individuals camped outside overnight to get the best view of the couple and only a few arrived early in the morning. But just as hearts began plummeting that hardly anyone would turn up, people began to arrive en masse, filling the pavements and obviously excited at the chance of seeing the royal couple. It was guessed that the crowd amounted to about 20,000, nowhere near the number that would turn up for a traditional royal wedding but a good enough show to prove to her critics that she definitely wasn't being snubbed by the public.

The heir to the throne and his obviously nervous bride arrived on time for the 12.30pm service in a Rolls-Royce Phantom VI lent to them by the Queen. A second car full of police officers followed. Just as Charles and Camilla stepped out of the Rolls, the sun appeared in what had been a grey sky. It was a welcome sign for the couple as they walked straight into the register office. The few boos were almost drowned out by the cheering majority shouting good wishes and waving the Union Jack. Someone in the crowd shouted, 'If Prince Charles is going to be king, I think we want a happy king and Camilla will make him that.' Neither of them responded.

Charles, however, must have been disappointed that the Queen and the Duke of Edinburgh decided it would be inappropriate to attend the civil service, Her Majesty putting her sense of duty first rather than making an exception for her son.

Although the overall intention for the wedding was to be restrained, Camilla's outfits managed to be both discreet and dazzling, an achievement that even the normally critical press praised. It was just as well as, if anything didn't go right, it would have been seized upon. Even so some newspapers, like the *Sunday Times*, couldn't resist a few sniping comments: 'If the ghost of a previous Princess of Wales hovered over Windsor, the couple didn't notice' and 'This was not a wedding where guests buy the couple three toasters and a duvet, but an Australian state did rename a garden bench after the couple.'

Camilla had chosen Robinson Valentine, a luxury fashion house now solely run by Anna Valentine, to make one outfit for the ceremony and another for the blessing. Work began on 21 February and finished a few days before the wedding. Camilla had two meetings to discuss what she wanted, followed by eight fittings.

Her outfit for the ceremony was an embroidered oyster silk coat over an oyster-coloured silk chiffon dress with a below-knee hemline that allowed her to show her slender legs. She had pinned a Prince of Wales feathers brooch, with diamonds and single grey pearl, on her coat's lapel. (She subsequently wore the dress again, at the opening of the National Assembly of Wales in 2007.) Her other choice of jewellery was earrings with pearl drops and a diamond bracelet. Her wide-brimmed cream hat overlaid with ivory French lace and trimmed with feathers came from Philip Treacy, one of the Royal Family's favourite milliners. Her beige suede pumps with a 5cm heel were from LK Bennett and she carried a leather clutch bag by Launer, the royal bag makers.

Prince Charles was dapper in a black morning suit with grey pinstripe trousers made by Anderson and Shepherd, a grey waistcoat, and stiff-collar shirt with a blue and yellow tie. As usual he had a flower in his buttonhole. This time he chose a hellebore, a flower that symbolises serenity, tranquillity and peace, from his garden at Highgrove. It was an outfit very different to the naval commander's uniform he wore at St Paul's Cathedral in July 1981 when he married Diana.

The Ascot Room had been prepared for the ceremony, but its size limited the numbers and only twenty-eight family members and friends were ushered in by a rather tense Sir Michael Peat, the prince's private secretary. Despite the lack of space, the couple, who are both keen horticulturists, couldn't resist filling the room with flowers. Camilla carried a small posy of yellow, purple and white primroses, along with lily of the valley, that has a spiritual meaning of rebirth, devotion, humility and happiness, and a traditional sprig of myrtle that is expected to bring luck and fidelity. The ceremony was conducted by Clair Williams, the superintendent registrar. It took just twenty minutes to break centuries of royal tradition.

The guests included both of the couple's children, Tom and Laura Parker Bowles, and Princes William and Harry. William and Harry wore black morning suits with grey and black pinstripe trousers. Harry's waistcoat was grey and William's pale blue, and both of them wore tiepins given to them by the Queen that had once belonged to her mother. It was a challenging day for the two princes, who must have thought about their late mother, but their jovial smiles showed they were coping well enough. The wedding also marked a more serious phase in both their lives. Harry would begin officer training at the Royal Military Academy, Sandhurst, in a month and William would be going back to St Andrews University in Scotland to revise for his final exams in geography.

Prince William was best man and responsible for keeping the wedding rings safe. He and Tom Parker Bowles also acted as witnesses. In keeping with a royal tradition that dates back to 1923 when the Queen's parents – then known as Prince Albert, Duke of York, and Lady Elizabeth Bowes-Lyon – married, the couple's wedding rings were crafted from 22-carat Welsh gold from the Glogau St David's mine in Bontddu. The design of the wedding rings was by Wartski, who have held the Royal Warrant to the Prince of Wales since 1979. Ironically, it is also the jeweller where King Edward VII bought presents for his mistress, Camilla's great-grandmother, Alice Keppel. There is no royal tradition for men to wear a wedding ring; Prince Philip and Prince William chose not to. Prince Charles and Harry wanted to, but Charles wears his on the shortest finger of his left hand alongside the gold signet ring that he has worn since the 1970s.

The ceremony was a huge relief for Camilla's father, Bruce Shand, who had been worried about his daughter for years fearing that she would be left on the shelf. At eighty-eight he was far from well but had put off going to see his doctor. You could tell from his proud, happy face that he felt it was worth waiting for. When he kept his appointment four days after the wedding, he was diagnosed with pancreatic cancer and died fourteen months later.

Camilla's younger sister, Annabel Elliot, and brother, Mark Shand, were there too. Ruth Powys, now Ruth Ganesh, who joined forces with Mark, a travel writer and adventurer, the year before the wedding and is now Chief Executive of the Elephant Family charity that he set up, said: 'He was absolutely thrilled about the wedding. It was a very happy moment for him. He even saved his portion of the wedding cake in a tin, often wondering whether he should eat it or never eat it.'

The moment the ceremony was over, Camilla, who walked into the register office as Mrs Parker Bowles, would in future be addressed as 'Her Royal Highness, The Duchess of Cornwall'. She took Charles's arm as they walked out into the street to cheering crowds and a jazz band playing 'Congratulations'. Charles had at long last married the woman he loved. There was no time for a walkabout as Camilla had to change her outfit for the blessing ceremony. Instead, she waved to the crowds as she was about to climb into the Rolls, accidentally hitting her hat as she did so. The newly-weds were then driven back to Windsor Castle for a Service of Prayer and Dedication at St George's Chapel where the Queen and Prince Philip were waiting.

For the service, Camilla wore an equally elegant floor-length hand-embroidered pale blue and gold coat over a matching chiffon dress. She had diamond flower pendant earrings, and a Philip Treacy-designed headdress adorned with gold-leafed feathers and Swarovski diamonds. Her shoes were again by LK Bennett, but this time, pale-grey silk pumps. She later loaned them to Laura, who wore them the following year when she married Harry Lopes.

Modest-looking private coaches took most of the guests to Windsor Castle. Prince Harry sat in a front seat and grinned at the crowds with his nose pressed against the window. It was very windy and many of the female guests held on tightly to their elaborate hats as they walked into the chapel. As well as the Royal Family, there was foreign royalty, the Prime Minister Tony Blair, other party leaders, religious representatives, comedian Rowan Atkinson, author Jilly Cooper, rock star Phil Collins and broadcaster Jonathan Dimbleby, who wrote the authorised biography of Prince Charles. Camilla's former husband Andrew, accompanied by his second wife Rosemary Dickinson, was there too. Andrew married her a year after his divorce from Camilla and lived happily with her until her death from cancer in January 2010 aged sixty-nine, two weeks after Andrew's seventieth birthday. Camilla is known to have been very supportive during Rosemary's long battle with cancer. Neither she nor her first husband bear grudges and Camilla in particular believes in turning former intimate relationships into friendships.

Charles took the opportunity to be unrestrained and had festooned the castle with 35,000 cut daffodils, a symbol perhaps of his strong connection with Wales. The decorations in the chapel were also breathtaking and included three flowering trees planted in wooden boxes specially made by a Highgrove carpenter. One was a flowering crab apple tree named after Edmund Hilary's conquest of Everest in the Queen's coronation year, 1953. Another was a Great White Blossom full of exquisite white flowers and the third a Prunus Hai Hauku, an ancient Japanese cherry blossom tree. Other flowers included cowslips, fritillaries, violas and narcissi that epitomised Prince Charles's love of flowering meadows and would be replanted in the garden at Highgrove after the ceremony.

The televised blessing was given by the Archbishop of Canterbury, Dr Rowan Williams, who had chosen to wear a simple choir dress, the ecclesiastical equivalent of smart casual. He told the author and commentator Lord Bragg that it was the first blessing he had conducted. The Dean of Windsor, David Connor, was also present. The music included Bach's Cantata *Nun Komm, der Heiden Heiland* and excerpts from Handel's *Water Music*, which was played by members of the Philharmonia orchestra, of which the Prince of Wales is patron. A young Russian contralto, Ekaterina Semenchuk, was specially flown over from St Petersburg to sing a Russian Creed as a wedding present from the Mariinsky Theatre Trust, of which Prince Charles is both a patron and benefactor.

Three of the couple's favourite hymns, 'Immortal Invisible',

'Love Divine All Souls Excelling' and 'Praise My Soul the King of Heaven', were sung, as was a verse of the national anthem. This was followed by a specially composed fanfare by the Welsh composer Alun Hoddinott.

The service's most solemn moment was when Charles and Camilla joined the congregation in reading from the 1662 Book of Common Prayer: 'We acknowledge and bewail our manifold sins and wickedness, which we, from time to time, most grievously have committed, by thought, word and deed' – lines that caused somewhat sarcastic comment in the next day's newspapers. Meanwhile Prince Harry, who at the time had a knack for taking the sting out of tricky situations, decided to ensure the Queen felt at ease in what could have been an awkward occasion. He kept making her laugh by imitating the facial expression she uses when seeing something she disapproves of.

Once the blessing was over, the newly-weds walked down the West Steps of the chapel with banks of glorious daffodils and jonquils on either side. Charles had looked rather serious but suddenly started to beam. At one point he looked at his bride in a way that revealed he, at last, knew what true love meant. Camilla too looked radiant and slightly disbelieving. It was as if a huge weight had at last been lifted from both their shoulders. 'I just can't believe it. I just can't believe it,' she kept saying. Significantly there was no post-ceremony public kiss at the top of the steps, which might have disappointed the 2,000 well-wishers who had been admitted by ticket into the castle grounds. Perhaps it was significant enough that the Queen smiled at Camilla several times. The couple did a quick walkabout shaking hands with as many individuals as they could reach.

Just outside the chapel stood representatives from the regiments Prince Charles is associated with and most of the charities he is involved in. Camilla was greeted by representatives from the

Wiltshire Bobby Van trust, a home security service for the elderly and vulnerable, and the National Osteoporosis Society, of which she was president.

The duchess's new assistant private secretary, Amanda MacManus, along with other members of staff, was waiting for the newly-weds to come into Windsor Castle when the ceremony was over. She clearly remembers: 'We all stood waiting to greet them, and they both came up the stairs crying. For the first time we said: "Hello, your Royal Highness." It was a very powerful moment and so emotional for us all. In the end we were all crying. There had been so much anxiety and tension but now it was over and they could relax and enjoy things. It is fairly terrifying if you've got tens of millions of people watching your every move on television.'

A two-hour reception hosted by the Queen followed in the castle's state apartments. If Charles had hoped for a gourmet display from one of the country's top caterers, he would have been disappointed. Instead, there was a relatively modest spread for such a significant occasion, catered for by Palace staff. Few of the guests were able to sit down while having an afternoon tea of smoked salmon, potted shrimp or roast venison sandwiches, followed by miniature scones with clotted cream and jam and strawberry tartlets.

The wedding cake was made by Dawn Blunden of Sophisticake and more modest than the one supplied when Charles married Diana. Instead of a five-foot high, five-tier cake, the newly-weds chose a large square cake with the shape of a small tent on top that weighed around 17 stone (110kg). The ingredients included 383lb (175kg) dried fruit, 139lb (63kg) sugar, 139lb (63kg) flour, 139lb (63kg) butter, 1080 eggs, 36 bottles of alcohol, twenty of which was brandy, 20lb (100kg) marzipan and covered with 220lb (100kg) sugarpaste. It took approximately 130 hours to coat and decorate the cake. Delicate sugar roses, leeks, daffodils and thistles (to depict England, Scotland and Wales) lay alongside royal iced lattice work, four of the prince's royal crests and the letter C, representing both Charles and Camilla, was all hand-iced in royal icing. Sophisticake were also asked to bake 2,500 slices of additional cake for special commemorative tins. To cut the wedding cake, the couple used the Prince of Wales's naval sword, which had belonged to his great-grandfather, King George V, and was normally used for investitures.

By chance the wedding date coincided with the Grand National at Aintree, and after the archbishop's blessing, the Queen, who looked striking in a cream coat, dress and hat, had quietly withdrawn from the ceremony into a side room with other racing fans to watch one of her favourite events. She emerged to make a speech at the reception. 'I have two very important announcements to make,' she began. 'I know you will want to know who was the winner of the Grand National. It was Hedgehunter.' This was met by immense applause. She waited for it to die down before turning to her son and his new wife and continuing: 'Having cleared Becher's Brook and the Chair and all kinds of other terrible obstacles, they have come through and I'm very proud and wish them well. My son is home and dry with the woman he loves. They are now on the home straight; the happy couple are now in the winner's enclosure.' The speech was a great success and although it wasn't effusive about her new daughter-in-law, it was complimentary enough. A positive feeling also seeped into the professional wedding photographs. The Duke of Edinburgh smiled mischievously while the Queen looked relieved and happy.

Prince Charles's speech was very emotional, especially when he toasted his new bride, saying: 'My darling Camilla, I can't believe that you married me.' He went on: 'She has stood with me through thick and thin and [her] optimism and humour have seen me through.'

The wedding had been a great success, described by one newspaper as a 'Fairy Tale for Grown-Ups'. Soon after 6pm the couple left Windsor for a low-key honeymoon at Birkhall. They drove off in a Bentley that had been decorated by Princes William and Harry. The words 'Prince' and 'Duchess' were sprayed on either side of the windscreen and 'Just Married' written on the back. Bunches of red, white and yellow heart-shaped metallic balloons were tied to the car, which was thought to have been Prince Harry's idea.

The car took them to RAF Northolt for the flight to Aberdeen. Their choice of honeymoon may have lacked the glitz of Charles's cruise around the Mediterranean with Princess Diana, but the peace and beauty of the Scottish Highlands and Balmoral (he once described it as 'a unique haven of cosiness and character') were more to his taste and somewhere he and Camilla could share their love of long country walks and fishing in the River Muick, which flows at the bottom of Birkhall's sloping garden.

It marked the end of one very long chapter of their love story and the beginning of a very different new one.

Chapter 11

HUGE CHANGES AT FIFTY-SEVEN

Following the ceremony the prince's new bride, HRH Camilla, The Duchess of Cornwall, was the most senior female royal after the Queen. As their wedding was unlike any other senior royal marriage, it is understandable that their honeymoon could be equally idiosyncratic. While most couples choose to spend their time luxuriating in each other's company, Camilla invited her sister Annabel Elliot and her close friend Lucia Santa Cruz to join them.

They all went to church the following day without worrying about the reaction they might have. Lucia remembers that the congregation was really enthusiastic to see them. 'It was such a welcome for her first day as a wife that Annabel and I cried,' she said. 'The honeymoon itself was so lovely throughout too because they were so happy. Prince Charles is one of my oldest friends. He went through a very, very difficult stage of his life [in his first marriage to Diana]. Camilla saved him. He looks transformed. Camilla was just what he needed.'

It was proof of sorts that the carefully planned, unprecedented campaign Mark Bolland, aided by Amanda MacManus, managed to execute had worked and successfully led to the pathway for their marriage. Prince Charles was now at his favourite place with the love of his life.

Camilla has often called Prince Charles a 'workaholic' and she isn't wrong. He works on behalf of the country and Commonwealth every day, from early morning often until well after midnight, and regularly falls asleep at his desk. So it was no surprise that there were various official engagements tucked into their honeymoon, including opening a playground in nearby Ballater. Camilla wasn't exactly going in at the deep end, but they were starting as they meant to go on.

Nor was it going to be easy. Camilla was very familiar with Charles's private life but less informed about his working days. It has been said that the first time she was asked to do some charity work she replied that she had an appointment on one day and was having tea with a friend on another, so could it be postponed for a week or so? No wonder her close friend Lucia was initially concerned about how she would adapt. 'When she married Prince Charles, I think she thought she wouldn't have to change her life very much and assumed she would take on one or two charities but would be able to relax and read in a happy and comfortable place. But getting involved with various different charities has really motivated her and she really cared about what she has been doing. It has stimulated her to do more and more and more. I don't think she or anyone understood how demanding it was going to be when she took on the job. I think it came as quite a surprise in the beginning. Yet she's got extraordinary focus for someone who appears to be very relaxed. And if she's going to do something she's going to do it well. I think the work gives her a real sense of achievement, which I don't think she was expecting.'

What surprised many of the people who know Camilla well was how, at fifty-seven, she could completely change her life. Some put it down to her love of Prince Charles. Camilla's long-time friend, the actress Dame Judi Dench, told me: 'I always think it is such a tribute to her, who didn't have a career or do much work, suddenly has to do all these engagements. Her work level is extraordinary. She even keeps up with Prince Charles and he works non-stop. It's her marriage that carries her through and gives her fantastic energy, which adds strength to both of them. There can be people you are in awe of and feel great respect for, but you generally feel restrained when you talk to them. But with her there is no kind of reticence, and you can treat her as a friend.'

Camilla was encouraged to take on royal duties for the first time. As this included accompanying her husband on engagements abroad, which he very much wanted to happen, she had the additional challenge of overcoming her fear of flying. Early on it was far from easy and she was also known to shiver when she did a walkabout in case someone in the crowd would shout abuse at her.

In addition, she would have to get used to not staying in any one home for long. Depending on the season and events, she and Prince Charles would move from Clarence House in London to Highgrove House in Gloucestershire, Birkhall in Aberdeenshire, and Llwynywermod in Carmarthenshire. A year after their marriage, Prince Charles extended his property portfolio by purchasing a rural farmhouse in Viscri, a small village in Transylvania, after falling in love with Romania during an official visit in 1998. He is, however, rarely there for more than a few days a year and rents the guesthouse out to the public most of the time. Other aspects of royal life were easy for Camilla, like remembering people's names and making small talk. According to Amanda MacManus, 'She always remembers faces, names, situations, dates and times.'

Prince Charles's life was equally transformed but in different ways. The intermittent loneliness that he had felt since childhood was lifted on his wedding day. Camilla was now officially his rock – someone he could trust to talk to about the inevitable pressures of being heir to the throne. Long official trips abroad would be different with Camilla by his side too, and something to share, but at the beginning of their marriage she often went home early through exhaustion, or to see her family. Despite that she supported him, boosted his self-esteem, giggled at the same things, even in public, and above all accepted him for who he is.

Jude Kelly, CEO and founder of WOW (Women of the World) Foundation has got to know Camilla very well. She says: 'It's very obvious she loves [Prince Charles] for who he is and what he is and has made a huge difference in his life. He was an absolute wreck, and she has saved him because she gave him tremendous support and encouragement. They also seem to bring out the best in each other, and that's exactly what one wants. She looks as if she has the security of being very loved and knows how to give love. It's fascinating because she went through such a terrible time when she was described as the most disliked and wicked woman in the world. And yet she managed to come through it. I know she said it's because of her family and her friends who loved her, but nonetheless, it's very interesting that she managed to overcome all that without losing the essence of herself.'

After the honeymoon comes reality when differences in lifestyles rise to the surface. When Prince Charles married Camilla, he also became stepfather to her daughter Laura and son Tom, to whom he was already godfather. Tom married fashion editor Sarah Buys that September. Princes Charles, William and Harry attended the wedding. Camilla in turn became stepmother to William and Harry, an awkward position but one she has tried hard to handle. After the wedding it became clear that Princes William and Harry weren't as keen on Charles's second wife as it appeared but were just being polite before and at the wedding. Instead, both William and Harry had arguments with their father that I've been told were 'hardly respectful'.

It is always difficult to take on the role of stepmother and William and Harry presented Camilla with an almost impossible challenge. They were both determined to hold on to their mother's legacy and didn't want their landscape to change with another woman taking her place, whatever she was like. They hugely missed the joyous way Diana embraced them but wouldn't dream of letting Camilla do the same. Charles had moved on and found happiness, which was largely out of range for his sons. The two princes had everything that money could buy but little emotional experience of being part of a relaxed and loving family. Living with parents who were increasingly at loggerheads had left its mark. Perhaps partially because of the turmoil at home the princes built up their own strong bond. In addition, their position in the Royal Family made it difficult for them to find out what being part of an ordinary family was like.

Sleepovers could only take place if the homes were first inspected by Royal Protection Officers, who then hung around, which in itself was embarrassing. Harry also told me when we spoke in 2018 that he had difficulty judging whether people liked him for who he was or for his position in the Royal Family. A complex combination for any stepmother.

Charles was used to having members of staff doing everything for him. He never has to worry about paying the London congestion charge, programming his day, sorting out issues with his computer and all the other mundane tasks that commoners are required to perform. Camilla, on the other hand, a single mother of two, was used to being there for her children; she ran her house and for years was wary of going out, even to the supermarket, in case she was verbally attacked. Charles never eats lunch; Camilla

Alice Keppel.

Camilla and her sister Annabel
as bridesmaids.

Prince Charles with Lucia Santa Cruz in April 1970, after they
had been to see a play in London's West End. It was during that
year that she introduced Charles to her friend Camilla Shand.

Charles and Camilla together at a polo match in 1972.

Camilla's wedding to Andrew Parker Bowles took place on 4 July 1973, after Charles went on a Royal Navy mission to the Caribbean earlier in the year.

Charles and Camilla remained close friends after her marriage, occasionally going to the opera together, as here in February 1975.

Charles asked Camilla to be an older companion to Diana Spencer, as his relationship with the daughter of Lord Althorp grew more serious. Here, in 1980, they both watched on at Ludlow racecourse as Charles competed in a race.

Camilla, with her husband Andrew and son Tom at the memorial service for her mother, Rosalind, in October 1994. A few weeks earlier, Prince Charles had spoken publicly about Camilla for the first time, in a television interview with Jonathan Dimbleby.

Camilla arriving at Highgrove House in July 1997 for her fiftieth birthday party, but the tragic death of Princess Diana the following month in Paris would have a big impact on her relationship with Charles.

Ray Mill House, Camilla's 'bolthole', bought for £850,000 from her divorce settlement, was just a fifteen-minute drive from Highgrove. (Right) Camilla shared Prince Charles's passion for hunting and was reluctant to give it up.

A significant moment as Charles and Camilla are photographed together for the first time, emerging from the Ritz after the fiftieth birthday party of her sister, Annabel. The event had been carefully choreographed by Mark Bolland.

In 2001, Camilla became President of the National Osteoporosis Society, a cause close to her heart after her mother had suffered from the illness. Here she is with her daughter Laura at an event at Somerset House to mark fifteen years of the charity. (Right) Camilla with Barbara Windsor, who was a patron of the charity.

Camilla with Queen Rania of Jordan in Lisbon, ahead of her first public speech as President for the charity, in May 2002 – it was a significant step forward for her.

At a gala dinner in Windsor Castle in February 2005, Camilla proudly displays her new engagement ring, which had originally belonged to the Queen Mother and had been passed down to her by the Queen.

Charles and Camilla leave Windsor Guildhall after their civil ceremony on 9 April 2005.

Camilla leans over to thank members of the public for wishing her well on her wedding day, 9 April 2005.

The Royal Family leaving the St George's Chapel at Windsor Castle after the blessing that followed the couple's civil ceremony.

needs to, in order to keep going. They have different temperaments, friends and hobbies. Charles is very sensitive and can easily get upset; Camilla lives from day to day and is naturally positive.

Yet they have been natural soulmates from the time they met. They love being together, understand each other's way of thinking and are accustomed to their trivial differences. They have shouting matches just like other couples, but their shared sense of humour usually clears the air. It makes sense that after all the battles they've had to face they are not going to look for more trouble.

About the time of their marriage Camilla had become patron of three charities. She has since gradually accumulated around one hundred patronages. She soon needed someone to look after her diary and deal with the thousands of letters that arrive each year. In addition to the patronages there are state banquets to attend, and meetings with a variety of heads of government and royals from overseas. She could no longer go out on a whim without a police protection officer. It was equally crucial she had a wide range of new, appropriate clothes – a very different wardrobe for someone who felt most comfortable in jeans and a baggy jumper.

Camilla had become one of the most scrutinised women of the modern age – as she took her place as an official member of the Royal Family. She was put to the test when she attended the Trooping the Colour ceremony for the first time in June 2005. Afterwards she made her first appearance on the balcony of Buckingham Palace, taking her place between Prince Charles and stepson Prince William to watch an RAF flypast, spear-headed by two Typhoon Eurofighters. If she was nervous it didn't show. Nor did the press find something to attack.

Camilla's royal duties had to be absorbed along with her role as mother, stepmother and grandmother plus trying to keep Tom and Laura and her five grandchildren out of the spotlight, which is what they wanted. They are not 'official' Royal Family members, hold no royal titles and attend very few royal events each year. It has enabled them largely to continue with their own lives as they would wish.

Laura, who is a mother of three and runs an art gallery, keeps well away from publicity. Tom is more in the public eye as he is a food critic. In his interview with Cassandra Jardine in the *Telegraph* a year after his mother's marriage, he said: 'People say we were mercilessly bullied at school. But for my first years at Eton, there was nothing newsworthy at all with my mother and Sir. [He, Laura and all their children call Prince Charles 'Sir'.]

He said he 'felt for my mother and for Sir' over the allegations and nastiness they went through. 'It was awful, totally immoral.' He and Laura coped, he said, because they were protected at home and at school. 'Of course, Oxford is a much more open society than Eton: there are people who might not agree with toffs or monarchy or whatever. Fine.'

Camilla tried to help her offspring when their home was besieged by journalists and photographers and suggested handling the paparazzi who were lurking in the bushes and reporters at the door with good humour. Tom said: 'If [my mother] can take it, we thought, we certainly can.' He loyally added: 'I can guarantee that anyone who meets my mum will like her because she's incredibly nice and honest, a proper person. She just gets on with it.'

He subsequently talked to *Hello!* magazine and said: 'All you care about with your parents is they're happy and my mother is exceptionally happy. I've always adored my stepfather; he's always been kind and good and a lovely man. He is a man of warmth, intelligence and humanity, and I think if it ever happens, he will make a fantastic king.'

Talent agent and equestrian Gavin Barker, who has known Camilla for a long time, believes there are advantages for Charles to have married a mature woman, but that it has been a more difficult change for her. 'I think the reason she doesn't like to be in the spotlight is a combination of just her and the residue of being unpopular before her marriage to Prince Charles. It's difficult when you get a profile like she has late in life. It's not like the Queen or Princess Anne who were born into it and haven't known anything different. Camilla was thrust into it and very unpleasantly. Being a normal person until fifty-seven, she knows a lot more about the realities of life than other royals. It's very helpful for the Royal Family. I think she will be a fantastic queen. She is devoted to both the future king and the country.'

Comments from the public seemed to be more in her favour as time went on. Looking back, it seems impossible that people could be so cruel, and even more remarkable that she stood her ground, didn't complain, stayed in love with Prince Charles and didn't walk away. One comment was particularly positive: 'When history judges her, she will not be seen as the woman who nearly brought down the monarchy but saved it.' Others were somewhat begrudging: 'I loved Diana. I don't love Camilla, but I accept her place in Charles's life and I do think that she works hard at her job. It's time to forgive.'

In a light-hearted New Year's Day article headlined 'Camilla the IT Girl', on the biggest likely influencers of 2006, the *Sunday Times* interviewed two futurologists who picked out Camilla as an unexpected trendsetter. American trend spotter Marian Salzman saw her as 'the next great lifestyle icon', while Tom Bentley, then director of the think tank Demos, foresaw a 'new golden age for the baby boomers', Camilla's generation. 'They have the money, freedom and confidence to enjoy life and devote themselves to the causes they really believe in.' This accurately summarised Camilla's situation. 'Camilla could definitely be a pin-up,' he said, 'an exemplar of finding fulfilment late in life.' Salzman thought Camilla was typical of 'a lot of women who were stuck in bad marriages . . . remarrying in their fifties'. She also fitted the bill in terms of health and looks – 'she is well put together and very healthy looking' – and even a sex symbol: 'symptomatic of the acceptance of sex beyond fifty'.

The article concluded: 'Another testament to the power of Camilla: we used to call her fat but as we look at her more carefully, in today's light, we realise she's not fat at all. We're going to start seeing a lot of books that tell women to embrace their inner size 12 because people are no longer interested in having the kind of fraught relationship with food that Diana had; they want to be great-looking and happy like Camilla.'

Even though Camilla was officially married, soon after the wedding the Queen changed the Order of Precedence, with the result that neither Princess Anne nor Princess Alexandra, the Queen's cousin and granddaughter of George V, would have to curtsy to Camilla when Charles was not with her.

A different kind of rebuff annoyed biographer Kenneth Rose, who had impeccable royal contacts. He wrote in his diary for 3 December 2005 that he had been asked to comment on the Queen's decision that Camilla, unlike Diana, should not be prayed for in church. He wrote:

I think this is wrong and that the wife of the Prince of Wales should be prayed for. I deplore the various ways in which Camilla is not allowed to take the same status as her husband, e.g. the present proposal that when Charles becomes King, she would become not Queen but Princess Consort.

Another entry on 23 December 2005 continues his support:

Prince Eddie [the Duke of Kent] tells me about the Royal Family Christmas lunch. 'I was lucky enough to sit next to Camilla. She is one of the best things to have happened for years. I like her down-to-earth good sense, total lack of airs, warmth, friendliness and sense of humour. She told me she loves Birkhall more than anywhere (good girl) though is not so keen on the Castle of Mey.'

August 2007 marked the ten-year anniversary of Diana's death and William and Harry, who were going to lead a thanksgiving service, had invited Camilla. But, shortly before the day dawned, Rosa Monckton, one of Diana's close friends, wrote in the *Mail on Sunday* that Diana would be 'astonished' and it would be 'inappropriate' if she came. Camilla hadn't wanted to attend but Prince Charles and her two stepsons wanted her to be there. She was unsure what to do so asked the Queen for advice. Her Majesty made it clear she would support her if she didn't go. An official statement from her was then released by Clarence House. 'I am very touched to have been invited by Prince William and Prince Harry to attend the thanksgiving service for their mother, Diana, Princess of Wales. However, on reflection I believe my attendance could divert attention from the purpose of the occasion, which is to focus on the life and service of Diana.'

Socially awkward dilemmas and etiquette issues at the royal level, such as curtsying and prayers, were an indication that Camilla's future life was unlikely to be stress-free. It is difficult for an outsider to blend easily into the British Royal Family and Camilla was no exception, even though she had been involved with Prince Charles for decades. New royals are under immense pressure about everything they say, do and wear. They also have to cope with restrictions emanating from the monarchy to hurtful comments from the press and the public, which is way beyond an ordinary person's experience.

Esther Rantzen comments: 'It's a strange job being a royal, because you suddenly have the most scrutinised public role to play in which every detail of your appearance and every word you say is analysed and picked over. Added to that we live in the age of the troll. So I think Camilla's a very, very strong person. She's had some vitriolic bad publicity over the years and found a way to survive it. In the end I think the public will recognise that it takes courage and strength.'

It was difficult for her to settle down in her new life of wealth and privilege when so many obstacles surrounded her. She knew too well that the Queen hadn't wanted her to marry her son and heir. It was also difficult to know how to live in harmony with the seemingly formidable Princess Anne who had also dated Andrew Parker Bowles. For years Anne kept away from Camilla as much as possible, which was unfortunate as they were a similar age and shared a love of horses.

It was bound to take time for her to ask for help when finding her way when she knew how her in-laws disliked her and the public insulted her. Every slip-up was bound to be noticed. No wonder she was initially fearful.

Overseas engagements were another challenge. They would put her in the spotlight, away from familiar surroundings, and needed to be sensitively handled and carefully planned. Amanda MacManus explained: 'Certain countries may want to get as much out of [the royals] as possible. I always tried to help put together a programme that was not going to be too exhausting because they could have been coping with engagements from morning until night in another time zone.'

Camilla's resistance to flying creates problems on long foreign tours. She once sat, terrified, on the steps of a tiny private jet during an overseas visit, refusing to get in, but at last was finally persuaded to board. On most flights she squeezes Prince Charles's hand on take-off. Despite being an experienced pilot himself, Charles is hugely sympathetic to her phobia: he was heard during one particularly bumpy flight to yelp loudly, 'Darling, please don't hold me so hard!' Playing Scrabble helps to occupy and calm her on long flights. Her friend, the artist Catherine Goodman, who often joined the couple on overseas trips to paint events and scenes, said, 'She always won.'

In 2013 she and Charles had a mid-air scare when their helicopter was forced to make an emergency landing. They were fifteen minutes into their flight from London to the Hay Literary Festival in Powys when a 'technical fault' aboard the chopper forced the pilot to divert the flight to Denham Aerodrome in Buckinghamshire. Camilla was terrified but was relieved to hear they could continue their journey by car. They were three hours late getting to Hay-on-Wye but at least by then Camilla felt much calmer.

Charles has always been delighted to have Camilla with him on his travels to share experiences that have ranged from the amusing – like the Queen, he quite enjoys it when things go wrong – to the heart-wrenching, in landscapes from deserts to rainforests. He previously had no one with similar interests with whom he could appreciate such journeys.

Joy Camm explains: 'Tours are exhausting with one engagement after another but great fun and usually a very hard learning curve. HRH has incredible intuition, which helps get her through. We also speak to the relevant embassy or the high commission and report back to HRH. It was brilliant to be able to get her honest feelings and thoughts. What was equally brilliant was that she didn't only take in the briefing for a particular event, but she could walk into a building and/or a room that she had never been into, in a country that she may never have visited, as if she had been there ten times before. I think on occasion she was quaking underneath, but I was always quaking more than she was.'

*

Between December 2005 and November 2006 Charles and Camilla

undertook three royal overseas tours and Camilla looked increasingly relaxed with each one. The first took place in December
when the royal couple went on an eight-day visit to New York,
Washington and San Francisco, plus they had a quick stopover to
meet aid workers and residents of hurricane-hit New Orleans. The
spotlight was bound to be on what Camilla did and how she did
it, partly because Americans were still smitten with Princess Diana,
who died eight years previously. The visit was billed by the British
government as an opportunity for the two countries to affirm their
'common bonds and shared tradition', but it was also the first
chance to introduce Camilla to the American people and hopefully
obtain their approval. The prince's aides wanted his first official
tour of the US since 1994 not to be eclipsed by memories of his
trip in 1985 when a radiant Diana danced with John Travolta at
a White House dinner.

On their first morning Charles and Camilla paid their respects
at Ground Zero in New York and unveiled a cornerstone in the
British Memorial Garden for UK victims of the 9/11 attacks by
al-Qaeda terrorists in 2001. Hundreds of well-wishers turned up
to watch. The couple subsequently met privately with the families
of some of the sixty-seven Britons who lost their lives. 'It was
terribly, terribly moving,' Camilla said later that evening at a
reception at the Museum of Modern Art. 'I think they're terribly
glad to have the garden.' She was asked if she talked to survivors
about their experiences. 'Yes, I always get straight to the point,
which I probably shouldn't.'

As a sign of unity, the Union Jack was flown alongside the World
Trade Center flag for the visit, but the day after their arrival the
New York Times carried an astonishingly disrespectful and mis-
ogynistic report: 'Since this is, after all, a marketing tour for
Britain, the big question remains: How is the 58-year-old duchess,
who has been viewed as an ungainly frump throughout her long

liaison with the prince, looking these days?' It continued: 'She had several strings of pearls around her neck, carried a black rectangular clutch bag and – this is most important – wore black stilettos, a sign, when worn by a middle-aged woman, that she is really, really trying.' There was even a snide comment about the way Camilla waved. 'The duchess beamed and performed a royal wave that appeared to have been practised to perfection.'

Describing the evening cocktail reception at which three hundred 'of New York's finest and richest turned out', the paper chose to concentrate on Camilla's choice of clothes. 'Her calf-length gown had a lace and pearl trimmed bodice, which revealed prominent décolletage – one area in which Diana could never compete.' But it admitted: 'Everyone wanted to talk to her, though', including, as it happened, artist Yoko Ono, widow of former Beatle John Lennon. The *Miami Herald* was just as unkind. 'It's an un-Diana tour,' it declared, 'for a couple of middle-aged, earnest eccentrics from the English countryside' – a very different reaction to Prince Charles's last trip twenty years earlier when he was with Diana. To make matters even worse, a CNN/Gallup poll showed 81 per cent of Americans were not remotely interested in their visitors.

On Wednesday the pair left for Washington for lunch and dinner with President George W. Bush and first lady Laura Bush at the White House. Despite the sniggering American press, British photographer Ian Jones, who was covering the tour, said it was obvious that they were enjoying being together and 'were full of fun. When they were in Washington, they had to sign something in a visitors' book and shared a pen. Prince Charles signed with his pen and gave it to Camilla. He then leant over her to take his pen back. She was about to give it to him and then snatched it back. He burst out laughing, which made her laugh too.' The couple subsequently visited farms, markets, schools and museums, which gave Charles a chance to highlight issues close to his heart

– organic food production, the environment and education.

The couple's second overseas tour together began on 20 March 2006. It was for two weeks and would include Egypt, Saudi Arabia and India and would focus on promoting tolerance between faiths, sustainable agriculture, and training and employment for young people. Egyptian security was tightened for the visit and the prince's team of bodyguards was on high alert.

While she was in Egypt, Camilla was escorted to the Commonwealth Cemetery in El Alamein where she paid tribute to two of her father's comrades who died in front of him in the aftermath of the 1942 battle. It was a turning point in the Second World War and convinced the British that they could beat the Germans and that Hitler was not invincible. The Axis defeat at El Alamein meant that North Africa would be lost to Hitler and Mussolini. Camilla's father, Major Bruce Shand, survived the battle and, at her father's request, she gently placed a bunch of roses on the grey-white marble tombstones of the two crewmen, Sergeant Charles Francis and Corporal Edward Plant who were with Captain Shand and died when their armoured car exploded. She also left a handwritten message from her father. He was by then a frail 89-year-old who was suffering from cancer. He died three months later, leaving Camilla devastated.

The couple were also photographed walking arm-in-arm, which the Queen would not approve of, when they climbed a path to the Temple of the Oracle in the oasis town of Siwa in the western desert region of Egypt. It was not normal royal protocol to show any affection when on royal duty, but it certainly made their climb safer. Camilla once again showed how unfussy she is by happily sitting on a floor with Egyptian seamstresses during a visit to a British start-up co-operative in the same town. She also enjoyed feeding a donkey with a carrot at the Brooke Animal Hospital in Cairo. The hospital treats about 160,000 working horses, donkeys and mules each year in Egypt alone. Camilla was so deeply moved by what she saw that she agreed to become the equine charity's first president. She revisited Brooke when she and Charles did their Middle East tour in 2021 and found to her horror that largely due to the pandemic many of the animals were in the hospital because the owners, many in the collapsed tourist industry, were too poor to feed them. Camilla has since appealed to the public to support the hospital.

The third royal visit was a five-day trip to Pakistan starting on 29 October 2006, which was a first-time visit to the country for both of them. It was obvious to see that after the first eighteen months of marriage Camilla was not only more confident but had developed a sense of style by the time she arrived in Pakistan and wore a very flattering salwar kameez with scarves to match.

There was a high threat of terrorist violence throughout Pakistan at the time. In March, a bomb had exploded outside the US Consulate in Karachi, killing several and injuring around fifty people. It meant that the security around the couple was extremely tight, and their visit was described as one of the most high-risk for some time. As a result, the royal couple had to travel around the country in a Pakistan Air Force helicopter, which would have been nerve-wracking for Camilla. Exclusion zones were enforced around each location, with anti-aircraft batteries in place wherever the helicopter landed.

The concerns were so strong that the UK High Commission refused to give details of the royals' itinerary in advance to local journalists. As a result, very few Pakistanis caught a glimpse of the royal couple, and those that did were carefully vetted. A local paper, the *International News*, commented: 'Security concerns might not allow the common man to interact with [Prince Charles] . . . [although] people in Pakistan always take great interest in his life, mainly due to the Lady Diana factor.' Nonetheless

Charles and Camilla managed to show on the surface at least that they were unconcerned about the danger and instead settled into a round of official engagements.

The main aims of the tour were to support the breadth of the partnership between the UK and Pakistan and highlight the countries' shared heritage. Despite the strict security, Charles and Camilla shared a light-hearted moment when Charles put on a traditional Pakistani hat known as a 'tasher', presented at a Youth Business International event at the Prime Minister's House in Islamabad much to Camilla's amusement. The couple saw some of the damage in remote northern parts that had been hit by the October 2005 earthquake, in which more than 73,000 people were killed, and visited Jaulian, a World Heritage archaeological site at Taxila, near Islamabad. A planned visit to Peshawar was cancelled due to a security alert after Pakistani forces attacked an Islamic school in the area.

Camilla's immersion into how royal engagements worked abroad opened her eyes to how demanding they could be, both physically and emotionally. Engagements at home had different demands, some of which were great fun while others demonstrated how she wanted to use her position to get across important messages.

Chapter 12

DANCE FOR OSTEOPOROSIS

The summer of 1994 was particularly challenging for Camilla. Her much-loved mother, Rosalind, who had suffered agony from osteoporosis, died on 14 July, only two weeks after Prince Charles allowed himself to be interviewed by Jonathan Dimbleby on BBC TV, and disclosed he had committed adultery with Camilla while still married to Princess Diana. This confession inevitably generated another wave of offensive comments for Camilla to cope with – something that Prince Charles would never have wanted. Rather than totally give in to her grief, she chose to help others, no doubt hoping it could take her mind off her bereavement.

Arrangements were made for her to visit the headquarters of the National Osteoporosis Society. It had been established in 1986 but hadn't yet made much of an impact. Camilla went along hoping that her own experience of watching how her mother and grandmother Sonia Keppel had suffered could be useful. Her offer to help was accepted with open arms, but she initially insisted on working behind the scenes as she didn't want to be accused of trying to emulate Princess Diana's charity work.

Three years later, Linda Edwards, the pioneering and formidable director of the charity, asked her if she would become a patron. She said: 'Camilla looked at me very directly and said: "Are you sure it would do you any good?"' A response that shows the verbal abuse that was continually thrown at her made her wary of bringing negative publicity to whatever she did. Edwards' answer was 'Yes.'

It was the first step on a journey that gradually transformed her to become one of the Royal Family's hardest-working and most valued members. It also helped set the scene for her and Charles to come out in public. Encouraged by Charles, she accepted the role and made her first public appearance in April 1997. Shivering with nerves, she gave a moving albeit somewhat rushed speech.

That same year Camilla and her sister Annabel Elliot announced an 'evening of enchantment' in Gillingham, Dorset. Tickets cost over £100, much of which would go to the National Osteoporosis Society. Journalists and Grade A celebrities, including Eric Clapton, Emma Thompson, Joan Collins and Mick Jagger were invited. It was part of a sequence of events that enabled Charles and Camilla to go to the theatre or concerts together or out with friends. The media responded positively. Mark Bolland felt 'the process of being open about things seemed to be working'.

In 2001 Camilla became President of the National Osteoporosis Society. That same year she and Charles took another step forward to public acceptance when, for the first time, Charles played a supporting role for her rather than the other way round, by going as her guest to Somerset House in London. Camilla was hosting a drinks reception for two hundred guests to mark the Osteoporosis Society's fifteenth birthday. The party took place under a steel marquee next to a set of fountains and guests were served with wine and canapes.

Mark Bolland planned the choreography of the occasion to get Prince Charles there so the couple would be seen together at a public event for the first time. It was risky as it could have brought yet another avalanche of criticism. 'We had a conversation about whether the Prince of Wales should come,' remembers Bolland. 'We all felt worried and anxious about it but then decided, why shouldn't he go? Even so, we were a little nervous.'

Other guests included Camilla's children Laura and Tom, her sister Annabel, ex-King and Queen Constantine of Greece, actress Wendy Craig and comedian Jim Davidson. Actress Barbara Windsor, who was a patron of the Osteoporosis Society, was also there. 'She was marvellous,' said Mark Bolland. 'She loved the Royal Family and was delighted to see Camilla and the Prince of Wales. She also talked to everybody. At one point, Camilla's personal secretary, Amanda MacManus, said, "Thank goodness for Barbara Windsor; she is the glue that is keeping everything together."'

The prince arrived with Queen Rania of Jordan, who was the president of the International Osteoporosis Foundation and a good friend. Camilla, who was wearing a pale-pink chiffon cocktail dress, curtsied to her but significantly did not curtsy to Charles. Instead, she greeted him with a smile. He placed his right hand on her arm and kissed her gently on both cheeks, then mouthed a loving 'Hello you'. Royal watchers said it was the first public kiss for the couple and it spoke volumes. Mark Bolland insists the kiss wasn't planned. 'I could never go as far as suggesting he kissed her, but he always wants to kiss her because they love each other.' It had taken almost thirty years for the couple to show their feelings openly and was the culmination of Mark's two-and-a-half-year campaign.

In May 2002 Camilla travelled to Lisbon for a conference organised by the International Osteoporosis Foundation and spoke movingly about her mother's final days. 'We watched in horror as she quite literally shrank before our eyes. She lost about eight inches in height and became so bent that she was unable to digest her food properly, leaving her with no appetite at all. The quality of her life became so dismal and her suffering so unbearable that she just gave up the fight and lost the will to live.' She went on: 'As a result of my mother's death, I became determined to find some way of helping people with osteoporosis from experiencing the same fate and general disregard that she encountered.' Her speech was a further step forward.

Camilla's involvement with the National Osteoporosis Society led to her meeting *Strictly Come Dancing* judge Craig Revel Horwood, who has developed a reputation for being the harshest of the judges on the show. Camilla and Craig first met on 20 October 2009 to mark World Osteoporosis Day and soon found they shared two important interests: dancing and osteoporosis. Craig's mother, Beverly Hallward, suffers from rheumatoid arthritis and he suffers from osteoarthritis – both conditions cause painful joints.

He became a patron of the charity and developed a campaign he called 'Boogie for Your Bones' to help children, especially in poor areas, to build bone strength. 'I was trying to enlighten the primary school kids, most of whom couldn't say or spell osteo-porosis,' he explained. 'I thought teaching them to dance was a great way for kids to learn that if they didn't like sport they could dance, which could help them with osteoporosis later in life. Up to the age of twenty-four you can make a difference if you build up a bone bank.'

He was in the middle of a teaching session at St Clement Danes Church of England School in Drury Lane, London, as part of the National Osteoporosis Society's 'Bone Factor Tour' when Camilla arrived. 'I suddenly felt very nervous and aware that I was quite hot and sweaty because I had been dancing. Nor did I look my best in a tracksuit. I also had no idea how to act around a royal.'

Camilla asked what he was teaching. 'I said the cha-cha-cha,' he recalled. 'And without realising it I added: 'Would you like to try it?' Camilla said: 'I'd love to. I know how to do the cha-cha-cha.' So we started dancing together. Wow! She was absolutely brilliant and danced like a dream. It was amazing. She has the best rhythm and could teach me a thing or two. I was also quite shocked as I thought a cha-cha-cha would be totally out of character, but it turned out not for her because she's so bubbly. We laughed so much together that from that moment on we've met frequently to promote the charity with a mission to get the world to understand what osteoporosis is all about and help people.'

As far as his relationship with Camilla goes, Craig makes sure 'I neither bow nor scrape. I was born in Australia and don't have the pomp and circumstance that others do. I always try to treat her as she does me: one nice person to another. I see her as a friend who is royal with an important job to do and completely respect her, but I call her "Camilla" or "Darling". Aside from Covid, when we meet we greet each other with a double theatrical kiss and a hug, which feels natural and normal.' Camilla didn't seem to mind his informality.

Craig said that the duchess was 'a massive fan' of *Strictly Come Dancing* and, following their meeting, Amanda MacManus, whom Craig describes as the 'ultimate diplomat', got in touch with Craig's agent Gavin Barker, and asked if there was any way she and Craig could do something together.

Gavin discussed it with the *Strictly* producers and the BBC and, after several meetings, the visit was approved and Camilla came to BBC Television Centre in Shepherd's Bush, London, on Friday 25 November 2011. The programme was about halfway through the ninth series, and a Friday was chosen as there is a weekly dress rehearsal prior to the live show on Saturday. Craig was asked to host her and willingly introduced her to the professional dancers, cast, crew and celebrities, and Bruce Forsyth and Tess Daly who were then the presenters. 'She was really interested in how *Strictly* was made,' he recalls. 'It was great for me to take her on a dream of a lifetime backstage to meet everybody. We also both judged a dance routine.' The former *EastEnders* actress Anita Dobson was one of the participants. Camilla went up to speak to her in the line-up and told her she was a great role model for older women and how healthy it was to dance. It was a skilful way to get the osteoporosis message across.

Six years later Camilla held a tea dance in the Buckingham Palace ballroom, which was filmed for the *Strictly Come Dancing Christmas Special* as a thank you to all the people who had helped with the series. A wide cross-section of about a hundred elderly people were invited plus the *Strictly* dancers. Camilla arrived when the tea dance was under way and went to talk to the guests at their different tables. One of them was Craig's mother, who had come from Australia to see her son. 'Camilla went to sit next to her, and they talked for about half an hour about where I grew up and my father's work in the Royal Navy,' says Craig. 'My mum said it made her life worthwhile. She just couldn't believe a senior royal would chat to her so naturally. What's so lovely about Camilla is that she is genuine, honest and normal. She also made me feel important enough to work for the charity with her and that's what we have done.'

When the professionals began to dance, Camilla and Craig slipped out of the ballroom to prepare a dance of their own. 'It had been prepared but, shortly before we were due on, I said, "Darling, do you want to have a practice before we dance the cha-cha-cha?" She agreed, so we found a corridor in the Palace we could practise in. It was hilarious but luckily no one saw us.'

When they returned to the ballroom, Craig's agent Gavin Barker said, 'It all went wrong. It had been very carefully choreographed that Craig would dance with Camilla at a particular time but that no one else could. Soon after they returned to the main room everyone was encouraged to get up and dance. It was then that Brendon Cole, one of *Strictly*'s professional dancers, found his way to Her Royal Highness and said, "Ma'am. Would you like to dance?" It was a very unprofessional thing to do. Craig stood there like a lemon as our hearts sank. Both of us and the producers were so shocked, we said to each other, "This is terrible. We're going to end up in the Tower."'

Craig wasted no time in coming to the rescue. 'Brendon was throwing her about at some speed while doing the cha-cha-cha, so I cut in and said, "Thank you, Brendon, I'll take over from here." We then had our dance together, which was fantastic.'

Gavin added, 'We didn't know what to do about what happened but luckily Amanda was there and said: "It hasn't fazed her, she's enjoying it." So I calmed down. I think Camilla is quite shy and doesn't want to do anything which is going to draw too much attention to herself. But she trusts Craig, who absolutely looks after her. He shepherds her around, makes sure she is in the right place at the right time, and that no one person hangs around chatting for too long.'

In February 2016 Camilla was awarded an honorary doctorate from Southampton University for her ongoing campaign to raise awareness about osteoporosis. Two years later the Queen gave permission for the charity to change its name to the Royal Osteoporosis Society. Camilla also instituted the Duchess of Cornwall Award, which recognises an outstanding contribution to the treatment of osteoporosis.

It was through *Strictly Come Dancing* that Camilla also met the retired ballerina Dame Darcey Bussell, who was a temporary judge on *Strictly* in 2009 and permanently between 2012 and 2019.

Dame Darcey has attended several osteoporosis events and has had 'nice chats' with Camilla, who is well aware that dancing and movement is very good for you. Darcey said: 'I really want people and especially the elderly to understand how important it is to keep moving. And the wonderful thing about dance, it's not just a physical exercise; the music that accompanies it provokes memories, which is wonderful.' Dame Darcey also supports Silver Swans, dance classes for over fifty-fives developed by the Royal Academy of Dance (RAD). Following the Silver Swans' routines helped keep Camilla fit during lockdown in 2020. Although she has always loved dancing, until lockdown she had never done ballet.

Dame Darcey, the television presenter Angela Rippon – who is an ambassador for Silver Swans – and Camilla set up a Zoom conversation in April 2020 during lockdown. Camilla described how she went along to the Royal Academy of Dance and was told she would see Silver Swans dance. She began: 'Oh dear, I thought, this will be a lot of very ancient people like me wobbling about on one leg, but I couldn't believe how good everybody was.' She also emphasised 'how important it is to keep active, otherwise we will seize up and not be able to get out of bed'. She revealed on the call that she likes to do a combination of Silver Swan, Pilates and lots of walking.

The idea of Silver Swans, Dame Darcey explained, 'is to create short ballets, so older women and men can learn the lovely basics of a routine. It's not extreme but just keeps the body in shape and helps with balance. The duchess very much appreciated that during the lockdown the Silver Swans' classes were online, so she could do them at home. It's also possible to do it with friends, which is important as the duchess probably doesn't get much time to see them, and this is a lovely opportunity to do so. When I talked to the duchess, who is a great supporter of the arts, she told me how much dancing has helped her posture, which is so important especially when she has to stand for a long time at events. She said: "Oh my goodness, my posture has changed so much. Nor do I feel so tired." Too many of us forget our physical form and posture, but because Her Royal Highness is photographed non-stop, I'm sure she's very aware of that.'

When a teacher asked Camilla if she would like a Silver Swans lesson she said, 'I asked three ancient friends so the four of us could clatter around. Initially I thought it would be a big laugh. There was a sort of feeling that we were all in it together and it was going to be very funny. But we had to concentrate so hard on what we were doing we didn't even know what our friends were doing. We also had to remember things like dropping our shoulders and breathing deeply so there wasn't time to laugh.'

She also liked it because 'you don't need a lot of room to do it and you don't even have to have special ballet shoes. There's a kind of comradeship in doing it. It doesn't matter how good or bad you are, it's just something that will make you feel better, give you a certain amount of confidence and a bit of discipline, which I think we all need in our lives. And you always feel so much better afterwards.' She added that after a year 'I might have improved a tiny bit but will probably always remain a beginner' and finds it 'really good fun'.

In June 2021 Camilla joined Dame Darcey for her first official engagement with the Royal Academy of Dance since becoming Vice-Patron. The Queen has been Patron of the Academy since 1953. The Victoria and Albert Museum was holding a display celebrating the RAD's centenary. Dame Darcey, who is President of the Academy, took Camilla round and told her about the organisation's history. Camilla revealed that she was 'completely hooked' on ballet. Prince Charles, Patron of the Royal Opera since 1975, became Patron of the Royal Opera House in 2015. He has been a lifelong fan of both ballet and opera and goes regularly to the

Royal Ballet with Camilla. In June 2021 they attended a performance by the Royal Ballet at the Royal Opera House to celebrate
the return of the arts and entertainment after lockdown.

Dame Darcey says, 'It is wonderful that she has become Vice-
Patron. She was fascinated with the tour, and I thoroughly enjoyed
talking to her about the beginnings of British ballet. I suppose it
must be even more interesting because she physically gets involved
as a Silver Swan. At one point a photographer asked her to do a
pose or two. She seemed slightly surprised, and I thought she'd
run away. But she was quite game to get into a ballet position and
was cheery about doing a couple of exercises at the barre. The
energy that she gives off to others when she comes to visit really
sets the bar high for a 74-year-old. She's incredible. Prince Charles
and the duchess nowadays give off a much happier aura; people
notice, and it is lovely to see. I also know she is always happy
when Craig gets hold of her to do a little waltz, but my favourite
image is to think of her and Prince Charles waltzing around their
living room when *Strictly* is on television.'

Almost a year later Camilla was driven right onto the red carpet
outside the entrance door of the brand-new state-of-the-art £19.5
million RAD headquarters in Battersea, south London. She was
wearing a stylish navy-blue dress by Bruce Oldfield and came out
of the car smiling. No wonder. The sun was shining and, for the
first time in 2022, it felt like spring.

She handed her private secretary a navy scarf and her handbag
and walked inside to be greeted by Chief Executive Luke Rittner
and Dame Darcey. At the reception desk were two huge vases filled
with blue and yellow flowers, the colours of the Ukrainian flag.
The Russians had just launched their invasion of Ukraine and it
was not going to be forgotten at the opening. Luke Rittner
mentioned the dreadful attacks later when he gave a speech in the

193-seat theatre and asked all the guests sitting there to keep a minute's silence. It was easy to work out those who had likely been dancers as opposed to donors and supporters by their posture, both standing and sitting. Other guests included the actor Sir Derek Jacobi, Angela Rippon and the world-renowned dancer and choreographer Carlos Acosta, who kept praising the building, saying, 'This is amazing.'

The 60,000-square-foot building is an international home for dance with seven large dance studios, all with barres, to cater for different age groups. Nearly all the would-be dancers were females. There is also an accessible archive that has 75,000 artefacts, books, programmes, letters, relics and costumes. Several of the studios had young or very young dancers, whom Camilla watched with a smile. Her face lit up when she walked into the Silver Swans class. She proudly told the dancers she had been a 'Swan' for eighteen months but had not danced during the previous few weeks due to contracting Covid. Prince Charles had a second bout at the same time. She also mentioned she couldn't yet get rid of her cough. She was feeling so unwell that a couple of days later she took some time out. She had been due to attend the showpiece horse racing festival at the Cheltenham Festival and present a trophy to the winning owner, jockey and trainer of the Queen Mother Champion Chase. It must have disappointed her to miss it. At a later event at Clarence House, she said of her illness: 'It's taken me three weeks and I still can't get shot of it.'

It was perhaps why she also declined the offer of joining the Silver Swans dancing, saying: 'I'm rather impressed by all of you. You're much better than I am', and that she would 'have to do a lot more practice'. She did however pose with all the dancers for a photograph.

As part of the tour, Camilla also met participants from the RADiate programme, which provides subsidised classes to help children and young people with additional learning needs. Specialised dance artists worked with the children, some of whom were on the autism spectrum and/or had behavioural, emotional or social difficulties. Others were non-verbal. It was very moving to see them take part in the carefully created exercises. In between exercises Camilla went over to speak very gently to a young girl in a wheelchair who was non-verbal and an obviously rather disadvantaged boy.

The finale was a dance presentation in the new theatre that gravitated from ballet to hip-hop. The audience were told with a smile that getting everything organised had taken years but many of the items for the guests would only last five minutes. When the dancing was over all the contributors formed a semicircle. The smallest children stood in first position with ankles together and feet apart and didn't move during three speeches, albeit quite short ones, and while Camilla unveiled a commemorative plaque to mark the official opening of the building. She ended the hour-long visit saying, 'Having had a very short tour of it, I have seen its complete magnificence and it's just doing so much for so many young people – and old people like me,' which prompted laughter from the audience. As she left the building, everyone who had crowded into the reception area cheered and clapped. She glanced round to see who it was for and looked rather surprised, then hugely happy when she realised it was all for her.

The more work Camilla took on the keener she became. It did not, however, stop her from indulging in her childhood passion.

Chapter 13

HOMES, GARDENS AND
ELEPHANTS

Gardening has always been a source of escapism and peace for Camilla. She wanted to garden even as a child. Her family home, The Laines, in East Sussex, had more than five acres of country garden, and once a year her parents would open it for the local Conservative Party Association's summer party. Camilla's mother Rosalind Shand was influential in teaching her how to tend to her first garden. 'She taught me how to prune, she taught me how to plant, she taught me how to weed. There's a great art to weeding,' Camilla told Monty Don during an episode of BBC2's *Gardeners' World* in August 2021. The passion has grown with age. 'It's not actually until you get a house of your own that I think your interest [in gardening] is really sparked. I remember the first house I had, looking at this garden and actually then saying to my mother, "Help!" You know, where do I go from there? And she came and sort of talked me through a lot of the basics. I'd be out in my garden all day, every day if I were allowed,' she went on. 'I love to get my hands dirty.'

Camilla even had a rose named after her. Called the Rosa

Duchess of Cornwall, it is soft pink in colour and described as having a spicy fragrance. Someone must have thought that 'spicy' rather than sweet-smelling would suit her best. She was presented with the flower at the Gardeners' World Live show in Birmingham in mid-June the year she and Charles were married. A donation from the sale of each rose bush is given to the then called National Osteoporosis Society.

She is also fond of arranging flowers at Highgrove House, with all blooms coming from the garden. It is a skill she learnt at finishing school. Prince Charles is just as passionate about his gardens. He works in it when he has time, is very keen on building hedgerows and used to be mocked for talking to his plants. Between them they share an affinity with nature and the joy it can bring.

Prince Charles bought Highgrove House – a Georgian-style nine-bedroom, six-bathroom home – in 1980, before he married the then Lady Diana, from Maurice Macmillan, the son of former Prime Minister, Harold Macmillan. Diana didn't much like it, preferring Kensington Palace, but every Friday morning for several years the family and some of the staff would leave Kensington Palace to spend the weekend there. Charles loved being in the countryside, as did the princes, as they could enjoy more outdoor activities in the estate's fifteen acres of garden. Harry also liked going round the garden holding hands with his father who pointed out various plants and flowers. 'Harry loves animals and plants,' Prince Charles once observed. 'I tell him all about them and that they have feelings too and mustn't be hurt.'

It has now become the private country home for him and Camilla. Yet she has kept Ray Mill House, the home she bought in the late 1990s, to this day. It is her hideaway and where she can relax. The normal routine is that Camilla travels down to Highgrove with Prince Charles at weekends but spends much of the time at Ray Mill House. Other times they take it in turns

– one night together at Highgrove and one night together at Ray Mill.

I've been reassured by someone close to the royal couple that it doesn't for a moment mean that they don't still like being together. Quite the contrary. She uses Ray Mill as sort of 'decompression area' where she can recover from her royal duties and be 'a regular Wiltshire housewife in a way she can't anywhere else'. It's a place where she can do what she wants, wander around in her dressing gown or sit and read by the fire. She has someone who lives close by who helps with her dogs and anything else she needs. I was told 'she has an enormous workload, particularly as Harry and Andrew are no longer working royals and the Queen is doing less. It's really exhausting, especially all the formal occasions', and she recovers there.

At Highgrove, Charles has been so proud of his extraordinary garden that he wrote the introduction to *The Highgrove Florilegium*, a magnificent two-volume book of botanical illustrations of the plants that grow there, published in 2008 and 2009. All royalties have been donated to the Prince's Foundation.

He wrote: 'From the start it was my intention to try and create a garden that warmed the heart and soothed the soul; a place, if you like, of beauty and peacefulness; a garden based upon organic principles that would mark the turning of the year and the abundance and fruitfulness of nature in her many guises.' He remains proud of his fifteen acres of garden, all of them organic. When former Home Secretary David Blunkett, now Lord Blunkett, who has been blind from birth, was a guest at Highgrove, Charles took him round the cottage garden so he could smell and touch the flowers and plants.

Camilla agrees with what Prince Charles wrote in the introduction to *The Highgrove Florilegium*, that plants can have a uniquely positive effect on the human spirit as well as looking good. She feels that during the Covid pandemic, especially during lockdown, gardens could be a life-saver for those lucky enough to have them. 'I think gardens got people through Covid,' she said to Monty Don. 'They realised how special a garden was and what they could do with it. They could become inventive, even if they hadn't been before. They could start growing vegetables.'

She believes: 'It was a sort of spiritual experience for them; they discovered an affinity with the soil – you can go into a garden and you can completely lose yourself; you don't have to think about anything else. You're surrounded by nature, you've got birds singing, you've got bees buzzing about – there is something very healing about gardens.'

Prince Charles's favourite flowers are delphiniums. When I visited Highgrove innumerable pink, blue and purple delphiniums looked majestic in full bloom. He also loves colourful meadows full of wildflowers. Camilla's favourites are lady's mantel, lily of the valley, English lavender and the primrose.

Camilla spoke enthusiastically to Monty Don about Highgrove, where she has a woodland area that she looks forward to building up. 'I would love to put down swathes of bulbs, and I would also like to have a proper wildflower meadow. At the moment I've got a bit, but the grass has sort of taken over and we're going to have another go in 2022 planting more seeds, because I think, especially now, it's even more important to have these wild flowers if we're going to keep on attracting butterflies and bees.'

Of course, no garden can be controlled even by the greenest-fingered royal. 'I'm very lucky,' she added. 'I've got a big vegetable garden, but you get the mice, and the voles this year ate all the asparagus roots and then got into the strawberries, so you can never win. There's always something.'

Visitors regularly come to Highgrove House and the prince likes to take his own guests round his garden where eleven full-time gardeners try to keep up with his new ideas. He enjoys choosing different themes and colours in specific areas. When I was shown around, one particular area was pointed out to me. It was entirely filled with flowers that had the Queen's racing colours of red and purple and the nearest goldish-coloured bloom that could be found.

The garden is also home to all sorts of knick-knacks and gifts that for various reasons don't quite fit indoors. These include a slate bust of himself and Camilla, that isn't a very good likeness, that has been fixed onto a beech tree stub and a gnome given to him in Ireland. He even bought 'a wife' for his gnome after he married Camilla.

The garden has been slightly altered for his grandchildren. In July 2015 he refurbished the tree house once played in by Princes William and Harry for Prince George to play in. He also installed a £20,000 hand-made artisan shepherd's hut in his wildflower meadow that has a bed and woodburner for George and his siblings to enjoy. Best of all, when George was only two, he, with Grandpa's help, planted a balsam poplar tree that you can see from the main house. It is one of Charles's favourite spots.

Another part of the Highgrove garden is a dedicated memorial to Camilla's late brother Mark Shand. A tall stone entrance into the New Cottage Garden has a vibrant colour scheme of yellow, pink and blue, inspired by Tibetan silks. It has been renamed Shand Gate in Mark's memory. It is of course a special place for Camilla whose charismatic innovative youngest sibling died unexpectedly in April 2014 when he was sixty-two. His death followed a fatal fall after he tripped and hit his head on a pavement in New York just after an auction he had hosted, which raised almost £1 million for his charity, Elephant Family. The charity lives on, however, largely thanks to Prince Charles and Camilla who became its joint royal presidents.

*

Mark was the rebel of the family, but Camilla adored him, as did her sister Annabel and her mother. Annabel recalled that a few years before their mother died in 1994, she and Camilla were having lunch with her when she asked: 'Darlings, I've always been completely fair between the three of you, haven't I?' She and Camilla were open-eyed and both disagreed. Annabel added: 'Literally, Mark could do no wrong . . . Mark, having been worshipped by my mother, was spoiled by women his whole life.'

Camilla felt that 'he metamorphosed from rather a bad-tempered, fat child into a golden boy, blessed with good looks, charm and a devil-may-care attitude to life'. She was devastated by his passing and wrote a personal eulogy for him in *The Times* in September 2014. It marked the day of his memorial service, which was held six months after his sudden death. The terrible day occurred, she wrote, 'on a glorious early spring day in Scotland when the phone rang and an anguished voice on the other end told me that something terrible had happened to my brother; my indestructible brother, Mark. Surely nothing could have happened to him? He was in New York raising money for his beloved elephants, but an unfamiliar pavement had claimed his all-too-short life following a hugely successful auction for Elephant Family, a charity he co-founded in 2002. My charismatic and sometimes infuriating brother, who had survived tsunamis, shipwrecks, poisoned arrows and even the fearsome Komodo dragons, was no longer with us.'

In her eulogy, Camilla also wrote of the event that transformed his life: 'In 1988, on a visit to India, something happened that was to change my brother's life. Mark arrived in Bhubaneswar, the capital of Orissa, in eastern India and rescued a beautiful female elephant from a life of begging and misery. Her name was Tara. They embarked on a thousand-mile trek across the north of India [which he recalls in his bestselling book, *Travels on my Elephant*], and by its finale he was in love. This was the start of his lifelong passion for India and his quest for the survival of the Indian elephant.'

Mark had no interest in a conventional career and developed a reputation for roguish behaviour with beautiful women. His friend Don McCullin, the war photographer, said: 'Women fell like autumn leaves into his arms.' He was reckless and unreliable, and unlike Camilla wasn't tied to a diary. Camilla didn't have that sort of freedom but like many others found him intoxicating. It was second nature to her to support Mark in any way she could. The feeling was mutual. Despite Mark's rebellious nature he was intensely proud and protective of Camilla, admired Prince Charles deeply, a feeling that was reciprocated, and enjoyed being a welcome guest at Highgrove. He could also be relied upon for complete discretion and rarely spoke about his sister's royal relatives.

Mark married Clio Goldsmith (a niece of Sir James Goldsmith) in 1990 when he was forty, and their daughter Ayesha was born four years later. He adored Ayesha but his passion for Tara was stronger. 'She is the love of my life,' he confessed, with Ayesha second. Clio and Mark divorced in 2009.

In 2002 he and Ruth Ganesh set up Elephant Family. Ruth became principal trustee and the creative powerhouse behind the charity's iconic fundraising events. They were an unlikely couple who worked hard together, and at one point had an intimate relationship. 'I wanted to do something worthwhile, and Mark seemed a wonderful figure full of excitement and adventure,' Ruth explained to me. 'He was wonderfully unstructured and didn't see any boundaries to anything happening. I would just come up with some creative ideas, give them to Mark, he would roar them into life, take a long draft on his cigarette, phone a friend and make these ideas happen in a sparkling incredible way.'

The first big fund-raiser Mark and Ruth organised was Elephant Durbar at the Petersham Nurseries in Richmond in 2006. Camilla was delighted to attend, and Prince Charles came too.

'Mark was incredibly happy that they were supportive of Elephant Family,' Ruth continues. 'It was our first-ever fund-raising event and it was a really big deal that they came. We had dinner in long Victorian glasshouses while two elephants made of grass stood nearby. The pull factor was immense. Three hundred people came including Kate Moss, Angelica Houston and Rob Lowe, and many others who all donated to the charity. There was also a wheelbarrow of elephant dung at crazy prices, which was auctioned. It was a glorious English summer occasion and gave Elephant Family a great lift off.'

Other fund-raising opportunities followed. In July 2013 Prince Charles and Camilla hosted Elephant Family's Animal Ball, with drinks at Clarence House followed by dinner next door at Lancaster House. 'Camilla described it as a mad Ascot,' Ruth laughs. 'She looked out of the window and could see her back garden full of four hundred people, each one dressed as a different animal by different fashion houses. I had to introduce the people in the garden to their Royal Highnesses, which was very difficult as I had to work out who was behind the giant butterfly, snow leopard or arctic fox mask. Luckily, I never felt afraid of putting a foot wrong in Camilla's company. She always made you feel relaxed. In Mark's family there is zero snobbery. Instead, there is warmth, humour, incredible generosity and a big heart.'

That November Camilla and Charles went on an official tour of India. Mark wanted to show them some of Elephant Family's projects and how the charity also tries to support the poor rural communities who live alongside the elephants. Camilla was so keen that they carved out some time from their busy schedule. 'There have been occasions when we have relocated a whole village that found itself in the middle of a migratory route with elephants constantly going through and causing a lot of damage,' Ruth added. 'Sometimes when we relocate them, we give them better homes with more facilities, so they are out of the elephants' way.'

Tom Parker Bowles has said: 'My stepfather [Prince Charles] adored [Mark]. They were very similar in their views. They just got on. And when they went to India, Mummy said, "Thank God for Mark. I've never been happier to see my little brother in my whole life." The feeling was mutual.'

There was a plan to collaborate with the CoExistence campaign and a group of Adivasi artisans in Tamil Nadu, southern India. The idea was that a herd of one hundred elephant sculptures would appear across London from the Royal Parks to the King's Road. They took about five years to make after Mark's death and each of the sculptures was an anatomically perfect recreation. They were made from *lantana camara*, an invasive weed, so its removal from protected areas further benefits wildlife.

Because of Covid, the open-air exhibition was postponed. Ruth didn't know where to keep a hundred elephants and Camilla came up with the fun idea of starting an elephant adoption agency. In the summer of 2020, she wrote to lots of friends saying there was a bit of an elephant emergency and asking them to adopt one of the sculptures. She ended up successfully placing most of the herd in the gardens or country estates of different friends like author Jilly Cooper and broadcaster and farmer Jeremy Clarkson. The idea was if the people had the elephants – the smallest cost £6,000 and increased according to size up to £30,000 – in their garden they would probably fall in love with them and buy them. She was right.

'Everyone wanted to adopt them in the end,' Ruth told me, 'so it gave us an enormous headwind by raising £4 million and saved us from keeling over when it felt like everything was lost. Camilla and Prince Charles bought several, which I saw looking magnificent and very approachable in a special spot in Highgrove Garden.' The wonderful-looking elephants comprised of a family with parents and children has pride of place in the grounds. They give Camilla comfort and a closeness to Mark.

Highgrove House itself was designed by the admired and very expensive interior designer Robert Kime, who in the late 1980s and early '90s created what is called 'a lived-in, classic English look'. Unlike the garden it is not open to visitors. It has been described as rather grand, and has a lot of rich reds, lush Afghan carpets and a broad art collection, some from the Royal Collection, others from friends given to him over the years. There are also a lot of photographs of his sons, but various friends who had recently been there did not see any of Diana.

Nothing much has changed over the years as far as decor is concerned. Nor has Camilla tried to add her own taste to the rooms, apart from changing what was once Harry's bedroom into a dressing room for herself, something Harry was said to have recently complained about. Camilla's sister Annabel, who has helped Charles design the interiors of many other properties, has never been called in to work on Highgrove. The respected interior designer, who also deals in antiques, started to work for her brother-in-law soon after he married Camilla. Clarence House, however, did not put the work they wanted done out to tender and instead gave it straight to Annabel. There were grumblings about nepotism, but as no public money was involved Prince Charles was entitled to make his own decisions with his own money.

There have been many more refurbishments, including a sustainable building at the Duchy of Cornwall Nursery in Lostwithiel in 2011, twelve Duchy of Cornwall cottages, Dovey Castle in Devon, and various projects in the grounds of Dumfries House, Ayrshire. It might have been thought that because of his busy life Charles might have left everything to Annabel to sort out, but not at all. Speaking on a 2012 ITV documentary, *The Royal Restoration*, Annabel revealed that Prince Charles has incredible attention to detail. 'He will look at everything. His eye for detail is quite extraordinary. I don't think I've ever worked with anybody who is so interested in the detail.' She added: 'He always likes to be completely involved and know what's being suggested. He's looking at every piece of material – 'What's this for? Is that for a chair? Where's that sourced from? Has it got nylon in it?' When Charles was questioned in the documentary about where he learnt to pay such attention to details, he said it was from his grandmother, the Queen Mother.

Camilla is far too wise to ask for redecorations at Highgrove and accepts it as it is – unlike Diana's stepmother Raine Spencer, who alienated the Spencer family with her tasteless, vulgar remodelling of Althorp, the Grade 1-listed stately home where Diana and her ancestors lived. She began what she called 'the renovations' soon after she married Earl Spencer in July 1976, and I exposed all that she had done in my 1993 book *Raine and Johnnie: The Spencers and the Scandal of Althorp*.

However, modifications have been made so that Highgrove reflects Prince Charles's views on the environment. He has installed a series of measures to heat rooms and provide hot water to save energy. One green measure includes the installation of solar panels and woodchip boilers. Rainwater is collected and used to flush lavatories and irrigate land. The estate also has efficient double-glazing and a reed-bed sewage processing system, and all electricity used on the estate has been sourced to a green energy supplier.

Security is also vital. In the unlikely possibility that someone breached the tight security in place, Prince Charles and Camilla have a secret room they can escape to. According to some experts the steel panic room is so strong that if the Gloucestershire manor house was targeted in an air strike or terrorist attack, the royals inside would survive. Author Brian Hoey let the secret out in 2011, in his book *Not in Front of the Corgis*, in which he says the 'iron room' measures 20ft by 20ft. 'Inside are medical supplies, including containers of Charles and Camilla's blood group, long-lasting food and drinks, an armoury, radio transmitters equipped to obtain a signal even within its steel walls, air purifiers and chemical lavatories.' Hoey claims the prince and the duchess would be able to survive for weeks inside the room if needed.

According to royal expert Ingrid Seward, the panic room has never been used except for when a visitor made a wrong turn and got locked in. Apparently, Rory Stewart, then MP, got trapped inside after excusing himself to use the bathroom and could not be heard shouting for help. Eventually Prince Charles rescued him from the room and burst out laughing when he saw Stewart's face.

Camilla's love of plants and gardens drove her to make a well-publicised visit to some guerrilla gardeners' work in 2011, a name that makes them sound more aggressive than they really are. These gardeners usually work at night planting flowers or growing vegetables on public land on which they don't have the legal right to do so, with the intention of turning neglected public space into an attraction. It sounds a furtive engagement for a royal to get involved in, but royal aides were, I was told, 'very careful to take note of the places that were okay for the public to see and kept well away from others where people weren't allowed. We didn't want to aggravate anyone.'

The plan was that Camilla would go by day to see what the gardeners had planted the previous night. Several journalists were taken by a red Routemaster bus on a tour to see the results. One destination was an area in south London where a leader of the guerrilla movement showed Camilla where he and other activists had planted vegetables and flowers around trees, on traffic islands and by roadsides. She told them she thought their work was 'fantastic'. Originally, they worked without the consent of local authorities and other landowners, but it seemed their positive efforts were beginning to be accepted.

Camilla visited one such project, Walworth Garden Farm in Southwark, south London, that was established by local residents in 1987, on semi-derelict land. Camilla prefers actions to words and unexpectedly produced some shears. 'Anyone need a haircut?' she laughed. As she was shown around the smallholding, she stopped to chat to a group of schoolchildren who were examining living creatures in a pond. A nine-year-old girl handed her a toad. Camilla held it in the palm of her hand without cringing and, as she put it back under a log, joked: 'There you are, toad in the hole.' The *Daily Mail* reported on her unusual engagement using the cheeky headline: 'If I kiss you, will you turn into Charles?'

Camilla and Charles are regulars at various garden shows around the country including those organised by the Royal Horticultural Society, Hampton Court and, less frequently, the Chelsea Flower Show. The highlight in the royal gardening calendar is the Sandringham Flower Show in Norfolk, in the Queen's country home of sixty acres of stunning gardens. About 20,000 people visit on opening day, which helps raise money for charity, but inevitably it had to close for two years because of the pandemic.

It's traditional that the royal couple arrive and leave in a horse-drawn carriage and, according to the weather, usually have either a large umbrella or a small lace parasol beside them. Aside from looking at the plants, Camilla appreciates discussing them with the expert gardeners who can be found in marquees in the grounds. An aide told me, 'There's always a lovely atmosphere in the grounds and their Royal Highnesses are very well received.' Unlike most senior royals, Camilla takes money with her when she is out and about and is often tempted while at garden shows to buy a plant or even a slice of ginger cake from a charity stall to eat on the way home. They were, however, temporarily traumatised in 2015 when introduced to Zephyr, an enormous four-year-old bald eagle, who suddenly flapped her wings out to their full span and very nearly hit both of them in the face. The eagle's handler found it rather amusing, the royal couple looked terrified. An indication perhaps that they are always alert for their safety when they are out and about among people.

While gardens are just the sort of thing Camilla thoroughly enjoys, she has also built strong foundations for her new royal identity by championing particular causes that are more heartfelt and personal. It is where she has come into her own.

Chapter 14

A ROYAL TREAT

When Camilla is on an engagement, she always seems to gravitate to the neediest person in the room. She adores children and is heartbroken when they are seriously unwell. She could avoid such an experience but accepts those challenges when she feels she can help. Not to please members of the royal family who have doubted her, but to prove her own worth. One example is her hosting an annual Christmas party for children with terminal illnesses. She invites the children and their families to Clarence House, her London home, to have fun, lots of food and help decorate a huge Christmas tree. 'It's one of the most special things we do all year,' she enthused. 'I wouldn't miss it for the world.'

She had the idea in 2006, and the parties have been running annually since 2007. The only year that Camilla didn't host the party herself was in 2008 when she had a nasty cold and felt it would be wrong to mix with children who were so vulnerable. Prince Charles, who had fortunately been present at a previous party, stepped in to save the day. Joy Camm recalls: 'He arrived after doing an investiture and did the whole thing for her.' I was surprised, as the prince has so much work of his own, but Joy corrected me. 'His Royal Highness and Her Royal Highness help and support each other,' she said firmly. 'It's a natural thing for partners to do. For example, His Royal Highness always goes to her late brother Mark's elephant charity if it is having an event because he knows how important it is for her, like the Christmas party is. Her Royal Highness made an appearance at the end of the party, waving from the top of a flight of stairs.'

Camilla likes to get involved and personally serves up sausages and mash, often in the shape of smiley faces, for all the children and pours out the squash. Chocolate Christmas trees and decorated biscuits come later. She ignores any bits of food that fall on the floor, readily sits down to play with some of the children, makes sure she talks to them and their families and listens to their often heart-rending personal stories. Sadly, each Christmas party is likely to be the child's last and makes the occasion particularly emotional but Joy, a former nursing sister, insists: 'It is not heart-breaking, it's heart-warming. These children are ill, there is no secret about that. What the party does is give them a fabulous time. It is also an incredible memory for the parents. We usually have about fourteen children and their families and use all three drawing rooms at Clarence House. The children get very excited while the parents are often nervous waiting for Her Royal Highness to come in.'

Camilla thinks through every aspect of the party – from the food the children eat, to the present they take home and a special treat they can relish no matter their age or health. She always likes there to be an assistant equerry at the party who comes dressed in his Welsh Guards ceremonial uniform, complete with bearskin hat, scarlet tunic and sword. He salutes Her Royal Highness and the children, who usually look amazed, as they are unlikely to have ever seen anybody in that sort of uniform so close before. There is also an enormous sparkling Christmas tree to marvel at. All the decorations for the tree are laid out and the duchess helps every young visitor place their own brightly coloured decoration on the tree.

Joy continues: 'Her Royal Highness also helps the equerry get each decoration on his sword. He then has to tip the decoration on its string onto a little branch without dropping it. It's a tremendous challenge that needs a lot of practice.'

The children come to Clarence House from the Helen and Douglas House Hospice in Oxford, which Camilla became patron of in 2007. The hospice is known as the benchmark for hospice work around the world and relies entirely on voluntary donations. Ten years after the parties were under way, Camilla also became patron of Roald Dahl's Marvellous Children's Charity. It provides specialist nurses for a range of medical conditions to ensure all seriously ill children and their families receive support. Since 2017 a nurse brings a child who needs constant support to the annual party.

Various treats for the children include trying on a Welsh Guard's bearskin hat, which is usually far too big for them and makes them laugh. Camilla helps them pose for photographs while they are wearing it. There are festive tunes by the Band of the Welsh Guards. Father Christmas sometimes arrives with two live reindeer for the children (and Camilla) to stroke. On one occasion a nine-year-old girl held the duchess's hand and looked at the animals in wonder. 'A reindeer, a serious reindeer!' she exclaimed. There is also a fleet of black cabs, sometimes decorated, to take the children home. On one occasion, to the children's delight, one of the taxis was covered in fur and had a flashing red nose just like Rudolph the red-nosed reindeer.

It looked as if there could be no Christmas party during lockdown in 2020, but Camilla was determined that an alternative arrangement was made. 'We couldn't have a gathering of hugely vulnerable children, so we did it virtually,' Joy explains. 'The duchess sent the decorations to the children's houses and, when we went interactive, she would watch them putting the decoration on their own tree, while she decorated hers. She had a conversation with them all about Christmas and then sent them gifts. It was a really special time.' Camilla gets great satisfaction from giving the children a happy time. She tells them: 'It is one of my favourite things to do each year and seeing your faces as the door opens is magical.'

It was also touch and go whether the 2021 Christmas party would go ahead, but after careful consultation with the charities, they decided to have the party amid strict protocol, including lateral flow tests for all those involved. Camilla was photographed with a face mask decorated with holly. She was pleased and hugely relieved that the party had been given the all-clear and said to the children: 'I didn't think it was going to happen but thank goodness you all decided to come. I just really wanted to wish you all a very, very happy Christmas.'

She then revealed that she leaves her own Christmas present buying rather late. 'The tree decorating for me is always the start of Christmas,' she said. 'I haven't thought about it before today, but I come in and see the tree and the children and everything and it just gets me in a Christmas mood.' She turned to the reporters present: 'It's just magical to have them here. Such a special, special event for me. It makes my year.'

Camilla enjoys making self-deprecating jokes and there are usually a few at every engagement as it also relaxes the mood. Just before the pandemic lockdown in March 2020, she visited Barnardo's charity that cares for vulnerable children. She chatted to a young girl who showed her a squishy toy she said she used to help her cope with anxiety. Camilla held it for a while then, with a broad smile, said she might need the anti-stress toy herself, and advised the girl, 'You'd better take it back otherwise I may steal it.'

Camilla is keen to help children who have different problems and is dedicated to the Ebony Horse Club in south-east London, which was founded in 1969. She became president in 2009. The club doesn't just teach young people, who largely live in council estates, how to ride, but also helps them to develop skills from their experience to give them a broader future. In 2011, Camilla opened its new centre in a deprived part of Brixton, which was built on a site between tower blocks and overground railway lines. Two years later, she persuaded the Queen to come along to see it. Her acceptance was a welcome confirmation of her support for Camilla's public role. It was also a powerful confidence boost for Camilla that her suggestion was a good one and that the Queen enjoyed herself.

Camilla's hands-on approach led to her inviting some of the children from the horse club to a reception at Clarence House. She also invited Splash, a ten-year-old cob, a type of pony, to join them. It was an ice breaker. Laura Boland, Ebony's chief instructor, said: '[The duchess] is lovely . . . the kids still talk about seeing her. They get really excited that somebody who isn't from the same background as they are has the same love of horses, and feels connected in that sense.' One of the boys there said: 'I was telling [the duchess] how much I enjoy riding Splash. Before, I used to be antisocial. I would sit in the corner. Now I can ride I am more open with people.' It was just the sort of comment Camilla wanted to hear.

In November 2019 Camilla invited several of the young riders for a Saturday event at Ascot. They had the fun of joining her in the royal box, which gives a great view of the racecourse and particularly the winning post. She arranged for them to watch a race. They were also given a VIP tour, which included the room where the jockeys weigh in, and the changing room where all the colours are hung. In addition, they had the chance to see the horses in the paddock, the pre-parade ring, where they get saddled, and down at the start where you can hear the jockeys talking to each other.

Clare Balding adds: 'It is a really good example of the duchess supporting something that is not going to get big headlines and affect us all but is going to deeply affect a small number of people. The duchess's patronage has made a real difference too, and the fact that she has supported Ebony so well has lifted its status, so they now have a really successful fund-raising campaign and have managed to survive and even thrive through very difficult times.' Camilla doesn't seek headlines for herself. She prefers to quietly get on with what she has to do and use her position and contacts for those who are disadvantaged.

Living with a workaholic is not easy and Camilla had to choose whether to live a different life with her friends or try to keep up with her husband. She chose the latter. In an interview with *Vogue* magazine she said: 'Sometimes it's like ships passing in the night, but we always sit down together and have a cup of tea and discuss the day. We have a moment.'

Chapter 15

WORKING WIDER

The duties of senior royals are wide-ranging as they represent both themselves and the Queen. Camilla is always deferential to Her Majesty, despite her early efforts to block her relationship with Charles, and takes a step back out of respect when they are on a royal engagement together. The Queen has, in turn over recent years, handed over many patronages to Camilla, when they have become too much to manage. There are also foreign tours to cope with, meeting visiting heads of state, occasions like the State Opening of Parliament, hosting parties and receptions galore. There is a lot of standing and, when Charles and Camilla are abroad, they have to cope with different time zones and weather.

Closer to home they can't pick up any cause; they are expected to find something they genuinely care about and research it thoroughly so when they talk publicly, they can say something meaningful and make an impact. For example, if it's something delicate, like domestic violence, it is important to understand the experiences of the victims and the context of what happened before venturing out and addressing the public.

Camilla has chosen a wide range of charities that include health, literacy, supporting those in need, the elderly, victims of rape, sexual abuse and domestic violence, empowering women, food, animals, dance, heritage and the arts. When a charity's focus is rather sensitive, or a subject people would rather not talk about, she gives them a platform that will help reveal the issues. She declines charities she isn't drawn to or when she feels she can't make a difference.

The broadcaster Dame Esther Rantzen, founder of two charities, hugely admires Camilla: 'I think she has done a brilliant job of finding things that she really cares about and that really matter without treading on Prince Charles's feet. She is a strong woman but there is also softness there. Sometimes the story she hears is so heartbreaking that she cries. Hers is not an easy job; it can be very intense and draining when people talk to her because they trust her to know about their suffering. It's a good thing that she and Prince Charles support each other.

'She also gives her support to charities that help family relationships, understanding how hard it is to be lonely and how different it is to feel you are part of a team. Prince Charles has been transformed by having her support him, help calm his distress and accept him for who he is.'

Camilla has gradually become more comfortable with being the centre of attraction, when she's making a positive impact on something she wants to highlight. Amanda MacManus explains: 'Her Royal Highness has taken on so much. She's usually quite careful not to push herself forward but she seems to do more and more with Prince Charles, and in a sort of non-stop way like him as he never stops working. I think the more she continues to work with causes where she's making a difference, and that she really cares about, the more satisfaction the job will give her. And the more respect she will command.'

Constitutional expert Professor Vernon Bogdanor thinks the life of a royal is not easy. 'Contrary to what many people think, it's not glamorous [to be a senior royal]. It's hard work and it's painful. Inevitably Camilla meets a diverse range of people and has to be careful not to express any political opinions, which isn't as easy as people think. She might meet someone who says the reason that certain children don't get better treatment is because we've got a dreadful government, and she can't say, "Yes, I agree" or "No, that's unfair". What would happen to any of us if you couldn't express any opinion at all on something controversial?'

While Camilla is expected to always remain impartial and dignified, certain members of the general public can be quite the opposite, expressing their opinions in ways that can be downright dangerous. On 9 December 2010 there was a security blunder that led to rioters trying to harm Charles and Camilla. They were in their 1977 Rolls-Royce Phantom VI on their way to the London Palladium for the Royal Variety Performance, escorted by three police outriders and an unmarked police car. As the car turned into Regent Street from Piccadilly Circus the couple happily waved at passers-by and chatted to each other when suddenly a crowd began to close in around them.

This was swelled by four- to five-hundred protesters who had been demonstrating outside Parliament about the rise in university student fees. The royal car became separated from its police escort. The protesters quickly saw who was in the limousine and began kicking the vehicle, throwing bottles and paint bombs over it, and cracking the windows. The Rolls-Royce suddenly stopped altogether when a large bin was thrown in front of it. Many of the rioters surrounding the car were wearing balaclavas and scarves over their faces and banged on the windows shouting, 'Tory scum' and 'off with your heads'.

One protection officer, dressed in a dinner jacket, who was travelling in convoy with the royal couple, managed to get out of his car and tried desperately to clear a way through the mob. Camilla's usual composure left her, she screamed and gripped Charles's hand. Terrified for her safety, she then slipped down to the floor of the car. One witness said Charles pushed her down in an attempt to protect her. The prince, however, defiantly remained sitting in his seat and continued to wave at the crowd. The car managed to move away from the crowd, but the couple looked very shaken when they finally arrived at the Palladium. However, Camilla, who is renowned for turning fear into laughter, said about the experience as she left the theatre, 'First time for everything.'

Neither of them was hurt but the potential risk to their safety raised worrying echoes of the 1974 kidnap attempt on Princess Anne. It wasn't something that could be shrugged off, especially as the demonstration became more dangerous when they threw rocks at the police, attempted to smash into the Treasury and the Supreme Court building and surged into the National Gallery's Impressionist rooms. At least eight police officers were injured including one seriously. According to the Metropolitan Police, nearly forty protesters were hurt and twenty-six arrested. The force opened a full investigation.

The Queen obviously heard about the incident and was relieved that Prince Charles and Camilla were safe, and that Camilla had largely retained her dignity and even made a joke about what happened. She is naturally cautious but was well aware of how well Camilla was coping with royal demands.

David Cameron, prime minister at the time, condemned the violence as 'unacceptable'. He added: 'It is shocking and regrettable that the car carrying the Prince of Wales and the Duchess of Cornwall was caught up and attacked in the violence.' Home

Secretary Theresa May said: 'I utterly condemn the increasing levels of violence and disorder that some of the protesters have been, and still are, involved in.' The incident highlighted just how difficult it is for royals to try to be close and accessible to the public while remaining secure, particularly as incidents can flare up very quickly and a road that seemed relatively open in one minute could become a danger point a few seconds later.

There are some occasions, however, when being dignified becomes tricky. On one trip to Canada in July 2017 Camilla and Chares breached royal protocol when they had a fit of giggles. They were at the city of Iqaluit, as Inuit throat singers put on a performance for them. But the sounds from the singers – which involved a lot of heavy in and out breathing left the pair in stitches. They tried to cover their faces but every time they looked at each other their shaking shoulders gave the game away. Fortunately, it didn't affect how much better Camilla was getting on with the Queen. It had been a while since her marriage to Charles in 2005, and Catherine's marriage to Prince William in 2011, and in March 2012, the Queen decided it was time to invite the two women who would, one day, follow in her footsteps, on a girls-only outing.

The three royals, dressed in various shades of blue and with different hemlines – only the Queen wore a hat and gloves – visited Fortnum and Mason in Piccadilly for some delicious treats. The Queen's Diamond Jubilee year had just started and there were hundreds of cheering well-wishers outside plus a jazz band to welcome them. There was also a much smaller crowd protesting about Fortnum's selling foie gras. It was the first time the three women had carried out an official duty together and was a sign the Queen was keen to have both duchesses close by as she celebrated sixty years on the throne.

Charles and Camilla helped the celebration by visiting Norway, Sweden and Denmark in March 2012 on behalf of the Queen, followed by a four-day trip to Canada. In November that year they also visited New Zealand and Papua New Guinea for a two-week jubilee tour. During the Australian tour, they went to see the 2012 Melbourne Cup, which is the country's premier horse race and one of the highlights of the social year. Camilla was delighted to present the Melbourne Cup to the owner of the winning horse. It was an impressive example of her sense of duty over her lasting dread of flying.

It wasn't totally obvious at the time, but the Queen was giving Camilla the necessary credentials so that, when the time came and Prince Charles became king, she too would be accepted. The Queen also showed her appreciation of Camilla's work by marking her seventh wedding anniversary by awarding her the highest personal honour of Dame Grand Cross of the Royal Victorian Order.

In April 2018 Prince Charles was delighted and relieved to receive the news that he had been voted by Commonwealth leaders to be the ceremonial leader after the Queen, who is the current patron. There is no set term of office and the role itself involves no part in the day-to-day governance of any of the member states within the Commonwealth. Instead, it is an important symbolic and unifying role. Although the title has so far been held by the reigning British monarch since its establishment in December 1931, it is not hereditary. When Prince William went with his wife Catherine Duchess of Cambridge on a tour of the Caribbean in March 2022 to celebrate the Queen's platinum anniversary later in the year, the Jamaican Prime Minister Andrew Holness made it clear that Jamaica wants to cut ties with the British monarchy. Shortly afterwards, Prince William, in an unprecedented speech, said that he didn't want to tell 'countries what to do'; he may also not lead the Commonwealth. It was not by any means a hint that he may not wish to be king when the time came.

Later in 2018 Camilla became the first Vice-Patron of the Royal Commonwealth Society, which also marked its 150th anniversary. In her acceptance speech she said: 'I'm delighted, and honoured, to . . . celebrate this significant milestone. Over the past one hundred and fifty years the Royal Commonwealth Society has done so much to promote both the value and the values of the modern Commonwealth . . . you have much of which to be justly proud.'

Camilla stays conscious of the monarch's heritage, and when she has an engagement representing the Queen she always adds 'on behalf of Her Majesty' to any speech she makes. She had gained enough confidence to not worry too much about doing exactly what the Queen would do; she just feels proud and duty-bound to the continuation of the monarchy.

The Queen's Commonwealth Essay Competition, established in 1883, is the world's oldest international writing competition for schools. Each year, young people are asked to write on a theme that explores the Commonwealth's values and principles, fostering an empathic and open-minded world view in the next generation of Commonwealth leaders.

Recent themes have focused on the environment, inclusion, the role of youth leadership, and gender equality. Each year, winners are invited to travel to the United Kingdom for a week of educational and cultural activities, which culminates in a special awards ceremony that is now hosted by Camilla. I attended one in October 2021, held in St James's Palace, excellently compered by Camilla's lifelong friend Gyles Brandreth. A record-breaking 25,648 children from the Commonwealth entered the competition in 2021 on the theme of 'Community in the Commonwealth' but, because of Covid, not all the winners or runners-up were able to come to London.

Camilla wore a smart navy suit with white collar and cuffs and greeted one-time *X Factor* winner Alexandra Burke and the former Spice Girl Geri Horner, who are both Royal Commonwealth Society ambassadors. A very slim Geri, who made a speech, asked after Prince Charles. Camilla told her he was 'fine' and still a 'complete workaholic'. Geri then mentioned a book she had read which claimed that working is the key to a long life. Camilla agreed. 'Don't retire,' Geri said. Camilla wryly replied, 'That's not my problem.' She subsequently gave out certificates to the winners for their excellent writing and paid tribute to the 'unity, purpose and friendship' of the Commonwealth, saying those who belong to it are 'incredibly privileged'. She went on: 'Our Commonwealth community gives each of us 2.4 billion friends.'

The winning essays were profound but their authors as individuals were quite shy. Camilla chatted to them one by one and managed to get them all smiling. It is something she is very good at.

Occasionally a trip abroad makes history. On 26 March 2019, Prince Charles and Camilla became the first members of the Royal Family to set foot in communist Cuba when their RAF Voyager plane landed in the capital, Havana. The aim of the historic four-day royal tour was to strengthen UK-Cuban ties. It was part of the couple's twelve-day tour of five Caribbean countries involving more than fifty engagements.

Within an hour of touching down in Havana Prince Charles had laid a wreath at the monument to revolutionary poet José Marti, Cuba's national figurehead, who became a symbol of the country's bid for independence against Spain in the nineteenth century. Charles and Camilla stood at the base of the memorial, a star-shaped tower made of Cuban marble, said to be the largest monument in the world to a writer. The couple were flanked by a guard of honour while a military band played the two national anthems (the words to Cuba's were written by Marti). Prince

Charles and Camilla next visited the old quarter of Havana, much of which had fallen into disrepair but was slowly being restored, where they were mobbed by press and public.

A busy schedule sometimes planned more than a year in advance makes it difficult to find time even to squeeze a short visit like the one Dame Judi Dench and Camilla arranged on the Isle of Wight in July 2018. Dame Judi wanted to show her friend the restoration of a special room of Osborne House in East Cowes. It was bought by Queen Victoria and Prince Albert in 1845 and was one of Victoria's favourite places to stay. She once said: 'It is impossible to imagine a prettier spot.' The house was given to the state after the Queen's death in 1901. It is now cared for by English Heritage and open to the public all year round. Dame Judi is a patron of Friends of Osborne House. She has also played Queen Victoria in two films, *Victoria and Abdul* and *Mrs Brown*.

It was a glorious summer's day and both Dame Judi and Camilla wore cream-coloured clothes. Judi greeted Camilla as she arrived at Queen Victoria's private beach, where she was also welcomed by a group of schoolchildren. Judi said: 'You must be so careful of the house because it's been preserved so beautifully.' She particularly wanted Camilla to see the newly restored Durbar Room, which was used in the filming of *Victoria and Abdul*. Judi admitted she and Camilla 'don't talk about films that much. When you play Victoria as a Royal Queen it's a bit awkward to mention. I just hoped that if she had seen the films, she liked them. I did, though, show her the desk which Queen Victoria sat at because it was used in the film. She was fascinated and excited about it.'

Dame Judi has been a 'huge admirer' of Camilla since they met in 2008. 'I think it was at the Sandringham Flower Show,' she says. 'She's one of those people you feel you've known for years. She's got a fantastic kind of grace and ease of manner that makes you feel you could unburden yourself and tell her anything. I remember Prince Charles recently saying, "My darling wife," as he usually refers to her, "can get anything out of anybody, incredibly quickly."

'She isn't someone who holds grievances or is critical about other people and is not in the slightest malicious even when she has good reason to be. When I first met her, I would stand back to wait for her to speak to me first, but there's never been any of that. I could be absolutely open with her and say anything. I think we are the type of people who could be somewhere very solemn and get the giggles.'

She worries about the future for Camilla when Charles succeeds his mother. 'I often think how hard both their jobs are. It's not really a job but a responsibility that must be with them every single day. It's such a weight and the country is so unkind and always looking for the negative. Instead, I imagine a quiet life at Highgrove for the two of them. It would be ideal, but of course it's something they can't possibly have. It's a great plus as long as they're together. They are a wonderful couple, as you can see when they're out and about. They complement each other and are so at ease when they are together.'

Judi was right to be concerned. Princess Anne had slowly softened towards Camilla and had just about come to terms with Camilla using the term princess consort when Prince Charles became king, as had been agreed when they married. She was very put out, however, when she discovered that Charles had told their mother he would like her to be queen consort instead. A former member of Palace staff told me that she had no qualms about telling Charles and Camilla exactly what she thought. There was also a strong possibility that she would try to convince the Queen that the country wouldn't accept it and felt confident other members of the Royal Family would support her view.

Prince Charles remained firm, Camilla stayed neutral. She had faced so much stress before their wedding that she dreaded any more. Even so, it was an anxious time. Camilla got on quite well with Sophie, Countess of Wessex, but their relationship is civil rather than close. There were also rumours that Sophie had said that she knew a lot of people who 'didn't want her to be queen'. As for Prince Andrew, Camilla had as little contact as possible with him, as he had never cared about her. She hoped Prince William would agree with his father, but she couldn't take it for granted. She protected herself by not thinking about it too much and buried her head, not just in books but also by taking on one engagement after another.

Official state responsibilities and helping the Queen in her national duties are a priority. The Queen attended the State Opening of Parliament on 11 May 2021, her first major royal appearance since her husband died a month earlier. The Duke of Edinburgh usually sat close to her at this foremost state occasion until 2017, when he retired from all public duties and Charles stepped in. It must have been difficult enough for the Queen to be there, and all the more so to see that the Consort's Throne, where the duke always sat, had been removed from the House of Lords.

Camilla and Charles had to sit on the Chairs of State, some distance away, which made the Queen look very alone on the Sovereign's Throne. Traditionally the Queen would have worn the long crimson velvet Robe of State and the Imperial State Crown, but because of the pandemic, wearing the robe was cancelled to prevent any spread of coronavirus. She also last wore the crown, which is made of more than 3,000 gemstones and weighs two pounds and thirteen ounces, for the 2016 State Opening. Instead, it was placed close to her. Her chosen outfit was a grey jacquard coat with lemon flowers, and a grey and yellow silk dress and hat designed by her personal assistant Angela Kelly. She also wore pearls and two diamond and aquamarine clips that her father King George VI gave to her on her eighteenth birthday. It is very rare to see the Queen wear the same thing twice, and a sign perhaps that in her sorrow she didn't want to bother with a new dress. Perhaps too, what she wore had more positive memories of when she wore it for Ladies' Day at Royal Ascot in June 2019.

Camilla also wore a brooch that meant a great deal to the Queen. Called the Rock Crystal Brooch, it belonged to the Queen Mother and was a treasure that the Queen herself might have lent her daughter-in-law. Camilla wore it on the left side of her cream coat. Behind the crystals, the back is transparent, allowing the colour of the clothing beneath it to show through. It was a supportive choice for her to make. Camilla has also pleased the Queen by wearing other brooches that belonged to the Queen Mother. Earlier in 2021 she wore a diamond brooch in honour of Burns Night. It is shaped like two thistles and was once a favourite of the Queen Mother, who wore it on her hat. It is no doubt incredibly meaningful for Her Majesty to be reminded of her mother, whom she loved and admired, by Camilla's brooch choices.

Camilla makes sure there are also opportunities for fun in her full diary, and in September 2021 the smiling duchess appeared on Instagram holding a large, home-made, freshly baked cake. It was to celebrate the return of Poetry Together tea parties, an annual event that brings together elderly people in care homes with school-children who learn and then recite a poem to them. After that, everyone has tea and cake. Clarence House put out a slightly tongue in cheek explanation: 'The Duchess has shared her recipe for a Victoria Sponge for young and old(er!) alike to enjoy after reciting a poem by heart together.'

Poetry Together is a project Camilla has supported since it was launched by Gyles Brandreth in 2019 in partnership with Dukes Education and National Poetry Day. Her delicious-looking Victoria Sponge, also known as the Victoria Sandwich Cake, was named after Queen Victoria, her husband's great-great-great-grandmother, who liked cake with her afternoon tea. During her reign her favourite cake was usually topped with a dusting of caster or icing sugar and the middle filled with jam, and later with cream and fresh strawberries. Camilla revealed an innovation of her own with a mischievous smile, telling everyone that she often bypasses tradition and uses lemon curd or Nutella as a filling instead. Traditionalists were shocked, others were delighted. Her admission is a small but perfect example of the unique way she conforms with royal convention then often adds an original tweak of her own. But it took a few years before she felt confident enough to do so in public.

Camilla believes that learning poetry by heart is a lifelong benefit for children and is ready to get involved in something that encourages it. Hence, in her capacity of Vice-Patron of the Royal Commonwealth Society, she got together with her friends Dame Joanna Lumley and Gyles Brandreth, along with his daughter Aphra in June 2022 to launch the Commonwealth Poetry Podcast that will 'virtually visit' all fifty-four countries of the Commonwealth through poetry.

Camilla also skilfully uses her position and contacts to reach out quietly and with no publicity to those who are in need. Helping Catherine Goodman, a friend for twenty-five years, is one example. 'I have a disabled sister called Sophie and have been her carer for my family,' Catherine told me. 'Camilla has been incredibly supportive. Sophie needs twenty-four-hours-a-day care and lives in a care home. For the last fifteen years Camilla has invited her to watch Trooping the Colour from Clarence House. It's become the highlight of Sophie's year, as she doesn't get out much. Camilla also invites along her hat designer Philip Treacy, her private secretaries and other people who help her. Everyone is given a lovely brunch and we wave at the carriages as they pass. The duchess has been amazing with Sophie in other ways too: she writes to her regularly and always sends her a Christmas card. She is so thoughtful about lots of people who haven't had it easy.'

Catherine offered another example of her kindness, when Camilla helped Harry Parker, who was badly injured in Afghanistan. He was twenty-three when he joined the forces in 2009 and, three years later, when he was a captain in 4th Battalion, The Rifles, caught the full force of a booby-trap bomb, losing both legs. On his way back from a night patrol with some fifty men, he mistakenly decided to take a line of soldiers on a shortcut through a field rather than follow the longer path. He was rushed to the military hospital at Camp Bastion, during which time his heart was restarted five times.

Harry, son of General Sir Nick Parker, was flown back to the UK to recover and convalesce, and by chance Camilla was visiting the hospital he was in. She learnt that he had done a foundation degree at Falmouth College of Art before going on to study History of Art at University College London and then becoming a soldier. Catherine explains: 'She went to talk to him and said immediately afterwards that when he was a bit better, she'd pay for him to have a course at the Prince's Drawing School that Prince Charles and I founded in 2000, as it could help with his rehabilitation. I only heard about him when I had an email from her private secretary Amanda MacManus. I met him and, when he was ready, he came to the drawing school. The duchess paid for a couple of courses, and he then went on to our postgraduate programme. He has since had his prosthetics, and wrote his autobiography, *The Anatomy of a Soldier*, in 2016. He is also married with two children and his designs have been used for the medals that are awarded at the Invictus Games [launched by Prince Harry]. I am not saying that his success is all down to Camilla, but her thoughtful gift put him on the right road.'

It's said that good bosses have loyal and willing staff. They were certainly understanding when Esther Rantzen went to Clarence House in August 2016 to look at some of the rooms that had been opened to the public. 'As I was approaching the X-ray machine, I realised I had a gun in my bag,' she told me. 'It was a pellet gun, but looked like a revolver, and I owned it because Desmond Wilcox, my late husband, had an ongoing personal feud with grey squirrels. My then four-year-old grandson had found it and it somehow ended up in my handbag. I quickly told one of the rather well-brought-up young ladies from Clarence House who were around that I was terribly sorry to have a gun in my handbag. They called a policeman, who removed the gun and let me continue with my visit. When I had finished, a charming young woman loped towards me, put her hand deep into her pocket, pulled out the gun, which was wrapped in clingfilm with a Clarence House label attached to it, and put it into my handbag. I wrote to Her Royal Highness and said how grateful I was that a member of her household had treated me with such discretion, and [that] no one shrieked for me to be arrested.' No one knew at the time that there was a real danger just round the corner.

Chapter 16

COVID 2020

At the end of December 2019 news emerged of a virus named Covid-19 that was believed to have come from Wuhan City in China: it attacked the respiratory system and could cause pneumonia. Nobody thought that it would change lives in the UK and around the world, or that by the end of 2021 it would be responsible for nearly 200,000 deaths in the UK and an estimated 6.34 million globally.

The Duchess of Cornwall, like countless others, initially chose to carry on as normal. On 19 January 2020, she visited Prospect Hospice in Wroughton, Wiltshire, to help celebrate the facility's 40th anniversary year. It was a cold day, and when she arrived, she took off her black gloves to shake hands with the staff, dignitaries and volunteers, unaware, as was the nation, that this most common custom would soon abruptly stop and be replaced by bumping elbows, touching fists or merely bowing.

Prospect Hospice is highly regarded locally and each year cares for about 7,300 patients, carers and family members spread across Swindon, Marlborough and north-east Wiltshire. 'I know everybody thinks . . . a hospice is going to be a sad, depressing place,' Camilla said, 'but it is always the opposite. Prospect is certainly one of the most uplifting hospices I've been to and I'm very proud to be its patron.'

While there she spent time talking to the Bereavement Support Group and individuals who had recently lost a loved one and had spent their first Christmas without them. Camilla remarked how important such groups were. 'Everybody has experienced the same grief, probably, so you know exactly how everyone else feels,' she said. 'I think it is such a good idea to have group therapy to let it all out.'

Always a good sport, she then agreed to try out a virtual reality headset. It contained an app by Sir David Attenborough that shows a peaceful walk through trees that can help reduce pain and stress for patients. 'I can see you could get addicted to this,' she laughed when she handed the headset back. 'It relaxes you.'

The visit was going well until one of the reporters unexpectedly asked the duchess very loudly whether she was missing Harry and Meghan. Eleven days earlier, the Duke and Duchess of Sussex had announced that they were leaving the Royal Family and would no longer use their HRH titles or perform royal duties. Camilla looked as if she had been taken by surprise. She smiled enigmatically, paused, said 'hmmm', followed by the word 'course', then walked smartly away.

On 23 January 2020 the Foreign and Commonwealth Office gave the first of many warnings about a possible pandemic and advised against all but essential travel to Wuhan. Less than a week later British Airways stopped all flights to and from mainland China. Two days after that the first two cases of Covid-19 were confirmed in the UK.

Camilla, again like many others, continued with engagements

that had long been in the diary. On 27 January she went to Poland to attend the International Holocaust Remembrance Day, organised by the United Nations, that marked the 75th anniversary of the liberation of Auschwitz-Birkenau, the Nazi concentration camp. The Prince of Wales had attended the World Holocaust Forum in Jerusalem with other world leaders the previous week. It is estimated that a minimum of 1.3 million people were deported to Auschwitz between 1940 and 1945 and that at least 1.1 million were murdered there. Camilla joined Queen Letizia of Spain, Crown Princess Victoria of Sweden and Queen Maxima of the Netherlands, as well as heads of state and camp survivors from round the world. After the service, she walked seven hundred metres with others alongside the railway lines that brought prisoners to Auschwitz. At the end of the walk candles were placed at the main monument, paying tribute to the victims. Camilla has sometimes found it difficult to cope with emotionally draining engagements, but doesn't let it stop her.

Two days later she had a more upbeat official engagement. She is president of the Royal Voluntary Service, (RVS) which mobilises volunteers to support those in need, and went to the Cornhill Centre in Banbury, Oxfordshire, to hear of the assistance it provides for older people. There was a crowd waiting to catch a glimpse of her and she went on a short walkabout shaking bare hands again with many onlookers. Once inside she showed her goodwill by agreeing to take part in an Israeli circle dance class run by volunteers Avis Gallager, then seventy-two, and Joan Sprittlehouse, then eighty-two. She beamed as she followed the steps she was shown by other members. 'It was fantastic to give the Duchess of Cornwall a flavour of the fun we have in class,' said Avis after Camilla had gone. A clip of her dancing was shared on social media and fans praised her for both her commitment and behaviour. One said: 'The Duchess of Cornwall shows what being a royal is all about. Good on her.' Another commented, 'I really like her. She just seems like she is game for everything.'

Camilla gets on well with Catherine and William. An insider might call it 'a very grown-up rapport', which basically means their relationship works, but they are not in each other's pockets. February 2020 saw a rare event when the Duke and Duchess of Cambridge combined forces with Charles and Camilla to attend the same engagement for the first time since 2011. It was a welcome opportunity to show family unity and that they were happy and willing to lead the monarchy into the future now that Harry and Meghan had stepped away. The destination was Loughborough – to see the £300 million Defence Medical Rehabilitation Centre (DMRC). Among other things, the facility helps military amputees and those suffering from battlefield neurological illness.

It was a horribly cold, wet and windy winter's day and the royals arrived just after a heavy hailstorm. Prince William was the only one without a coat, while Catherine and Camilla were well wrapped up in thick coats and high black boots. All four appeared to be in good spirits as they were taken on a tour of the centre, visiting some of the therapy areas and observing patients at gym rehabilitation sessions. Several of them were taking part in wheelchair basketball and Prince William was encouraged to join in. He borrowed a wheelchair, missed five shots but succeeded on the sixth, explaining that it had taken 'a while' to get his aim in. At the end of the visit Charles and Camilla moved on to Leicester city centre to meet stallholders and members of a local women's charity.

Despite the increased anxiety hovering over the country about Covid-19, Camilla was unrelenting, keeping herself extremely busy and mixing with a wide variety of people without anticipating what was to come. On 19 February she hosted, as patron, a reception at Clarence House for Venus Arthritis, the UK's largest charity dedicated to supporting those with the disease. Next stop was Brent, in north-west London, to celebrate its status as the 2020 London Borough of Culture. She visited the Granville Youth and Community Centre in Kilburn, Kiln, (the Kilburn theatre formerly known as the Tricycle) and The Agency, a social change project that works to help young people take on projects that have a positive impact on their local communities.

At the end of February confirmed cases of coronavirus in the UK had crept up to twenty-three. Shortly afterwards the government published its action plan for dealing with the virus, warning that a fifth of the national workforce could be absent from work during the infection's peak. Warning was given that the virus's increasing impact could rise from moderate to big in the UK. A few days later the World Health Organization (WHO) declared that the outbreak was now a pandemic, and any traveller was potentially at risk of infection.

On 23 March social distancing became legally mandatory. Prime Minister Boris Johnson said on national television: 'From this evening I must give the British people a very simple instruction: you must stay at home.' Pubs and cafes were shut. All but essential travel to the United States was banned. UK retailers released a joint message asking customers not to panic-buy products like pasta, hand gel and especially toilet paper. Not much notice was taken. Police broke up wedding parties with too many guests and handed out fines, which included £200 each to thirty-one Metropolitan Police officers who broke Covid rules by having haircuts.

One nerve-wracking public announcement followed another. On 17 March Buckingham Palace announced that the Queen, whose ninety-fourth birthday was a month away, and Prince Philip, then ninety-eight, would move from Sandringham to Windsor a week

Camilla's first overseas tour with Prince Charles after her marriage was to the USA, where there was some scathing press commentary. The couple were pleased to meet with President George W. Bush and his wife, Laura.

Camilla's relationship with Charles' sons William and Harry has not been easy. Here they are at a Prince's Trust event in 1996. Over time her relationship with William has improved. It has been more complicated with Harry.

Camilla and Craig Revel Horwood enjoy a spontaneous cha-cha-cha at St Clement Danes School in London in 2009. A big *Strictly* fan, Camilla also joined the Silver Swans dance programme.

Walking round a display of elephant sculptures with her brother Mark Shand in 2010. He tragically died in 2014. Camilla has remained a keen supporter of the elephant charity he set up.

One of Camilla's favourite events of the year is also tinged with sadness, as she hosts a Christmas party at Clarence House for children with terminal illnesses. An equerry from the Welsh Guards decorates the tree with his sword.

At Charles's seventieth birthday party in 2018, Camilla greets the newly married couple. Camilla tried to advise Meghan on dealing with the pressure of the royal spotlight, but her words weren't heeded.

The portrayal of Camilla in *The Crown* is harsh and unfair, so when Emerald Fennell (who plays her in the series) was a guest at a celebration of International Women's Day in March 2022, she made sure to joke about her fictional version.

When Prince Philip formally transferred his role as colonel-in-chief of The Rifles to Camilla in 2020, it was a huge thank you to her and reflected how she had won over the senior royals with all her hard work.

Despite the request to discourage people from laying flowers, after Prince Philip's death in April 2021, a huge number did so, leaving Charles and Camilla visibly moved.

During the Platinum Jubilee celebrations, Camilla travels to the Trooping the Colour with the Duchess of Cambridge and her three children, George, Charlotte and Louis.

Camilla and Charles made an informal visit to the set of EastEnders, becoming part of the long-running soap series. Here Camilla meets Maddy Hill, Danny Dyer and Rose Ayling-Ellis.

The Queen was 'humbled and deeply touched' by the cheers she received when she came out onto the balcony of Buckingham Palace at the end of the Jubilee weekend celebrations. With Charles and Camilla alongside her, the future of the monarchy looked secure.

earlier than originally planned. The Palace added that she and the duke expected to stay at Windsor until after Easter and that every care would be taken to keep them safe.

Consultation followed between the Queen's medical household and the government, and it was decided her public events would also be cancelled 'as a sensible precaution'. Events would include the Maundy Service at St George's Chapel on 9 April and the three annual garden parties the Queen hosts at Buckingham Palace. The cancellation of the garden parties was thought to be unprecedented, with Palace officials unable to recall a similar occasion in recent memory. Investitures were postponed and other activities dropped to try and control the spread of the virus.

Lockdown arrived across the UK on 23 March and the public and the royals began to live a life some called 'a new normal' – but it was far from it. Diaries that were often full a year or more ahead of time became obsolete, including those of the royals. Camilla described her sudden empty diary as 'peculiar', adding with a smile: 'My husband . . . will work wherever he is.' Other public events that had been booked well in advance collapsed like a pack of cards. These included Charles and Camilla's planned spring tour to Jordan, Cyprus and Bosnia-Herzegovina, a state visit by the Emperor and Empress of Japan, and the Queen's favourite annual event, Trooping the Colour. In addition, the Royal British Legion called on the nation to mark the 75th anniversary of VE Day, only from home.

It gave Charles and Camilla the opportunity for a few well-deserved lie-ins, but their work ethic and sense of duty put that out of the question. 'The Prince of Wales and the Duchess of Cornwall kept asking us what they could do to help,' an aide told me. 'They were very keen to be as useful as possible.' After much talk about finding a solution to them being stuck at home, the conclusion was to go remote. It was a very different way of managing royal engagements, communicating with the public, keeping in touch with the elderly and vulnerable, and connecting with family and friends. Although initially it seemed a very poor substitute for face-to-face interaction, positive change came out of it at many different levels.

One thing was for certain: virtual meetings had never been on the duchess's agenda. She later told BBC News: 'I'm ashamed to say that I really hated the internet. I didn't understand it and I thought, *What's the point of this?* but since lockdown, it's been so brilliant because I've been able to communicate with family, my children, my friends.' Although virtual meetings were nowhere near as satisfying as the real thing, it was, the duchess and countless others admitted, 'much better than nothing and at least I could stay in touch'. But she added that she still missed her five biological grandchildren, plus the ever-growing number of royal grandchildren.

The negative effect of the pandemic on the country continued. On 18 March the pound sterling fell to its lowest level since 1985 and a few days later the Bank of England cut interest rates from 0.25 per cent to just 0.1 per cent, the lowest rate in the Bank's 325-year history. Chancellor Rishi Sunak was a ray of light when he announced that the government would pay 80 per cent of wages for employees not working, up to £2,500 a month, as part of 'unprecedented' measures to protect jobs. Two days later the government stated that all schools would shut from 20 March, except for the children of key workers and vulnerable children.

Members of the Royal Family rarely announce information about their health unless they are hospitalised or have had to cancel a public appearance. Even then they are usually vague about their condition. This all changed as a result of Covid. On 26 March

Clarence House revealed that the Prince of Wales had tested positive for coronavirus. He had had mild Covid symptoms for a couple of days and was tested by the NHS in Aberdeenshire. A positive result came through the following evening. A Palace source said that the medical advice the prince had been given was that it was 'unlikely to escalate into a more serious case'. He had also spoken to the Queen and Princes William and Harry and was 'in good spirits'. The Queen, for her part, was 'following all the appropriate advice with regard to her welfare'.

American royal biographer Sally Bedell Smith was more concerned. She thought it was 'a very big deal because Charles is the heir apparent, and if anything happens to him, then his son will become the heir apparent and will be next in line.' She also pointed out that even though the monarch has no overt power in a constitutional monarchy, the British monarch is still crucial to the functioning of the British government, as, for instance, being titular head of the military. 'If the heir to the crown is suddenly threatened, it's unsettling to say the least.'

One of the reasons why the public were so concerned about Prince Charles was that he was known to be very fit for his age and, if he was affected, what chance did the old and vulnerable have of avoiding the deadly virus? An aide who is less than half his years told me his staff found it hard to keep up with him when walking together to talk about royal issues. 'It's even more exhausting when I accompany him on royal tours abroad. I come back absolutely shattered and have to take a few days off, while he is up and ready for the next engagement. He doesn't stop at all.' His wife, however, does well at almost keeping up. They both exercise every day and eat organic food, largely from the prince's own gardens, that helps them maintain healthy immune systems. Camilla, who must have worried about how her own life could change if his condition deteriorated, put on a positive front. 'He is probably the fittest man of his age I know,' she told BBC radio. 'He'll walk and walk and walk. He is like a mountain goat – he leaves everybody miles behind.'

The news of him catching the virus was released at a time when Prince Charles's popularity was increasing, as was Camilla's, but more slowly. This was put down as partly due to the support the royal couple were giving the Queen and taking on more of her duties. She had cut back because of her age and to spend more time with the ailing Duke of Edinburgh, grateful that she now felt able to trust her son and heir and his wife enough to rely on him to represent her.

It proved difficult if not impossible to find out how and where Charles caught the virus as he meets more members of the public than virtually any other member of the Royal Family. A spokesman said it was due 'to the high number of engagements he carried out in his public role during recent weeks, but otherwise [he] remains in good health'.

Buckingham Palace said the Queen had seen Prince Charles on 9 March when they were both at the Commonwealth Day Service at Westminster Abbey. Charles was seen greeting people with the Indian 'namaste' greeting – a slight bow with hands pressed together in prayer pose – instead of shaking hands. Younger royals were seen greeting people with elbow bumps. Charles was also seen at a charity event on 10 March sitting across the table from Prince Albert of Monaco, who had recently announced that he, too, had tested positive for coronavirus.

The Queen and Prince Charles met briefly again after an investiture on 12 March. He later attended a dinner in aid of the Australian bushfire relief and recovery effort. Camilla was also tested. As a one-time heavy smoker, in theory she could have been more vulnerable to catching Covid, but she was not infected. A Clarence House statement read: 'In accordance with government and medical advice, the Prince and the Duchess are now self-isolating at home in Scotland.' Charles and Camilla stayed isolated in Birkhall for about two weeks while he recovered. A number of household staff also began self-isolating in their own homes.

Shortly after Boris Johnson announced the lockdown on 16 March, members of the public were asked to clap to thank NHS workers for their vital role during the pandemic. Countless people across the UK responded by standing by their front doors at 8pm once a week, clapping, cheering, ringing bells and/or banging saucepans. Camilla and Prince Charles joined in by opening their front door at Birkhall and, with broad smiles, joined in the clapping while a photographer recorded the moment. The clapping for all continued for ten weeks while life looked grim. Almost everyone knew someone who had contracted the virus and almost as many knew someone who had passed away because of it.

It was a time when both British and Commonwealth citizens needed someone who was wise, comforting and insightful. Who else but the Queen? Sure enough, on 5 April more than 24 million people tuned in to hear her speak from Windsor Castle. It was an extraordinary broadcast for an extraordinary time, as the Queen rarely broadcasts other than on Christmas Day. Her speech had a nostalgic feel in that the suffering people were going through due to the pandemic reminded her of her first radio broadcast in October 1940, during the Second World War. She was a young teenager then and addressed children during BBC's *Children's Hour*. Eighty years on, she said, 'Today, once again, many people will feel a painful sense of separation from their loved ones.'

Now, with the country tackling a new and deadly enemy, she acknowledged the grief and financial hardships people were facing, thanked those who were following the government's social distancing rules, paid tribute to key workers, and said the UK 'will succeed' in its fight against coronavirus but may have 'more still to endure . . . Together we are tackling this disease, and I want to reassure you that if we remain united and resolute, then we will overcome it . . . I hope in the years to come everyone will be able to take pride in how they responded to this challenge.'

Thirty minutes after her comforting and meticulously chosen words, sobering news was released that then Prime Minister Boris Johnson had been taken to St Thomas' Hospital in London. Ten days earlier he had tested positive for the virus, and he'd had a high temperature ever since. As a 'precautionary step' his doctors advised he went to hospital, but the public was assured it was not an emergency decision. His condition continued to deteriorate and the following day he was moved to the intensive care unit. It took until May to discover that contingency plans were made in case he died while in intensive care. They were not needed as his condition gradually improved. He was moved back into the ward and released from hospital to continue his recovery at Chequers, the Prime Minister's country house.

Meanwhile it was left to the senior royals, including Camilla, plus the welcome contribution from war veteran Captain Tom Moore, to try to create some sort of silver lining to help everyone through lockdown. Captain Tom, as he was universally known, made international headlines in 2020 when the 99-year-old began raising money for the struggling NHS by walking up and down his garden hugely helped by his Zimmer frame. By the time he turned one hundred on 4 April 2020, he had raised more than £32 million and no doubt made millions of other people smile. Camilla mentioned him in a video call. After saying that the pandemic was 'bringing out the best in people', she added: 'you know that wonderful man Captain Tom walking around and raising all that money. I mean, that sort of thing makes you proud to be British, doesn't it?'

Although Captain Tom's efforts made millions marvel at his

achievement, it didn't lessen the stress, fear and dread that loved ones could be next in line to be affected. They needed reassurance but places of worship were closed down and doctors and front-line workers were overworked and falling ill at a frightening rate. It was a call to arms for senior royals.

Chapter 17

VIRTUAL CONNECTIONS

The duchess was isolating with Prince Charles in Aberdeenshire at the time. She put on a brave front, but it was inevitably a cause of concern. She distracted herself by doing voluntary work for the Osteoporosis Society and tried to help others. In normal times Camilla would have usually done an engagement or two a day and a modest number of people would have been there to meet or greet her. Lockdown, however, changed all that. Instead, it offered an enormous platform where thousands could watch and hear her reach out to those in need as well as sympathise, comfort and promote the causes close to her heart. As a result, her empty diary soon filled up with all sorts of engagements that fitted with the extraordinary times people were living through.

The lockdown worked so encouragingly for Camilla that while life itself became progressively tough, she seemed to blossom as a growing number of admirers spoke very positively about her, feeling that at last she had come into her own and revealed her genuine interest in other people. Her low husky voice makes her sound sympathetic, and this proved ideal for anyone who felt scared and bewildered about how the pandemic and lockdown was affecting their lives. Even remotely she was able to make people feel she understood what they were going through and less alone. A Palace official was pleased that lockdown was a chance for the public to get a glimpse of the real Camilla through social media. She is popular with the courtiers, who described her as loyal, hardworking and fun. 'She has a real sense of humour,' said one.

She confessed early on that when she was on a work call, she made sure her top half was appropriate and looked businesslike, while her bottom half was usually jeans or tracksuit trousers, which nobody could see. Thousands of women were doing just the same and her revelation made her sound approachable and not at all snobby.

Meanwhile, the Queen recognised Camilla's worth, loyalty, and the fact that she had risen to the occasion by willingly taking on additional duties that could help reassure those in difficulty. It drew the Queen closer to her and seemed to be the trigger that led to her acknowledging that she was after all rather good for Prince Charles. She made him happy and less irritable, which would make him a better heir to throne. Fifteen years after their marriage, the cautious determined Queen had finally grown fond of her daughter-in-law. So much so Her Majesty was shown how the video communication platform Zoom worked, and the two women could develop virtual connections, be able to chat to each other and discuss what the future might bring. Surprisingly the lockdown was giving Camilla the opportunity to discover abilities she might not have known she had.

High on her contact list during these very difficult times was Dame Laura Lee, CEO of Maggie's, a renowned cancer charity that provides free cancer support and information. Camilla was very concerned for those suffering from cancer who had to endure a harrowing time in compulsory isolation. It was a great relief for

Camilla when lockdown eased and she could visit Maggie's Barts, a special cancer centre at St Bartholomew's Hospital in the City of London. She confessed to Laura that despite the virtues of remote conversations, she much prefers face-to-face encounters. Laura remembers her saying: 'As you know I like being with people.'

She was also involved with several charities that support older people in the community, as well as children and, since 2017, she has been patron of the Silver Line, a free confidential helpline for older people experiencing loneliness. Thinking ahead, she anticipated that elderly people, especially as so many lived on their own, would be badly affected by the lockdown. She was right. Silver Line normally receives about 10,000 calls a week. When lockdown began in March 2020, the number of people calling the helpline went up by 'an unprecedented' 1.3 million visitors to a newly established coronavirus hub.

Camilla tried to help by reaching out for a friendly upbeat chat and voiced what many of them felt by talking about how much she missed her own grandchildren during lockdown, and how she looked forward to the day she could hug them again. She also acknowledged the work Silver Line was doing: 'For many lonely people, the Silver Line represents a lifeline into the outside world . . . As its proud patron I am thinking about all the Silver Liners, the staff and the volunteers in these challenging times.'

Dame Esther Rantzen founded and launched the organisation nationally in 2013, and in 2019 it merged with Age UK. She is grateful for Camilla's involvement and concern. 'It can be quite difficult for an older person to think of things to say to a celebrity, and they can be quite grand and intimidating, but Camilla is very easy to talk to. She's so un-grand and they think she genuinely cares, which I am sure she does. She also has a very touching, sincere and authentic voice.'

Catherine and Sophie joined up with Camilla on 1 June 2020

to take part in 'Check in and Chat', an initiative launched by the Royal Volunteer Responders to make phone calls to various people thought to be high risk during coronavirus, which included the elderly and those with pre-existing conditions. It was an example of how despite Camilla and Sophie's rather formal relationship, such things had to be put aside for the sake of working together in an emergency to help those suffering during the pandemic.

That same month, Camilla was online with the Duchess of Cambridge to mark Children's Hospice Week – the one week in the year dedicated to raising awareness and funds for children's hospices and palliative care across the UK.

Families with a terminally ill child are very vulnerable, even when they have support, and lockdown understandably made them feel even more isolated. In a Zoom conversation the two duchesses talked to a family with a terminally ill child and members of staff at hospices. They had different styles of talking, with Camilla more emotional and Catherine more forensic, but both offered warmth and sympathy and listened carefully at what each other said. It was a combination that worked very well.

Camilla talked about a visit to the children's hospice Helen and Douglas House thirteen years previously, saying: 'I have to admit, I was filled with a certain amount of trepidation as I wasn't sure what I was going to find. When I arrived, I was totally amazed by what I found . . . warmth, laughter and happiness.' She also made a point of adding that the nurses and carers were: 'the most wonderful people'. Catherine said how much she admired the staff too, and asked how everything was going with the pandemic, saying: 'There must be lots of extra services to provide for the family.'

The Government's step four that lifted Covid-19 restrictions went ahead in June, and Prince Charles and Camilla moved down south from Scotland. They wanted their first visit in person since the pandemic took hold in the UK in March to be one of thanks to NHS staff at Gloucester Royal Hospital, which is close to Highgrove. The engagement – despite the threat of showers – was held outside in a quiet corner of the hospital campus to avoid attracting crowds. The royal couple expressed their thanks for keeping the healthcare and its emergency services going throughout the crisis.

The staff, whether nurses, doctors, paramedics or volunteers, stood on an individual yellow marker in the grass to make sure they were keeping the strict two-metre distancing rules. No one shook hands and each person moved forward in turn to talk to the royal couple while keeping the correct distance apart. The royal couple spent thirty minutes meeting around twenty healthcare workers. Camilla voiced what many felt when she said: 'They've done the most remarkable things . . . The way they've looked after people, they've kept control of the whole thing, a question of not panicking and getting on with it. They are Britain at its best.'

In January 2021 it was announced that the Queen and Prince Philip had been given a Covid vaccination by a royal household doctor at Windsor Castle. It was an unusual step for the Queen to inform the public of personal details about her health, but it was under-stood she did so to prevent inaccuracies and speculation. The following month Clarence House announced that Camilla, Duchess of Cornwall, seventy-three, and Charles, Prince of Wales, seventy-two – who were in the fourth priority group for the vaccine via the NHS – had their first dose on Wednesday 10 February 2021. Camilla was shortly afterwards at a pop-up vaccination centre in a mosque when she let slip that she'd had 'the AstraZeneca one', adding 'it didn't really matter. I didn't ask . . . because I hate injections.'

In March 2021, a year after the start of the pandemic, the Queen and Camilla happily joined forces for a video call to tell members of the Royal Voluntary Service (RVS) what a great help they were being supporting people during the pandemic. It also served to mark one year since it launched the NHS Volunteer Responders Scheme. The Queen, patron of the RVS, said they had done 'wonderful work' when she heard that more than a million new volunteers had signed up in a year, taking the organisation's total number of volunteers to an astounding 12.7 million.

She told them: 'Thank you very much indeed, very interesting to hear what you [have] been doing. I think it's wonderful work and I do thank everybody, and all the others too, who have been volunteering. It's been a great, great help over this very difficult year. Very nice to meet you all.'

Camilla, who is president of the RVS, told the volunteers: 'We couldn't have done it without you' − a phrase that came to be much used for NHS frontliners. Camilla mentioned that she had had 'lots of happy conversations' with Doris Winfield, eighty-six, whom she met through the 'Check in and Chat' scheme (and who has since passed away).

She thanked them again four months later, on Thank You Day celebrations that honour the work of doctors, nurses, volunteers and many other workers throughout the year. One fan wrote: 'Ah, Your Royal Highness, you are truly a gem! And thank YOU for your service, kindness and involvement in many important causes.'

On 24 March the couple went on an official two-day visit to Greece, which had been arranged at the request of the government after Greece's prime minister, Kyriakos Mitsotakis, invited their Royal Highnesses to join in the 200-year anniversary celebrations of Greece's independence. As well as attending the Bicentenary Independence Day celebrations, they would join a reception at the National Gallery of Greece, take part in a wreath-laying ceremony and watch a traditional military parade.

Prince Charles said it was 'great' that his working visit to Greece was able to go ahead during the pandemic, despite criticism by an anti-monarchy group whose spokesman compared him to a 'social media influencer', adding 'ordinary people' who are unable to travel will 'take a dim view' of the visit, which he demeaned was a 'nice jolly in Greece . . . As so often with the monarchy, it looks like one rule for the royals and one for everybody else . . . These royal trips are entirely unnecessary . . . It's going to cause some level of confusion about why there's apparently no risk of Charles and Camilla catching and spreading coronavirus, but for everyone else there is . . . The government needs to explain why they have allowed that to happen.' A response from government was not forthcoming.

They landed at Athens International Airport on a very windy day to be greeted by the guards of the Hellenic Armed Forces. Charles came down the stairs first but slowed several times to turn around and check that Camilla, who was treading cautiously, was okay. She was wearing a blue and white dress with a short white cape, and both wore coloured material masks. Camilla's was black and emblazoned with the Prince of Wales feathers, which had been sent to her by a member of the public. Masks were mandatory in all public places both indoors and outdoors, and Prince Charles maintained social distancing during meetings with dignitaries.

Handshaking was not allowed due to the pandemic, so the Prince of Wales and Camilla greeted people with a 'namaste' welcome. They both underlined how different the world seemed from their pre-pandemic visit in 2018 when the couple shook endless bare hands and walked through huge crowds in Athens chatting to passers-by.

After their arrival they changed clothes for the official state dinner hosted by the President of Greece, Katerina Sakellaropoulou. The duchess looked stunning in a floor-length blue-grey dress with gold embroidery, a gold lace shawl, and this time, a gold-coloured mask. The visit meant a lot to Prince Charles, which he mentioned in his speech.

'My wife and I could not be more delighted to be back in Greece, which has long held the most special place in my heart.' He saluted the 'strong and vital' ties between the UK and Greece, adding: 'After all, Greece is the land of my grandfather; and of my father's birth, nearly one hundred years ago, in the centenary year of Greek Independence.' (The Duke of Edinburgh, who at the time was recovering from heart surgery at Windsor Castle, was born on the Greek island of Corfu.) He concluded by saying: 'Your Excellency – today, as in 1821, Greece can count on her friends in the United Kingdom. The ties between us are strong and vital and make a profound difference to our shared prosperity and security. Just as our histories are closely bound together, so too are our futures.'

The following day the couple attended a wreath-laying at the Memorial of the Unknown Soldier and watched the Independence Day Military Parade, which celebrates Greece's uprising against the Ottoman Empire in 1821. The country was supported by Britain, France and Russia and eventually gained independence in 1830. It was a very cold morning and the Prince of Wales helped Camilla unfold a white blanket to cover her legs and then tucked the blanket round her. It was a gentlemanly and loving act and showed his priority was to put his wife's health and comfort before the normal royal conduct of ignoring the weather, however cold. It was a small, tender moment that showed anyone how important she was to him and how close they were.

Soon after her return the duchess went to meet some of the unsung heroes of the pandemic. Included in her engagement was going to Haringey, north London, to see how local communities had been supporting each other. One part of the visit was spent at the Tottenham Vaccination Centre, which had a team of volunteers and vaccinators from all health care backgrounds and medical students from across London. Camilla, who wore a white head-scarf, face mask and black gloves, met staff, volunteers and patients receiving the Covid-19 vaccine. At one point she had a brief encounter with a needle as she spotted a medical student volunteer holding one. Camilla took a quick step back, but the doctor there said, 'Don't worry, it's not going anywhere near you.' The duchess also asked if a precious bottle of vaccine had ever been dropped. She was told 'only one in 50,000'. She replied, 'That is pretty good.'

The London Islamic Cultural Society at Wightman Road Mosque was also on her list to visit ahead of the start of Ramadan when Muslims fast from dawn till sunset for four weeks. The duchess saw how the organisation was supporting their community through the pandemic. She was told members of the mosque were helping those in need by distributing food hampers and giving counselling to those who were struggling. She also met members of the area's Muslim community and gave them souvenirs from the Royal Collection Trust gift shop. In turn, Bibi Khan, the centre's president, gave Camilla a Koran inscribed to the Duchess of Cornwall and Prince of Wales. When she was told the gift was printed in English, Camilla said, 'Oh, good.'

She then added: 'I am deeply, deeply touched by this as I am sure my husband will be too. I would very much like to bring him here in the not-too-distant future. You are a shining example and I wish there were more places like this in the country bringing the community and all faiths together. I hope I shall be back again.'

Camilla likes to mention her husband when she is out working – a rather touching way of bringing him close. She also likes him to come along to her regular receptions at Clarence House if he possibly can. She usually invites representatives with similar aims hoping they will connect with each other. According to the occasion there will be cocktails, snacks, finger food or, if the gathering is for children, carefully chosen sit-down meals. But the get-togethers she seems to enjoy the most are those dedicated to literacy, involving books. Despite Camilla's initial reticence to use social media platforms, she was instrumental in launching an initiative that would go on to be a huge success and showed her to be a pioneer in promoting reading – a first for the Royal Family.

Chapter 18

THE DUCHESS'S READING ROOM

The award-winning novelist Hilary Mantel is known not to be a fan of the monarchy. In May 2021 she claimed that it was facing 'the end game', saying, 'I don't know how much longer the institution will go on.' She also claimed there was 'no legitimate public interest' in broadcasting events such as Prince Philip's funeral or pictures of royal parents leaving hospital to take their new babies home.

Mantel's observations were made just four months after Camilla launched the Duchess of Cornwall's Reading Room in January 2021, and Mantel's novel *The Mirror and the Light*, the last of her Cromwell trilogy, was one of the first four titles Camilla chose to publicise. Praising the book, Camilla said it was 'well worth the wait for the stunning conclusion to her brilliant *Wolf Hall* trilogy, depicting the final stages of Thomas Cromwell's dramatic rise and fall in the court of Henry VIII'. Her comments doubtless stimulated sales and showed how she doesn't bear grudges.

In October 2021 Camilla invited Mantel to a lunchtime reception at Clarence House to celebrate the first anniversary of the

Reading Room, along with a wide range of well-known writers, actors, friends and family. While Camilla and Mantel chatted at one end of the room, several guests at the other end lowered their voices to reveal how surprised they were that the novelist was there. Among the comments were, 'Why was Hilary invited if she doesn't like the monarchy?', 'Why did Hilary come if she thinks the monarchy is at its end?' and 'Doesn't Hilary look like Queen Victoria?' Nonetheless, it was a particularly enjoyable party as most of the guests were mixing with lots of other people for the first time since the pandemic began. Camilla, as she usually does, went round chatting to everyone. When it was my turn, she pointed at me and said loudly, 'She's writing all about me,' adding more quietly, 'How's it coming along?'

Prince Charles had an out-of-London engagement that morning but rushed back just in time to join the celebration. Both he and Camilla looked delighted that he had made it. Also present were her sister Annabel and Camilla's daughter Laura, who was full of smiles and had the distinction of being the only guest to wear jeans. She also brought her beautiful blonde daughter and twin sons along. If the children were bored, they didn't show it, and when they left politely kissed their step-grandfather on both cheeks, then bowed slightly and said, 'Sir'.

There is no doubt that Camilla is an excellent hostess who, with her mischievous glances and an open smile, makes you feel at home. Sasha Swire says as much in a diary entry dated December 2019: 'Camilla charms all the men: she clearly still has it. She was, after all, one of the sex bombs of her generation and retains her smoky-voiced humour and naughty twinkle.'

Literacy is one of Camilla's priorities and something she is passionate about. 'Reading is a great adventure,' she begins. 'I've loved it since I was very small, and I'd love everybody else to enjoy it as much as I do. You can escape and you can travel, and you can laugh and you can cry. There's every kind of emotion that humans experience in a book. It's also a lovely way of communicating with other people round the world.' She also believes that literacy can change people's lives.

The Reading Room came about after the success of Camilla's two recommended reading lists that she released during the pandemic. It exists entirely on Instagram and its aim is to celebrate books and the people who write them. During each season, there are posts of interviews with authors, their own recommendations and more. There are also kits for people who want to run their own book club, including a list of suggested questions for discussing titles of their choosing. It has been widely welcomed by the public and Camilla has been praised for emphasising the importance of reading in everyday life.

Once pandemic restrictions were relaxed, she encouraged well-known authors to share their tips and favourite books via video and, later, in person. She also recommends books she has most relished and explains why. In one video she said that once lockdown began, she 'saved up all the books I wanted to read and sat down and read them'. She concluded, 'You know, whatever other awful things came out of lockdown, I think reading has come out extremely well and I think it's revived, and we just want to keep that going.' Her goal is to find books that are 'something that everybody could delve into and find something that suited them and enjoy it'. The project has links to libraries and is also in time expected to include the classics and writers from the Commonwealth.

Camilla's idea of encouraging children and adults to read is, surprisingly, an idea that royal families have not put into practice before. Prince Charles reads a lot, mostly non-fiction, but has never promoted reading itself. Prince Philip read a great deal and widely but was the same. Camilla chose not to let reading be just a hobby but to try to get more people to find pleasure and wide-ranging experiences from doing so. She has particularly focused on encouraging children to read, because if they start the habit young, they are far more likely to continue throughout their life.

Years before she had the idea to recommend books to the public, she was invited to present the Orange Prize, now known as the Women's Prize for Fiction. The fact that she attended a literary award ceremony brought out some unjustified criticism that highlights the sort of opposition she has had to fight against. According to her friend, author Dame Susan Hill, 'The first time she made any sort of dent in the reading world was giving away the award. A person I won't name, but whom I was disgusted with, said: "These people just wanted to get a royal involved. I doubt whether she has even opened a book." I told him he was absolutely wrong, and that she is a huge reader and always has been. He remained cynical but she has staunchly proved herself not just by handing out prizes but by all the things she has launched off her own bat.'

For season three of the Reading Room, one of Camilla's four choices in July 2021 was *The Various Haunts of Men* by Dame Susan, and she noted it is the first in the *Serrailler* crime series. The series takes place in the cathedral town of Lafferton, and each book follows a different person's disappearance. Dame Susan was delighted. 'I know she enjoys my work. She often writes to me, "Let's have another one."'

Camilla somehow manages to find time for reading and Dame Susan says: 'She is a wide reader and will try things she thinks may not be for her. During the summer she loves sitting outside at Birkhall, and in winter sitting by the fire. When she introduces a book, she never needs any notes.'

To mark World Book Day in 2022 Camilla, together with Catherine, Duchess of Cambridge, launched a children's section of Camilla's Reading Room with a set of book recommendations from Catherine, along with a message that read: 'Regular reading can have a profound impact on children's wellbeing, literacy and comprehension, introducing them to almost 300,000 more words by the time they start school! A passionate advocate of the importance of early childhood development and children's mental health, Catherine has chosen for the Reading Room five children's books that she has enjoyed over the years.'

One of her choices was *Stig of the Dump* by Clive King, inspired by her love of nature. 'As a child I loved spending time outdoors, making dens, digging, discovering and making things out of odds and ends,' she said.

She also included *The Owl Who Was Afraid of the Dark* by Jill Tomlinson – a book she read on CBeebies *Bedtime Stories* in February 2022 sitting cross-legged on a rug. She began: 'I loved this book as a little girl and listening to my own children reading it has brought back so many wonderful memories . . . a comforting story to help children face their fears and grow in confidence with the help of others.' It was somehow reassuring to see the wives of the next two heirs of the throne working together.

Camilla joined in and revealed that one of her favourite books to read to her grandchildren is *Gangster Granny* by David Walliams, which centres around an eleven-year-old boy called Ben who goes to his grandmother's house every Friday while his parents go out dancing. At first, he dislikes going there until he discovers his grandmother is an international jewel thief and arranges to steal the Queen's Crown Jewels from the Tower of London. She added she loves watching 'their eyes widen as they begin to wonder if their own grandparents might have some interesting tales to tell'. Camilla has a grandmotherly way of telling a story, which is gentle and warm with lots of pauses for effect. She'll also tell the children the names of her own six grandchildren and what their favourite books are.

Camilla's aim of passing on her passion for reading led to several literary patronages. The first in 2010 was for the National Literary Trust, a charity that works with schools and communities to give disadvantaged children the skills they need to succeed in life. She has since added several other charities that focus on reading, including Beanstalk, BookTrust – passed down to her by Prince Philip – First Story, the Roald Dahl Literary Estate, and the Wicked Young Writer Award. 'I've got involved in a lot of literacy programmes and patronages,' she admits. 'I just feel very strongly that all children should be taught to read.' She has also presented Britain's most prestigious literary award, the Booker Prize.

Jonathan Douglas is chief executive of the National Literary Trust, whose mission is to improve the reading and writing skills of children all over the country, an aim close to Camilla's heart. They first met in 2010 after one of Jonathan's colleagues went to the Orange Prize award ceremony to represent the charity. 'She phoned me from there because Her Royal Highness had just spoken about family literacy and family reading, and she said it was just as if she was speaking on behalf of our charity. It was extraordinary.'

The Trust contacted Clarence House and invited her to visit one of their projects that was about to take place in a local library in Wiltshire. 'It wasn't about teaching or pedagogy but instead about the way families are with books,' Douglas explained. 'Her Royal Highness walked in and within seconds she was on her knees with the children and the parents, talking about books.

'What came through so profoundly from that first event was that she has a natural empathy with the families we were most concerned about. These poorest families lacked confidence, but they weren't in the least intimidated by talking to Camilla about reading, despite her being a member of the Royal Family. It was amazing. I think people recognise her authenticity and respond to it, which is the foundation for how she communicates. Shortly afterwards we asked her to be our patron.'

Camilla subsequently went to Stoke-on-Trent, Middlesbrough and Swindon, which have high levels of child poverty and low levels of literacy. 'It's where,' Douglas says, 'a royal visit means so much. When the duchess went to a family network centre in Swindon in January 2019, it was one of the most moving things I've ever seen. The kids frequently have significant issues, and the parents have a lot of challenges in their lives. The characteristic that shone through was Her Royal Highness's ability to create a natural rapport with families from very diverse backgrounds. She shared stories with them, talked to them about books, and they talked to her about their lives. At the end she produced a basket of Highgrove goodies and Duchy Originals that went down very well.'

The charity also arranged for her to visit prisons. In February 2016 she went to HMP Brixton, a men's prison in south London, and in January 2018 she went to HMP Styal for female adults and young offenders in Cheshire. 'For security reasons we couldn't explain who the VIP visitor was until literally two minutes before Her Royal Highness walked through the door,' said Douglas. 'Prisoners love taking part in conversations about reading and books, because a lot of them just don't speak when they're in prison. I remember a conversation in HMP Brixton with the Duchess of Cornwall and a group of prisoners which was all about what reading meant to them as individuals. It was brilliant.' Some of the conversation was recorded by National Prison Radio.

To mark Camilla's seventieth birthday the Literary Trust wanted to do 'something for the families she cares about', and along with other reading charities developed a project called The Duchess's Bookshelves. Seventy primary schools around the country with very low levels of literacy received specially designed bookshelves filled with seventy children's books. In July 2017 a selected number of primary school children and children's authors travelled to Clarence House for her birthday garden party. They arrived in style on a vintage bus. The actor and bestselling children's author David Walliams took on the role of bus conductor in a 1950s uniform. Camilla was presented with a set of the bookshelves and during the party the children sat in the garden and talked to her about their favourite books and listened to storytelling with various authors.

Always ready to promote reading in every way she can, in January 2020 Camilla wrote about the Books for School campaign run by the *Sun* newspaper and supported by the National Literary Trust. This time she chose to write about some less-known advantages of reading: 'We all know how important reading is for our children,' she began, 'but it might surprise you that a good reader can also improve their skills in maths and science. There are other untold and astonishing benefits. Research has shown that reading for pleasure improves how children think, explore and figure things out.' She also mentioned how much she took pleasure in taking part in the Trust's 'book-nic' – a picnic with books instead of food.

Her article continued: 'Finding the right book can be the key [to convincing young people to read]. It might be opening the door of the wardrobe into Narnia, training an owl with Harry Potter, or plotting to steal the Crown Jewels with Gangsta Granny. Or it could be a factual book about computer coding, climate change or cookery that catches their fancy and ends up sparking an obsession that lasts for a lifetime.'

In January 2022 Camilla placed lots of books signed by their authors in local telephone box libraries. Dressed warmly in a khaki jacket, brown jeans, long green socks and black lace-up walking boots, she was photographed beaming, standing in the doorway of a red phone box full of books near Birkhall. It was one of several disused historic red telephone boxes bought by Prince Charles from BT to be used for local good causes, such as libraries.

Dame Esther Rantzen is a trustee of the charity Silver Stories and hoped Camilla would get involved. 'I wrote to the Duchess of Cornwall and said, 'Look, I know you love reading and encouraging children to read, and I know you care about older people. Would you be interested in this small new charity in Cornwall that was registered in March 2020? She was. If you say the word "old" to the media they instantly run for the hills, and it's thanks to the duchess, who has such a great impact, that a small charity like this gets coverage.'

The charity encourages primary school pupils (Silver Readers) to read stories once a week to isolated elderly people (Silver Listeners). The aim is to give young people more confidence when reading aloud and to cheer up older people who are often on their own. It is a typical example of how Camilla picks small charities as well as large. She doesn't have an ulterior motive or show off how caring she is when accepting a patronage. But these readings will make such a difference to a small group of people.

In one Zoom call Camilla revealed how reading has even helped her to improve making speeches. The call was to two children in Cornwall aged eleven and ten. She first listened to them reading excerpts from Roald Dahl's *Charlie and the Chocolate Factory* and David Walliams's *The Ice Monster*. The children talked about learning how to read slowly when they read out loud. Camilla confessed: 'I used to read very, very fast. When I made a speech, I used to talk very, very fast. Then you have to take a deep breath and slow down and look at the commas and full stops.' She also told them they were doing 'an absolutely brilliant job' and how much they were helping the older generation by reading to them.

Camilla even managed to squeeze in a reading session during her and Prince Charles's packed three-day visit to Canada in May 2022 in honour of the Queen's Platinum Jubilee. During her time in Ottawa, she visited The Assumption Elementary School and kept the children spellbound reading them *The Library Book* by

Bahram Rahman about a woman and her daughter who deliver books by bus to girls in Afghanistan. An assistant sat next to her and held up the pages so the illustrations could be easily seen.

Encouraging children to read is as important to her as much as gathering people together.

Chapter 19

THE BIG LUNCH

When Camilla was asked by the Queen to take over another of her charities, The Big Lunch, she accepted immediately as its aim is to help bring all types of people together. It also supports Prince Charles's concern for the environment and climate change. What The Big Lunch is not really about is eating. Led by Executive Director Peter Stewart, who has responsibility for the Eden Project's charitable mission, it began as a small initiative in Cornwall. It has been such a success that it has also played an important role in the Queen's Platinum Jubilee celebrations in June 2022.

Stewart explained: 'The Big Lunch came about in 2009 when we wondered what it would be like if you could stop the whole of the UK for about four hours and encourage people to sit down and have lunch with their neighbours. We wouldn't give a reason for the meeting but just send an invitation that says "Come in and sit down and you'll have fun".'

This distinct way of bringing people together soon aroused the curiosity of Buckingham Palace, who, in June 2012, asked

Eden if they could make a 'Big Jubilee Lunch' to celebrate the Queen's Diamond Jubilee. They also wanted someone to represent Her Majesty and suggested Camilla. Not least because her title 'Duchess of Cornwall' gives her a special connection with the area. It was also another indication that, although it had taken a while, the Queen's relationship with Camilla, who gracefully accepted the request, was now firmly established. Her regular work with The Big Lunch over ten years shows that when she takes on a charity, she stays with it, comes up with ideas and is supportive.

The celebration took place on Sunday 3 June, with more than eight and a half million people taking part around the country. Charles and Camilla attended the lunch in London's Piccadilly. It was pouring with rain and quite cold. Prince Charles was in a smart suit with his signature silk handkerchief in his jacket pocket. Camilla wore a beige trench coat, cream gloves and carried a see-through umbrella. Every seat on the long table was occupied and the table was decorated in red, white and blue. The road and pavements on both sides were also crowded with onlookers. Strangers talked to each other as the smiling couple walked up and down the length of the table chatting before taking their places. When they did, a vast cake iced with a Union Jack was placed in front of Camilla to cut. The event was a huge success and timed to finish before a flotilla of a thousand boats made their way up the Thames, followed by a concert at Buckingham Palace, lighting beacons and a National Service of Thanksgiving. Unfortunately, it poured with rain during the flotilla and Prince Philip became ill and sadly couldn't attend any more of the celebrations.

Former Prime Minister David Cameron described it in his auto-biography, *For The Record*:

The highlight of the Jubilee came on Sunday 3 June, when a celebratory flotilla of a thousand vessels sailed down the

Thames. Barges, cutters, sailing boats, gondolas, canoes, dinghies, even the Dunkirk little ships were led by the royal barge, The Spirit of Chartwell. And it poured with rain. Incredibly, the Queen and Prince Philip, aged eighty-six and ninety, stood on deck for four full hours. Duty, tradition, stoicism – their profoundly British behaviour matched the profoundly British weather. I was at the end of the route at Tower Bridge to greet the shivering royals. The Duchess of Cornwall made a beeline for the cups of tea and told me she had thought she would expire out there. No one wanted to go against the Queen's example, so everyone spent the proper amount of time on deck.

Sir Roy Strong had a different viewpoint and wrote in his diaries on 5 June 2012:

I saw the service from St Paul's Cathedral on television, an impressive spectacle with a superb sermon by the archbishop . . . I then went off for a tough training session . . . at the gym and returned in time for the carriage procession, the Queen travelling with the Prince of Wales and Camilla. As usual it looked beautiful. Then after a gap came the balcony tableau, which struck me as significant: the Queen was flanked to her right by Charles and Camilla and to her left by William and Kate. What it seemed to say to me was that the future of the monarchy depended on the women, as indeed it had done through the twentieth century.

Another Big Lunch was part of Camilla and Charles's three-day visit to Ireland in May 2015. Camilla made a solo visit to East Belfast, where a Big Lunch had been arranged at the Skainos Centre. It was quite a responsibility. She was met by community activist Linda Ervine, who greeted her in Irish. Camilla gave her a mischievous smile and quietly asked her how to say 'thank you' in Irish, admitting she had tucked a piece of paper with the correct words up her sleeve, but it had dropped out, and she was keen to learn how to say it again.

The aim of The Big Lunch was to help bridge religious divides. There had recently been some unrest, and security was tight, but Peter Stewart, who accompanied Camilla, said: 'Her Royal Highness wasn't afraid to go among the people. She was disarmingly calm.' In keeping with how The Big Lunch works, everyone was asked to bring something to the table. Camilla helped prepare a salad and iced a cupcake, confessing the cupcake was not as good as her son Tom's. Camilla presented the cupcake to Jackie Upton from Pitt Park Women's Group, who wanted to bring residents from both sides of the peace-line. Ms Upton said: 'She was a very nice lady, very down-to-earth and seemed to really know what she was talking about when it came to Northern Ireland and was very interested in the cross-community event.'

The Big Lunch's achievement is as unexpected as it is successful. Peter Stewart spoke of his surprise at the extraordinary effect it had in some of the hardest to reach areas in the UK. 'In the early days of 2012, although you couldn't say that a Big Lunch sorts out knife crime, it created an atmosphere among neighbours where people felt happier, safer and less lonely. This resulted in some attendees not reverting to crime and instead doing more positive things. The mood enabled problems like knife crime to be discussed, with the result that it just didn't flourish.'

Unfortunately, a Big Lunch event in June 2016 to celebrate the Queen's ninetieth birthday didn't go quite as smoothly but was saved by Camilla at the last minute. Stewart was well into preparing for the occasion, when the Queen's grandson, Peter Phillips, came up with the idea of having a 'Patrons' Lunch' for his grandmother in The Mall, and was paid £750,000 for organising it. According to Phillips's website, The Mall would be 'transformed for its largest street party to celebrate the Queen's patronage of over 600 charities and organisations on the occasion of her 90th birthday . . . it will be an iconic event recognising the unrelenting support and service our Monarch has given to the community over her 63-year reign. The Queen's commitment to this service is cause for a national and Commonwealth-wide celebration.'

The royals were out in force, umbrella in one hand to protect them from the rain and shaking hands with hundreds of well-wishers who were lining the streets with the other. White plastic raincoats were handed out to individuals who wanted to wear one. Prince Charles and Camilla were noticeable by their absence, which triggered some to wonder if all might not be well between Camilla and the Queen. The truth was quite different.

'Communication between Buckingham Palace and Clarence House wasn't at its best,' Peter Stewart began tactfully. 'I had had an email from Peter Phillips, who said he'd been asked to contact us to tell us about the Patrons' Lunch and that he had sponsorships for the event. This clashed with our sponsors, who had already put money into The Big Lunch to celebrate the Queen's birthday, and who all of a sudden found they had been gazumped. We told Clarence House what was happening, and although they were incredibly empathetic, it was awkward for a while as we tried to fit in our Big Lunch with the Patrons' Lunch and expand the celebration nationally and internationally.

'I decided not to do anything about it as Peter's idea was a good one and he is also the Queen's grandson. Then, a month before the event, Clarence House rang us to ask if we could look for possible locations within Gloucestershire, close to Highgrove where Prince Charles and the duchess live. Her Royal Highness and Prince Charles wanted to take part in The Big Lunch, but within their neighbourhood. It was a great rush, and ten days before the event we finally found the village of Brimpsfield in Gloucestershire, which is thirty-five miles from Highgrove and seemed perfect.

'No one knew their Royal Highnesses were going to come, so it was a huge surprise when the duchess arrived and brought her husband with her. They sat on bales of hay to talk to the villagers and moved from table to table that [was] covered with food and Union Jacks. I believe the duchess wanted to convey the very simple message that to make The Big Lunch authentic it is important for it to be close to home and with your neighbours. It was truly brilliant. Even the sun came out. It was incredible that she showed us such loyalty that we didn't have to play second fiddle.' She obviously didn't approve of Peter Phillips's tactics.

In November 2018, Prince Charles and Camilla went on a nine-day visit to West Africa on behalf of the government, which coincided with Prince Charles being appointed the Queen's designated successor as Head of the Commonwealth. It was the first time that The Big Lunch had been tried out abroad. The Commonwealth Big Lunch in Kigali, Ghana, turned out to be a mammoth event attended by more than three hundred people. This included a cross-section of high-profile dignitaries, Ghanaian celebrities, such as the multiple award-winning singers Becca and Stonebwoy, plus schoolchildren from both the public and private sector.

It was a huge challenge for the Eden Project to be asked to help host the G7 two-day summit in the popular destination of Carbis Bay in Cornwall in June 2021, when the Covid-19 pandemic was still raging. The specific focus of the summit was the pandemic and climate change. The leaders of the free world descended on the resort, headed by Prime Minister Boris Johnson and his new wife Carrie, US President Joe Biden and First Lady Jill, President of

France Emmanuel Macron and German Chancellor Angela Merkel, along with the Queen, Prince Charles and Camilla, and the Duke and Duchess of Cambridge. The Prince of Wales, with Prince William's backing, also brought a delegation of CEOs from some of the world's largest companies to work with the G7 leaders on tackling the climate emergency and environmental sustainability.

The summit was launched with a reception to promote The Big Lunch, hosted by the Queen and the rest of the royal party, and attended by the world leaders. Stewart admits: 'It was a massive task as, due to the pandemic, we only had four weeks to organise it, get everyone accredited and arrange the security. At the time Cornwall was on a high alert about the virus and we worried about the Covid constraints and whether everyone could get ill. We tested ourselves so many times that, overall, everything felt incredibly safe. Among our other concerns we needed to make sure that no one got too close to each other. Nor could there be more than thirty people in any one place.'

Camilla, who likes to be kept informed of what's happening, came up with an idea that would have been close to the late Princess Diana's heart. Camilla didn't want The Big Lunch to be attended only by prominent individuals and royals and suggested it would make the event more genuine if the royals could meet local people who had had difficult times during the pandemic.

Peter Stewart invited several people from all walks of Cornish life for the royals to talk to. One lady told Her Majesty the Queen and the Duchess of Cornwall that she'd worked in a care home throughout Covid, caught the virus and gave it to her husband, who unfortunately died. The empathy Her Majesty had was incredible. At the end the lady said, 'Well, I don't need to tell you about this, Your Majesty. You've had a tremendous loss yourself with the Duke of Edinburgh passing.' Her Majesty said, 'Yes, we are very similar in that regard.' The duke had died only two months previously.

After the long months of lockdown, everyone seemed both delighted and relieved to see people face-to-face rather than remotely. Camilla stood chatting to Emmanuel Macron while holding a large glass of red wine. She is a connoisseur – something she inherited from her father who worked in the wine business. The food consisted of various cold dishes and salads. Stewart explained that it was the least complicated to arrange. Most royals don't eat during engagements, which left plenty for others. Camilla gave a short speech to say how touched she was to be there and what a particularly moving visit it was for her. Not an easy task. 'I'm thrilled to be here today,' she began. 'It would have been the birthday of the Duke of Edinburgh and tomorrow would be the day of the death of my father and I'm very honoured to be here today doing something I know they would have appreciated.'

It was all relaxed and friendly and a boost to see the free world work together. The highlight came when it was time to cut an enormous oblong cake bearing The Big Lunch logo in green icing. The Lord-Lieutenant of Cornwall, Edward Bolitho, handed the Queen a ceremonial sword and joked that she might like to use it to cut the cake. Stewart recalls: 'The atmosphere was so relaxed, and Her Majesty was so pleased to be out and about with people, having been in lockdown for so long, she turned to me and said, "Do you think it's a good idea?" I replied, "I can't possibly comment, your Majesty, I think you should do what you'd like to do."

'An aide then offered Her Majesty a conventional knife as an alternative, but she refused, saying, "This is more unusual."' The Duchess of Cornwall looked nervous and gave the Duchess of Cambridge several anxious, questioning looks – one assumes about whether or not she should intervene and help her mother-in-law. The Queen is very determined, but there seemed to be a subtle change in their relationship as Camilla showed a caring concern for her ageing mother-in-law.

Camilla kept putting out her right hand as if she was about to take the sword from her. Initially, the Queen rejected her offer of help with one of her indomitable looks but cutting through the thick cake turned out to be harder than she thought, and she finally let Camilla help press the massive sword down to the bottom of the cake. At that moment another aide arrived with an ordinary knife to hand to the Queen, which she agreed to use to cut a second slice of cake. She took a moment to observe her handiwork then remarked: 'That looks very good.' Catherine and Camilla laughed, partly no doubt from relief that the knife didn't slip.

Chapter 20

EMPOWERER OF WOMEN

Before Princess Diana arrived on the scene, royal patronages were confined to relatively uncontroversial charities, all of them worthy but limited to a fairly narrow spectrum. Diana changed all that with her well-publicised support for edgier causes, in particular Aids/HIV charities and landmine clearance. Her unprecedented handshake with an HIV sufferer may have done more than anything else to create a wholly new public sympathy for Aids victims, while the photographs of her walking through an area recently cleared of landmines in Angola, kitted out in the appropriate protective gear, went round the world and brought the reality of the issue home to a previously rather indifferent public. She had also produced the heir and a spare and boosted the whole Royal Family by her huge popularity.

How could Camilla compete with that? She wouldn't do so by visiting old people's homes and animal sanctuaries, the sort of charities patronised by royalty for a century or more. With Diana's spectre hovering over her, and her determination not to step on her husband's toes, Camilla's options for which charities to support made her own seem limited.

Going on joint engagements with Prince Charles was more purposeful and, by 2015, she had become much more accustomed to royal life and was up and ready when the British government asked the couple to go on a four-day trip in March to America. It was their first time in the USA for ten years and would be a test to show how she coped and the public's reaction to her. The press had been unpleasant about her first-time round, but on this occasion, she knew what to expect and felt more confident. Nor did the press take such a negative stand. Instead, the initial comments were that Charles was much more at ease with himself. During an interview he said how proud he was of Camilla: 'She is brilliant in the way she has tackled these things.' Charles was jealous of Diana's people skills but is very proud of Camilla's.

It helped too that Charles genuinely enjoys visits to the USA, especially when the programme covers the needs of the Foreign Office, in terms of reinforcing Britain's connections with policy-makers and opinion formers. These trips also give him an opportunity to speak out on issues that are very important to him such as the environment.

Before he married Camilla he seemed to be almost eclipsed by his mother, his first wife, his sons and his daughter-in-law. This time around the mood seemed to be that he had clearly taken on more of his mother's role and really was Britain's next king. As a result, the attitude was respectful that he had made time to talk to a very important ally.

Their trip was timed to mark the 800th anniversary of the Magna Carta and the 150th anniversary of the end of the American Civil War. They also visited monuments to Abraham Lincoln and Martin Luther King Jr and were joined by figures from the American civil rights movement, Jesse Jackson and Congressman John Lewis. Later, speaking at an environmental conference, the prince called on governments and businesses to end the dumping of plastics into the oceans.

They met President Barack Obama and then Vice-President Joe Biden at the White House who generously told the couple of the 'fondness' of American people for the Royal Family. Prince Charles replied, 'That's awfully nice to know.' Obama even joked during the White House meeting that some 'liked them much better than their own politicians'. Charles was later presented with the 'exceptional leadership in conservation honour' from the International Conservation Caucus Foundation.

Once home, Camilla and Charles privately celebrated their tenth wedding anniversary at Birkhall, their Scottish honeymoon destination. An intimate but informal photograph marked the occasion and showed them taking a stroll together – a couple wrapped up against the cold who were at ease with each other. She told *Vogue* magazine: 'It's lovely to catch up when we have a bit of time. You know when we go away, the nicest thing is that we actually sit and read our books in different corners of the same room. It's very relaxing because you know you don't have to make conversation. You just sit and be together.'

There were other positive things happening too. Prince William and Catherine's second child Princess Charlotte Elizabeth Diana was born. William described her as a 'little joy of heaven', while a statement from Kensington Palace said: 'The Queen, the Duke of Edinburgh, the Prince of Wales, the Duchess of Cornwall, Prince Harry and members of both families have been informed and are delighted with the news.' That September Queen Elizabeth, aged eighty-nine, became the longest-reigning monarch in UK history, by surpassing her great-great-grandmother Queen Victoria, who spent sixty-three years and 216 days on the throne.

By now Camilla bravely felt she was ready to take on what had previously been taboo to a royal. It was the immeasurable issue of violence against women, something that affects women of all ages and classes but one that has been resolutely pushed under the carpet by politicians, royals and the public for centuries. Not until Erin Pizzey opened the first British shelter for battered women in 1971 did society become aware of one of the biggest hidden scandals of Western society. Yet more than half a century after Pizzey's pioneering action, violence against women continues unabated, with police and other public bodies all too often reluctant to intervene until it is too late. Certainly, no royal had deemed it a cause worthy of their support. It became an opportunity to open doors that had previously been firmly shut, especially for the royal family, that Camilla seized with both hands, and which has been hugely successful and much admired. It has also helped her to forge a new and more powerful identity.

That same year I was invited to spend a day with Camilla visiting three rape crisis centres in London. It struck me as a rather astonishing thing for a royal to want to do. I felt there wasn't much chance of any connection between her and the survivors, and that small talk might be an embarrassment.

First stop was the Rape and Sexual Abuse Support Centre in Croydon, south-east London. The protocol is that you always arrive before the royal, so it was quite a shock to watch from inside the building as the wife of the heir to the British throne climbed up a metal fire escape, which looked tricky for anyone in heels, and only slightly less so when she bent almost double to avoid hitting her head against the metal frame of the narrow glass door.

There was good reason for her unorthodox means of arrival. Although she had first visited the centre in 2009, no one wanted the abusers to be able to trace the location of the women it serves. Camilla's staff had said that as she was more well-known now, she could draw attention to the nondescript building and asked if there was another way to get in apart from the front door. It was agreed she would enter through the back of the building. Rather than looking perturbed, she smiled broadly as if she had enjoyed the challenge.

When I asked whether she thought it was a rather unusual visit for a senior royal to make, she told me that one of her roles was to 'shine a light on the violence hiding in the dark corners of our society'. I asked if the brutal stories she heard stayed with her. 'I think about them a great deal, and they stay at the back of my mind all the time,' she replied. 'Sometimes it is quite harrowing.'

The Croydon centre provides victims with long-term counselling and support with the aim of helping 'turn them from a victim to a survivor'. It also helps homeless women and those who have been involved in prostitution and are trying to stop. It was informal and comfortable, more like a living room than a medical base, with magazines and snacks dotted around. Every abused woman arrives by appointment as they attempt to put the past behind them.

A staff member at the centre told me that prior to Camilla's interest neither the government nor police had done enough to tackle the problem of sexual abuse and rape. 'I have been working here for twenty years,' she told me. 'Laws have changed since the duchess came here and raised the profile. It could have been co-incidence, but I very much doubt it. It's also very difficult to explain sexual violence to the public. They believe that if a woman gets herself into a situation and is raped it's her fault, and we have to dispel that myth.'

There were about thirty women of various ages in the centre that day, all of whom had suffered serious sexual abuse, such as gang rape, sometimes as children. Their faces were strained, and they were extremely wary. When I talked to them before the duchess arrived, they showed little interest in her visit. It quickly changed. The retinue waiting for Camilla included the then Home Secretary Theresa May, who gave the best curtsy.

Camilla immediately showed her sense of humour when a photographer asked if he could take a photograph of the two women together. Mrs May is much taller than Camilla, who looked up at her, grimaced slightly, then asked the assembled crowd, 'Should I stand on tiptoe?' It was a smart way to break the ice. Her natural warmth and maternal instinct that was neither patronising nor pitying was key to making it easier for these devastated women to soften and open up. Several of them told me that the short time they had with her did more for their self-esteem than months of therapy, because they felt they had been properly listened to.

Camilla was wearing a sober blue-grey suit with two delicate dragonfly brooches on one lapel and did not seem at all unsettled by the rings in the noses of some of the women she met, or by their tattoos. Nor did she seem to mind that most of them didn't curtsy or address her as 'ma'am', as royal protocol demands. She was introduced to each woman one by one, and leant forward towards whoever she was talking to, which made any interaction seem more intimate. A member of staff told me: 'She puts everyone at their ease . . . she doesn't ask pointed questions, which is no good for survivors because it takes them back to a bad place. Instead, she has been very warm, has a maternal instinct and looks people in the eye.'

After leaving Croydon, Camilla and her entourage drove to Nelsons, a British manufacturer of health care products in Wimbledon. It was Camilla's idea to provide female rape victims with a washbag of toiletries, which she described as a 'crumb of comfort'. The women would be given the items following the trauma of post-assault forensic tests at London Havens, specialist centres for people who have been raped or sexually assaulted. Staff at Nelsons had organised a pop-up assembly line. When she was asked if she would she like to help assemble the washbags, a look of anxiety flashed across her face. 'Oh, no,' she said at first, looking vulnerable, then agreed. She fumbled at getting the right product in the correct place in the three interlaced transparent washbags, possibly feeling awkward about performing a manual task in front of photographers. 'I wouldn't get ten out of ten for them,' she said apologetically. 'I can see it takes a bit of practice.'

It was curious to note that although she seemed confident when talking to the women at the centre, things seemed less easy when other people were hovering nearby, and she looked nervous when standing in a production line putting things in plastic holders. For most people it would have been the other way round. She relaxed a little when one of the victims confided to her that she felt very low, and that having a nice product like shower gel and lip balm made a big difference.

Having gone from strength to strength it's hard to believe that the Camilla she is today is the same person whose teenage goal was to go to three parties a night. Her aim to shine a light on hidden violence has grown stronger over the years and expanded to cover domestic violence and coercion. It's possible her resolve is connected to her own experience of being verbally attacked, as some of the pain that has stayed with her has made her ever more passionate to help women who have experienced abuse of any sort. Her goal is to end violence against women for good and she chose two charities to help her.

In January 2016 she became involved in SafeLives, a UK-based charity dedicated to ending domestic abuse. It involved a trip to a SafeLives event at the Oval, Kennington, south London, to hear about the charity and listen to women tell their stories about how they survived violence – and to learn about other women who had been killed by their partners. It could have been too traumatic for some, but Camilla will listen to even the most horrifying stories despite the effect they have on her.

In spite of her stoicism, she was overwhelmed by what she heard. One woman spoke of how she endured eighteen years of living with her violent husband who, when she told him she had filed for divorce, beat then shot her. Their teenage son couldn't bear it and killed himself six weeks later. Another mother revealed she had lost her daughter to her violent, abusive husband when he killed her with a hammer. Camilla is not embarrassed about being emotional or even crying in public, even though both have been frowned upon within the Royal Family. When she recalled the story, she said: 'I don't think any of us could believe what we were hearing. I could feel the tears starting to drip down my face. It was so moving and so horrific. Afterwards I met her mother, a grandmother who had taken charge of the children and brought them up herself. I just remember saying to her that: "I don't know what I can do but if there's anything, I promise you I'll try and find a way."'

Suzanne Jacob, Chief Executive of SafeLives, told me: 'The duchess cried in front of everybody, not privately. The women who didn't know what to expect or had felt slightly nervous or sceptical, felt very moved by the duchess and her obvious emotion. It was particularly difficult for each woman to reveal such intimate details as, in general, survivors of domestic abuse who have been denied both a voice and their autonomy for decades, in some cases feel that if they do speak out no one is going to believe them. Yet on that particular day, the duchess connected so strongly with them that they felt able to say what they wanted to say, in their own way, to a member of the royal household who not only believed them but validated what she had heard and told them that they were of huge value.'

Despite hearing the 'most harrowing experiences', and the nightmares Camilla experienced after her visit, she was determined to stick to her promise to help all she could and invited a range of people connected with the charity to Clarence House where she spoke about the accounts of abuse she'd heard. She said: 'I had the privilege of hearing incredibly brave women . . . standing up to tell their stories. Harrowing stories that reduced many of us listeners to tears. That memorable day fired my interest in domestic abuse. I did know of people who had suffered from it, but I was both shocked and horrified by just how many thousands of people across the world live with it.'

Camilla, who became patron of SafeLives in 2020, has revealed she has friends who have been victims of violence and coercive control, admitting 'no one knows what goes on' behind closed doors. Coercive and controlling behaviour became a legislative offence at the end of 2015, but arrests and charges remain rare. Camilla was shocked to hear that one of the early coercive prosecutions focused on an adult son who had confined his mother to certain parts of the house and only allowed her out at certain times of the day. If she didn't obey there were punishments about when and what she could eat and when she could go to the toilet.

By March 2020, when the pandemic and lockdown struck, it became apparent that couples who were in abusive relationships had to stay at home together for twenty-four hours a day with only tiny amounts of respite. 'SafeLives was also very concerned that although the government had let children of key workers stay in school during lockdown, specialist domestic abuse workers weren't seen as key workers. Camilla asked what she could do and, with the help of her contacts, enabled SafeLives to take the argument to the government, who agreed that frontline specialist workers had to have their children in school to do their job.'

Camilla realised that the one way she could reach out to more people was to overcome her dislike of making speeches. She put her inhibitions aside, which wasn't easy, so she could speak frankly and forthrightly. She talked about female genital mutilation (FGM) and showed her support for female empowerment at WOW (Women of the World), a global festival movement that, to Camilla's relief, also believes women's equality is nothing to do with not loving men, as her priority has always been to support Prince Charles.

The WOW movement was founded in 2010 by Jude Kelly, former artistic director of the Southbank Centre in London. She is now its director. Camilla has asked Jude to join her on several overseas visits, including to Nigeria, Ghana and Jordan, to help her fight FGM and expand WOW's work. The visits are usually neatly fitted into official foreign trips with Prince Charles, during which each of them briefly goes solo. The format is to invite about a hundred women to lunch, who wouldn't normally meet, for a 'Think In', where they talk about what matters to them and look at the obstacles that stop them from achieving their potential. Jude said, 'Camilla always gravitates towards people who have probably got quite a difficult story to tell in their own lives. What is key for her is to be of real service to people who have no voice, as she believes she can help give people who have no voice, a voice.'

Although Camilla's confidence in her public speaking has grown, she is more comfortable keeping most speeches short and to the point. Jude adds, 'The duchess doesn't need to be a great orator. When you have somebody of her status and situation speaking directly about violence, like FGM, people realise that it is okay to talk about these things. The fact that she's so candid also makes an impact with people. Any number of women have said to me, "I can't believe she is speaking about women like me."'

In October 2021 she gave what was described as the most powerful speech of her royal life at the Wellcome Trust in London as part of a collaborative effort by the WOW Foundation and University of London Birkbeck's 'Shame' project. I attended the reception, largely filled with smartly dressed young women and a sprinkling of men. Camilla was wearing a long black dress and a bright pink WOW badge and pushed royal barriers even further away by talking about the murder of innocent women.

One of them was Sarah Everard, a 33-year-old marketing executive who was abducted as she walked home from a friend's house in Clapham, south London, on the evening of 3 March 2021 by Wayne Couzens, a serving Metropolitan Police Officer, who went on to rape and murder her. Camilla urged her audience to renew 'our commitment to do everything we can to end violence against women' and to help victims release the shame they might feel after they are attacked. 'Shame is one of the most powerful emotions felt after sexual violation,' Camilla said. 'The victim feels invaded and dirty; weakened by having been put in a position of helplessness by someone stronger – possibly by someone whom she previously trusted.'

In a rallying cry for both sexes to join together in the community to combat a violent spate of horrific crimes against women, she went on: 'We need to get the men in our lives involved in this movement. We do not, in any way, hold all men responsible for sexual violence. But we do need them all on board to tackle it. After all, rapists are not born, they are constructed. And it takes an entire community – male and female – to dismantle the lies, words and actions that foster a culture in which sexual assault is seen as normal, and in which it shames the victim.'

After her speech Camilla was introduced to many among the audience, including Carrie Johnson, the Prime Minister's wife, who had been practising her curtsy before Camilla arrived and had since been hovering near the podium. Camilla was overheard asking 'How's this coming along?' as she gestured to her baby bump. Carrie's answer was lost in background noise.

There was more banging of the WOW drum abroad in November 2021 when the couple became the first members of the Royal

Family to take part in a major overseas tour to Jordan and Egypt since the Covid pandemic started. It included a solo event in Jordan enabling Camilla and Jude to promote WOW. Queen Rania accompanied Camilla for most of the visit to show her support. Afterwards Camilla was presented with a picture of herself framed with the words: 'Women Empowerer'.

Camilla and Prince Charles enjoy each other's company but are also in harmony when they feel pain.

In March 2022 they both went to the Ukrainian Catholic Cathedral in London to show their support for Ukraine as Russia escalated its war in the country. They arrived with representatives of five charities, including World Jewish Relief and the British Red Cross, for people to donate to. The couple were welcomed to the church by the Right Reverend Kenneth Nowakowski. They met with a group of schoolchildren who sang them a song, were introduced to Ukrainians of different faiths and people who were helping to provide relief.

Camilla, who has shown great fortitude in her life, was again moved to tears as she heard the appalling stories of what the people at the church and their family and friends had endured. There was no attempt to keep a stiff upper lip. Nor did she adhere to the usual royal physical restrictions. Instead, she hugged the visibly distraught wife of Ukraine's Ambassador to the UK, Vadym Prystaiko, telling her: 'We are praying for you.' Charles is understood to have made personal donations to two charities. Camilla made her own sizeable donation too. Prince Charles gave an off-the-cuff speech, saying: 'My wife and I have been deeply moved by everything we have heard today during our visit and above all by the extraordinary bravery, generosity and fortitude of the Ukrainian community in the face of such truly terrible aggression. So, if I may say so, our thoughts and prayers, however inadequate they may be, are with you all at this most critical time.'

Some people criticised them for being political and believed they shouldn't get involved, but most felt it was a humanitarian rather than political issue. The Queen, who is renowned for staying above politics, also gave a financial donation.

In any event, on the second day of their May 2022 whirlwind three-day Platinum Jubilee tour of Canada on behalf of the Queen, they both visited a Ukrainian cathedral in Ottawa as a gesture of their support for the war-ravaged country. According to Clarence House, Canada is home to 1.4 million people of Ukrainian descent – one of the world's largest Ukrainian populations. They attended a service and recited a prayer. Father Ihor Kutash told the couple: 'Your country is truly a friend of Ukraine, having extended a helping hand, not only militarily but also as fellow citizens of our planet. We will never, never forget that.'

A distressing engagement that was made easier when you are a couple and can comfort each other. Nor was the day all gloomy. Outside the cathedral was Iryna Bloshenko, who arrived in Canada from Dnipro in the besieged country a month earlier. 'I am very happy, very excited to see the royals,' she said, waving a Ukrainian flag. 'We appreciate the royals' support for Ukraine.' While Ruslan Rovishen, a Ukrainian who lives in Ottawa, said: 'It has been my dream since childhood to see the British Royal Family. I am excited they are here.'

A crowd quickly gathered, and by the afternoon the couple was surrounded by well-wishers and royal watchers at Ottawa's ByWard Market. Kiki Malia said he had goosebumps in anticipation of meeting Prince Charles. Camilla tried a beer made from icebergs thousands of years old and looked as though she was enjoying it. There were, however, a few anti-monarchist protestors who demanded an apology from the Queen, which Charles declined on her behalf, for the horrific death of indigenous people in residential schools decades ago. Others present were pleased that the prince 'listened to' and 'acknowledged' what had happened. Overall, their welcome was more positive than for Prince William and Catherine's recent visit to Caribbean countries, where they were faced with protests decrying the Royal Family's close historical link to both slavery and colonisation.

Sometimes age and experience can triumph over youth or at least be a good example to follow. Shortly afterwards, as well as making financial donations, the Royal Family were reportedly providing accommodation to Ukrainian families who have been forced to flee their homeland. The individual royals wanted to stay anonymous, but they showed what is expected from the monarchy, which is humanity and a shining example for others to follow.

Chapter 21

A ROLE MODEL

Camilla has been a role model in many ways. Most significantly she has proved that ageing, especially for a woman, should not be the defining factor of her being. Nor should it negate any achievements or strip away a woman's identity. Instead, Camilla's message is that growing old can be a privilege and very liberating. By being herself and maintaining an enthusiasm for life she has become inspirational for young women and a comfort to older ones in that they don't have to accept being erased as an individual.

This is the conclusion of several of her friends and associates who have told me their personal view of the impact Camilla has made – her work ethic, loyalty, help for those less privileged than herself, keeping fit, dressing in your own style and, if you really love someone whose in-laws don't warm to you, be patient as time can bring them round.

Camilla's sister Annabel believes: 'She has stepped up to the mark wonderfully. I am so proud of her. My parents would have been so proud. Mark would have been so proud. We are a very close-knit family. We have families who have grown up together. Our children are virtually brothers and sisters.'

Dame Susan Hill thinks Camilla is a good role model for older women and has shown what they can achieve. 'The more so because she hasn't been someone who had a family when she was very young and gone into business, became head of a company and worked 24/7. She was an army wife whose husband was away a lot and had two children. She hunted, rode horses, and had her friends, but she wasn't that kind of glass-ceiling breaker. So, once she'd married [Prince Charles], a lot of people expected her to not do any more but just carry on as she was. Or think, *Here I am, I have a position as wife and have a voice*. She didn't just charge in and try and take over. Instead, she's done everything carefully and always let [Prince Charles] be first, of course. What is so lovely is that Catherine [Duchess of Cambridge] is doing the same: finding their own things to do which are just theirs and doing things together too.'

Camilla was already fifty-seven when she married Prince Charles and when her life totally changed. She has since defied those who hold the notion that any female over fifty is neither seen nor heard. Instead, she has proven the positive sides to getting older, like being wiser, calmer, more knowing and having perspective. Regrettably she hasn't fully escaped verbal abuse, and now that she is in her seventies, trolls are using her age as a target. She has been referred to as a 'splendid old trout', which is not only shocking in itself, but is also solely directed at women. Her looks are also still being compared to those of a young Princess Diana, who was breathtakingly beautiful but, sadly, a very damaged person. Looks are not all that matters, even for a prince.

Her friend Dame Judi Dench agrees: 'I think people still push aside women over a certain age. But Camilla can prove that you can change and learn and do things. She's a great example for older woman. Her sense of duty is overwhelming and quite phenomenal, but I do get very upset when she or Prince Charles are verbally attacked.'

Camilla puts in a great deal of effort representing the Queen, and particularly working for the disadvantaged. Her close friend Lucia is full of admiration and told me that Camilla once said to her, 'You know, I started working when everybody else around me was retiring.' She works so hard now. It has made her a marvellous role model for the older woman, because they can start their life in one way, and then when things happen, they can change. You don't have to keep going down the same path or do everything at a said age. Life today has many different stages, and at one stage Camilla was a wonderful mother with a wonderful relationship with her children. She's been very close to her daughter Laura and her children. They see each other and talk the whole time they can. She's also involved with Tom and his children. When she married Prince Charles, I think she thought she wouldn't have to change her life very much. Instead, she has accepted it as her role.'

Camilla gives the impression she would do anything for her children and grandchildren, but she doesn't let them define her. The only hint of her true feelings came during the pandemic, when she, like thousands of others, admitted how she longed to hug her offspring.

Esther Rantzen admires the fact that Camilla does not follow a lot of older women who choose to defeat ageing. 'They pretend ageing isn't happening and are extremely vague about their actual age. The duchess celebrates her big birthdays, talks about being a mother and pays attention to the vulnerability of people who are older. I think it's really important that she is not allowing the public just to say that once you've passed your sell-by date, you're invisible, inaudible and we don't care about you. Instead, she makes it clear that she cares about older people, and that's important.

Royals don't give up just because they reach retirement age, and the duchess continues to contribute.'

Jude Kelly, founder and president of WOW, states: 'As an older woman she has really grabbed the right to be loved, the right to be attractive, the right to have fun and the right to keep on developing intellectual curiosity. In that respect, she's a great role model because she lets you know there's lots of life left, and we should use it very well.

'I have found that young women are really excited to meet older women who have had a life . . . and are still trying to make change happen. They don't expect older women to be interested in them, so when someone like Camilla comes along and wants to find out about . . . the work they do or the issues that they've dealt with, for example, rehabilitation, they're absolutely amazed and thrilled, because they didn't know that they mattered. Camilla and I talk a lot about how to get young women to be confident and then hold on to that confidence and not let it get diminished by circumstance. We know issues like being post-menopausal, when women are marginalised because they have past their prime. I think there's now a bit of a fightback from women over seventy, who say, "I'm definitely here. I'm a happy, active woman with lots of life about me." I think having a sense of purpose is something we all know matters, and Camilla has had a growing sense that she matters now and uses it well.'

Many women would leap at the chance of changing all their clothes at any age, especially if there is no limit to the cost, but Dame Judi feels sorry for her. 'Camilla has had to change her way of dressing as well as her work. That's quite hard if you like to go around in jeans and a T-shirt.' As a mature woman Camilla has chosen not to follow fashion trends, wear British brands to promote them, or resort to extreme dieting or surgical interventions to make herself look younger. She believes that style has nothing to do with age, that worrying about wrinkles is a total waste of energy and that getting older and wiser can be more satisfying than being young.

Instead, she's carefully chosen her own image by having sorted out who she is first, looking at the demands made on her, and then dressing to match. Apart from formal ball dresses for special occasions, she's gathered a smart working uniform. The one thing she can be extravagant with are her hats, which are usually large and decorated with feathers or flowers or both. They suit her well and make it easier to find her in crowds. Daytime engagements usually see her in navy, with a dress that has vertical pleats from bust to stomach. It's slightly stereotypical but neatly avoids her being criticised for wearing something that is too fashionable or too dowdy. Nor does anyone expect her to constantly change her hairstyle or wear stilettoes. Even her shoes look comfy. She revealed how determined she can be when she agreed to a photoshoot for *Vogue* magazine in June 2022. Usually all the magazine's stylists sort out what will be worn from top to toe, but Camilla insisted on bringing her own choice of clothes.

Her favourite designers are Roy Allen, Dior, Fiona Clare and couture designer Bruce Oldfield. Bruce says, 'When she comes for a fitting, I listen to all the niggles about how she perceives her body shape and what she wants to show and not show. They are the sort of niggles of most women of her age. Few women want to flash their upper arms after they reach forty. It's easier to make things for someone once you know them well, but when I have sometimes tried to make little more radical clothes for the duchess it usually backfires. I don't think it's due to nerves. At a certain age you know what you like and what suits you, and if you are going to stand on the Palace balcony, or go to a very special event, you don't really want to take a chance.

'The duchess likes creams, soft blues and greens. I did persuade her to try pale pink, a colour she was not used to wearing, but she agreed to try it and later told me her husband liked it, so I scored there. For formal occasions the duchess likes georgette silk, because she has sensitive skin and soft silk crepes and chiffon clothes are more fluid and floaty. She can also move more easily in them.

'In her position she has to wear something that also makes her stand out, so the public knows she is there. She also has to look like she has made an effort, and that her garments go together in a thought-out way without looking stuffy. Another good thing about the duchess is that she always gives me plenty of time [to make what she needs]. For example, when I am doing something for the State Opening of Parliament, it has to be very formal, but nowadays the dress is allowed to be a little looser, even for the Queen. It's a different world today.'

She looked stunning in the sparkling light-blue dress with silver sequins that Bruce made for the world premiere of the Bond film *No Time to Die* at the London Albert Hall in September 2021. There was no beating tall, beautiful Catherine, Duchess of Cambridge, in her Jenny Packham glittering gold sequin dress. Nonetheless, a commentator who also admired Catherine added: 'I'd like to raise a glass to the Duchess of Cornwall, the blue, grey and silver are just perfect for her.'

Bruce adds: 'The Duke and Duchess of Cambridge towered over the Prince of Wales and the duchess, but in my aqua blue she shone like a beacon. It suited her so well it was a no-brainer.'

Mark Bolland confessed that when he was newly employed by Clarence House, he himself tried to update Camilla's look. 'I felt Camilla always looked middle-aged in the way the Queen Mother had to look old. Even now, in her mid-seventies, she looks like a country lady in her mid-fifties. She has very good legs but, as the

Duchess of Cornwall, you can't show your legs off all the time. Overall, physically, she is much more attractive than people give her credit for. Even as she ages, she will go on looking the same, with that mischievous look in her eyes. She doesn't feel [whatever happens] is all about her. She likes to think of others. I think she is the least vain and narcissistic person you could ever meet. Once Amanda MacManus, a charming force to be reckoned with, arrived, I stopped advising Camilla on how to dress and concentrated on other aspects.'

There is no doubt that keeping fit and having a good posture helps clothes look their best. Camilla, who does a lot of walking, Pilates and dance classes, is another good reason for her to have become a role model for this. She has even impressed Dame Darcey. 'It is very important to hold yourself well as you get older, which is both better for you physically and the clothes you wear. Nothing looks worse than crunched-up clothes. Having such a good physical image makes such a difference for the charities Her Royal Highness supports. She is very aware of the importance of health and wellbeing for both the young and elderly, and how she has set a very good example. I think she dresses immaculately and has a very distinctive style of her own. I noticed her posture when I saw her arrive at the James Bond premiere. She was standing beautifully.'

Another of Camilla's attributes is her sense of loyalty to the monarchy and the country. Friends and courtiers admire 'her hard-working ethic', believe 'she is fun', and enjoy her 'real sense of humour'.

Amanda MacManus feels Camilla's loyalty and trust has fundamentally changed her. 'I worked for Her Royal Highness for over twenty years, so long that I felt she really trusted me. It's an extraordinary validation, and when you have it you have freedom of thought and freedom of expression because you're not fearful about your job. It enabled me to think outside the box for her.' She recalls writing to Camilla where she said: 'You trust me to do things for you. You believed in me, and it gave me such an enormous sense of pride. I am a different woman from the woman I was because my employer was so supportive.'

Camilla's loyalty has led to loyalty in return. She has been going to the same London hairdresser, Jo Hansford, for nearly thirty years. Jo admitted to the *Daily Telegraph*: 'I don't talk to the duchess about personal things. I don't want to know. Whatever she wants to tell me, that's fine, but I don't ask. We get on incredibly well, because our children are the same age, and we both have grandchildren. She has a fantastic sense of humour, she really does. You're not best friends, but you build a rapport, and you know their hair. When the texture changes, you know how to alter the colour, but in a way that nobody notices there's been changes.'

I'm told by an insider that if you tell her she is a role model she laughs. She's too pragmatic to be interested in being any kind of hero. Instead, she wants to use her position to help those whose lives are difficult, and the more difficult they are the more she is driven to help. She has a nurturing side that comes to the fore with women and also animals, and that especially includes horses and dogs.

Chapter 22

DOGS AND HORSES

When one of Camilla's aides called me in October 2015 to ask if I was free the following afternoon, I had no idea why. At the time I was writing a magazine feature about Camilla, and they told me she wanted to surprise me, but it might not happen. I arrived, as instructed, at the Royal Mews at Buckingham Palace early the following afternoon. When Camilla appeared she said, with a mischievous look in her eyes, 'I think you will enjoy this if it happens.'

Not long afterwards a surprise visitor turned up. It was the Queen. She and Camilla greeted each other with a kiss on each cheek followed by a curtsy from Camilla. She introduced me to Her Majesty, who also had a rather mischievous gleam in her eyes. The Queen went on ahead and Camilla came up to me and said quietly that she thought I'd like to see her and the Queen together so I could decide for myself how they got on. Her Majesty, it seemed, had slipped away from hosting the four-day state visit of the Chinese President Xi Jinping to see something that was bound to interest her much more. [The following May, the Queen was caught on camera saying Chinese officials were 'very rude'.]

The event had been organised by The Brooke, a charity that takes care of working horses, donkeys and mules that Camilla first visited in Egypt during her and Prince Charles's Middle East tour in 2006. An ambassador for the charity, Monty Roberts, then eighty, and a world-famous American horse whisperer, had come along to demonstrate his innovative techniques with a five-year-old horse that had had minimum contact with people, never worn a saddle or been ridden. His goal was to show how the horse could be trained in a mere twenty minutes to accept a rider, rather than the usual six weeks. Camilla, who is patron of the charity, shares Monty's passion to bring non-violent training to the equine world.

It was a little chilly and both women sat with rugs over their legs looking transfixed as Monty made clucking and kissing sounds, waved his hands and then a long stick with a plastic bag on the end. The horse responded by turning one way then another before coming to Monty just within the twenty-minute time limit. Monty stroked him, then gently put a saddle and stirrups on him. Finally, one of his team mounted and rode the horse, by now completely docile, round the ring. Throughout, the Queen and Camilla chatted enthusiastically to each other and, when the amazing display ended, went over to Monty first to congratulate him and then to ask a series of questions. The Queen, who, as usual, was wearing gloves, stroked the horse's face. Gloveless Camilla tickled his nose.

Camilla loves horses partly because they bring back happy memories of time spent riding with her father. It's a passion she shares with the Queen and one that helped make their relationship less tense and formal both before and after her marriage. She can always find something to talk about in the horse world. Her own knowledge is vast, but she still marvels at the Queen's expertise. Speaking to ITV Racing in June 2021, she said, 'This is [the

Queen's] passion in life and she loves it. She can tell you every horse she's bred and owned, you know, from the very beginning. She doesn't forget anything.' The Queen has been patron of Royal Ascot since she came to the throne in 1952, and Camilla is likely to take over from her when the time comes as she is the Royal Family's strongest supporter of racing. In 2015 Camilla said: 'I hope [royal patronage] will continue. Royal patronage of racing is extremely important for the whole industry.'

Camilla cares deeply about the hundreds of horses enlisted by the British Army and the dangers they face. In October 2011 she donated her own self-painted watercolour of a famous horse called Sefton, badly injured by an IRA nail-bomb attack in July 1982, to the 'War Horse: Fact and Fiction' exhibition at the National Army Museum in Chelsea. It is a rare glimpse of her artwork and reveals her genuine artistic talent, which she usually dismisses.

Clare Balding, author and broadcaster, has close family links to the world of horses and was a leading amateur flat jockey. She speaks highly of the duchess: 'She has always been incredibly warm and friendly and open. Her behaviour doesn't change. Some switch it on and switch it off, but she has never done that. She knows a lot about it, loves riding, and she enjoys the racing scene. It is also an opportunity for her to see people she knows.'

Camilla also loves dogs, which is another throwback to her childhood when she found them great companions. She has since owned several. In 2010 she readily accepted an invitation to visit Battersea Dogs and Cats Home, the famed animal rescue centre in southwest London, to help celebrate its 150th anniversary. The then newly appointed chief executive Claire Horton was delighted. 'I knew the Duchess of Cornwall was such an animal person that, when she came along, she might also agree to open a state-of-the-art cattery that offers refuge to lost and abandoned cats and kittens.' It was the beginning of a strong relationship between Camilla and Claire. 'The thread that has run throughout my relationship with the duchess has been her great sense of fun, and her wish to get things right.'

Camilla herself has rehoused two rescue puppies, Beth and Bluebell, from Battersea. Beth, a Jack Russell terrier, had been brought to Battersea when she was three months old because her owners couldn't continue to care for her, and she won Camilla's heart in 2011. Bluebell, a cross between a Jack Russell and a Chihuahua, was adopted one year later. She had been found wandering in a London park when she was only four weeks old. Camilla described her on BBC News as having 'no hair on her, covered in sores, virtually dead. Battersea nursed her back to life and her hair grew again. She's very sweet, but a tiny bit neurotic.'

Claire wondered what Prince Charles felt about having two dogs, and found out at Camilla's seventieth birthday party at Highgrove in July 2017. 'His Royal Highness came up to me in the garden to say hello. I'd never met him before and when I told him who I was, he said, "Oh, so you're responsible [for the dogs], are you?" I said, "Yes, I'm sorry. It's my fault you've got two of them." And he said "No! They are absolutely part of the family. We wouldn't be without them."' Camilla complains when the dogs bring mice into the house but otherwise says she allows them 'to pretty much do whatever they want except they aren't allowed to sleep on the bed'.

The coronavirus pandemic brought about a tremendous demand for dogs from all sorts of people, including Charles and Camilla, seeking comfort and company during such difficult times. When Charles recovered from Covid and was reunited with Camilla after fourteen days of isolation, they celebrated their joint relief at his recovery and their fifteenth wedding anniversary on 9 April 2020 by releasing a touching new photograph of him and the duchess, who was casually dressed in jeans, seated side by side in the front porch of their Scottish country retreat, smiling broadly and each trying to hold a terrier in their arms, both of whom looked as if they were ready to make a run for it. It was not a set royal picture – just one of a happy couple.

The duchess was delighted to take over from the Queen, who was patron of Battersea from 1956 to 2016, another sign that she trusted her daughter-in-law to do a good job. Claire says, 'We couldn't have wished for anyone better and were absolutely over the moon. Thousands wrote to us to say "We've lost the Queen, but the duchess is brilliant. She'll be good for you." And she has been.'

Camilla likes to bring one or both of her terriers back regularly to visit Battersea. In December 2020 Beth made a special appearance at the official opening of the new kennels at Battersea Old Windsor, which has been open since 1979. It operates in the same way as the flagship London centre but on a slightly smaller scale. Camilla, who was jovially wearing a paw-print face mask, because of anti-Covid restrictions, picked Beth up and said: 'They say you should never work with animals, and now, with the help of Beth, I'm going to attempt to unveil a building with the help of a dog.' Royals regularly unveil plaques, but the way Camilla did it made it much more fun. Amanda MacManus thought it might be a good idea to involve Beth in the unveiling, and Camilla agreed. A sausage was attached to the blue curtain covering the plaque, and when Camilla picked Beth up, she immediately tried to grab the sausage and kept tugging at it until the small curtain fell away and the sausage was firmly in her mouth. Camilla roared with laughter, as did everyone else around her. Turning to Beth, she said, 'Anyone would think you've never been fed.'

She then thanked everyone for asking her to open the Duchess of Cornwall Kennels, saying: 'I'm extremely touched that they have been called after me. Every time I come here I'll be able to look at my very own kennels. I would also like to thank everybody here, because I know how tough Covid has been for all of you. Hopefully with the vaccine etcetera, we're seeing the light at the end of the tunnel, so things will start to improve. But I suspect as they do, more and more dogs and cats will start coming in and you're going to be busier than ever. So these kennels are going to be worth their weight in gold, and they're pretty luxurious kennels. I wouldn't mind spending a night in them – air conditioning and everything you could possibly hope for.'

There was another tongue-in-cheek joke on International Dog Day in August 2021 when Clarence House tweeted: 'We are highlighting the tail-wagging work of the duchess's canine patronages and charities' with a picture of a casually dressed Camilla striding across the moors with Beth leading the way.

Camilla's can-do spirit and generosity have always been a part of her personality. Over the years she has earned a wealth of respect from people from all walks of life who have come into contact with her sincerity and zest for life. When it comes to helping new royal arrivals familiarise themselves with the way the Royal Family operates, there is no person better placed than Camilla, who has been tireless – against all the odds – to demonstrate her value and loyalty to the Crown. In 2018 she extended that offer of help to include Meghan Markle, a beautiful American divorcee and not widely known actress that Harry had fallen for. But would it be appreciated?

Chapter 23

WHAT TO DO ABOUT HARRY

More than 6,500 people gathered to drink lemon barley water or tea and eat delicate sandwiches and creamy cakes in the gardens of Buckingham Palace on 22 May 2018. It was just three days after Harry and Meghan's £33.5 million wedding at Windsor Castle and the occasion was Prince Charles's seventieth birthday. He was born on 14 November 1948, but celebrations began early in the year so the events could be staggered, and some held outside. This first party was the Birthday Patronage Celebration; the hosts were Camilla and Charles, and the guests were the prince's military affiliations and representatives from the four hundred-plus charities he supports.

There were growing rumours that the newly-weds might be there, which made it the hottest ticket in town. I was one of CNN's TV commentary team on the wedding day and my biography of Prince Harry had just come out, so I was delighted when the day after the wedding a royal aide said they had just heard Harry and Meghan would be there for their first joint royal engagement as a married couple and would I like to join the party.

Charles and Camilla were 'absolutely delighted' that the newly-weds wanted to come, especially as Prince William couldn't be there as he was in Manchester to mark the anniversary of the Manchester Arena bombing attack exactly a year previously when twenty-three people died, including the Islamist terrorist who set off the bomb, and 1,017 were injured.

The royal aide told me Prince Harry had said he and Meghan wouldn't stay long as it was his father's birthday and he didn't want to take the limelight away from him on such a special occasion, and if I wanted to see the couple, I had better come early. It was a glorious sunny day, just as it had been for the wedding. Not surprisingly, the conversations among the guests were a combination of how wonderful the wedding had been and how happy people were for Charles to reach this milestone.

The prince and Camilla came out of the Palace doors first with Harry and Meghan right behind them. At one point Camilla held Meghan's hand, a rare royal public gesture – perhaps to give her confidence and show the guests that she was accepted as one of the family. At the time Meghan was seen as a 'breath of fresh air' for the monarchy. There was also great joy that Harry had at last found someone to love and who could cope with a life in the spotlight.

Harry then gave a touching speech that was full of warmth and gratitude. He thanked his father for the caring way he walked Meghan partway down the aisle as her own father was unwell and couldn't make the journey from Mexico. Harry was equally grateful that Charles had taken Meghan's mother Doria's arm when she looked bewildered at the end of the ceremony and walked out of the chapel with her on one arm and Camilla on the other. Charles looked very moved.

'Pa,' Harry began, looking at his father. 'While I know that you've asked that today will not be about you, you must forgive me if I don't listen to you – much like when I was younger – and instead, I ask everyone here to say a huge thank you to you, for your incredible work.' He then turned to the crowd: 'His enthusiasm and energy are truly infectious. It has certainly inspired William and I.' He was then slightly distracted by a bee that kept trying to fly into his ear and he made several attempts to swat it away. Meghan and then Camilla started giggling and looked at each other like co-conspirators as they tried to hold back their laughter. 'What's going on?' Charles mouthed to Camilla. She whispered back to him, and he leant round to beam at Meghan, all of which showed how relaxed Meghan and her in-laws were together. After the speech the newly-weds came down the stairs into the garden to greet some of the guests, thanking everyone who congratulated them. Harry and Meghan kept their word and, after about forty minutes, prepared to leave. All four embraced each other before they parted, and the party continued.

Sometime afterwards, critical comments began to circulate on social media about the celebration – and have done so ever since. Prince Charles was alleged to have asked, if not ordered, Harry and Meghan to leave; most thought because of Meghan's behaviour, although what that was supposed to be hasn't emerged. The party was later described as the start of 'the fallout' between the Sussexes and the senior royals that resulted in them moving abroad. I have never believed it. I saw for myself how they left full of smiles. There was no obligation for them to come in the first place. They came because they wanted to and left when they said they would.

It is rarely easy for children to accept a replacement parent for their own and almost inevitable to avoid changing the organised dynamic of a family, rich or poor. Keeping a positive face for the new step-parent can't be easy if the children are rude and aggressive. It also takes a while for a step-parent to be accepted into the family, and although Camilla had met the two princes and had brought up children of her own, a dark cloud hung over the relationship as the princes knew their mother hated her. Deciding what to say and how to do it must have been like walking on eggshells. As Camilla was also trying to be positive with the rest of the Royal Family, whom she knew didn't welcome her, it must have been a very stressful time.

William, who had the same childhood experiences and similar scars as Harry, has a very different personality and an instinctive caution to protect himself. He was helped to deal with his troubles by the then Kate Middleton, whom he met at St Andrew's University. She and her family let him see what normal close family life was all about. As a result, he rejected what could have been his inevitable path and, with loyal Kate by his side, worked through some of his anxieties. Although he admitted to initially finding parenthood difficult, having a happy marriage and becoming a father to three children has given him a new positive perspective on the world.

Harry as a boy was often reckless: one moment he would be behaving and the next going off the rails. As he grew older a combination of lack of self-control, poor judgement and too much alcohol – he started drinking when he was twelve – resulted in Harry deciding to wear a Nazi uniform with a swastika armband at a fancy-dress party in 2005, taking off his clothes during a game of strip billiards in Las Vegas in 2012, and jumping from the balcony of the Goring Hotel in London the night before his brother's wedding. Harry has always been more emotionally vulnerable and thin-skinned than William, but it's unfair to blame his troubles solely on being a royal second son with no particular goal in life. Warring parents and the tragic and traumatic loss of his mother didn't make things any easier.

Romantically he had an on-off seven-year relationship with Chelsy Davy, until she decided she didn't want a life in the spotlight. Although he was good at putting on a front and being the joker at a party, his grief at losing his mother increased to overwhelm him. William suggested he seek help. Harry didn't listen at first, but told me he changed his mind when he was twenty-eight 'and the time was right'.

Another insider felt that being Harry's stepmother wasn't easy. 'The duchess always felt quite wary of Harry and used to see him out of the corner of her eye looking at her in a long and cold way. She found it rather unnerving. Otherwise, they got on quite well. She was always supportive of him and, when she felt the time was right, tried to help him understand the challenges of being young in the modern world, and in a world that was more open than the one the Prince of Wales had to cope with as a child. She never interfered directly or tried to be a surrogate mother. Instead, she was a supportive figure in the background. What I observed between them was always friendly. He was and still is a lost soul in so many ways.'

In practice, neither William nor Harry needed nurturing as they were twenty-three and twenty respectively when Camilla officially became their stepmother in 2005. She was more of a friendly grown-up who they saw occasionally at royal gatherings. She tried to be encouraging rather than influential. Nor has she tried to take over any responsibility as a step-grandmother to the Cambridges' children, Prince George, Princess Charlotte and Prince Louis, especially as Catherine's parents, Carole and Michael Middleton, are so close.

Amanda MacManus has a positive view about Camilla being a stepmother. 'Her Royal Highness is a very warm woman so I would imagine it would all be quite good. She has her own children and grandchildren so she wouldn't try to take other children away from anyone else. Having them around is more like having a bonus. She loves children and the more the merrier.' William nonetheless has made it clear that Camilla is the wife of his father, but not a step-grandmother to his children, and that Prince George, his sister Princess Charlotte and Prince Louis have two grandfathers, but only one grandmother.

Camilla knows more than anyone how difficult it is to become accepted into the British Royal Family and wanted to help any newcomer, especially if they, like her, had previously lived a more normal life. This worked well with the then Kate Middleton, who William wanted people to call Catherine. Camilla helped her familiarise herself with some of the customs, antiquated protocols and restrictions of royal life. She also took her out for a girls-only lunch some weeks before her wedding ceremony in April 2011, and on another occasion Catherine and her sister Pippa, plus Camilla's daughter Laura, to Koffman's, the Berkeley Hotel restaurant in Knightsbridge. One of Catherine's friends said, 'Camilla's exceptional warmth has really touched Catherine.'

Behind the scenes they got on well too, as they have similar stable loving backgrounds and enjoy the countryside. It was believed that Camilla gave Catherine a gold charm-style bracelet before her wedding. She discussed with her what sort of charities she thought she might like to be involved with and recommended initially that she took on just a few she could give a lot of attention to rather than spread herself too thin. She suggested she employed a personal dresser to help with her clothes and gave her some hints on living in a huge apartment, as she and William would be moving into accommodation with twenty-one rooms on four floors in Kensington Palace. William was grateful and Prince Charles was delighted they got on so well. In July 2022 Catherine, at Camilla's request, took delightful photographs of her step mother-in-law to celebrate her guest editing of *Country Life* to celebrate its 125th anniversary and her 75th birthday.

Camilla warmly greeted Meghan when she came to London to be with Harry. I was told with a smile by a senior royal that the fact that she came from a divorced family was a positive, as it would fit in well with the modern royals. Prince Charles enjoyed talking to her, especially about the theatre and arts. Camilla felt the experience she had from coping with public abuse, press insults and frostiness from the Royal Family put her in a good place to help Meghan adjust to the restrictions of royal life and was equally keen to help Meghan find her feet. They had lunches together and Camilla spent a lot of time offering advice on how to handle the pressure. She tried to be supportive, was happy to be her mentor and took her out for private lunches. A source at the time told me: 'She doesn't want to see anyone struggling and she is fond of Meghan.' Meghan, however, seemed bored, was unresponsive and preferred to go her own way, with the result that Camilla's advice landed on stony ground.

Meghan had a reputation for being a hard worker, and her first book, *Together: Our Community Cookbook*, was published in September 2018, after the tragic Grenfell Tower fire in London in June 2017. A group of local women from different countries, who had connections with the tower, had gathered together to cook food for those in need. Meghan joined them. She helped with the cooking, wrote the foreword to the book and held a launch party for it. Camilla and Charles wanted to show their support and invited Harry and Meghan plus their friend Lucia Santa Cruz to lunch at Highgrove. Lucia recalls: 'As a surprise, Camilla went out of her way to make sure the lunch consisted only of recipes from Meghan's cookbook, and that included a very hot salsa. It was a really nice gesture.' One that made no impact.

Although the relationship between Camilla and William, Catherine, Harry and Meghan was amicable, members of the Royal Family are kept very busy and it's not unusual for them not to see each other for weeks or months at a time. It was a shock when, in January 2020, Harry and Meghan stepped away from their senior positions in the Royal Family. Camilla behaved as she did when she was verbally attacked in the 1990s. This was to avoid talking about it and concentrate on supporting Prince Charles. One journalist told the *Sun* newspaper that 'Camilla is the sort who would refer to Meghan as "that minx"', which soon became regarded as a fact rather than speculation. Several insiders said Camilla wouldn't and hadn't ever talked like that about anyone. I was told: 'It's not her sort of word and she would never give her views of her in front of anyone.'

In March 2021 Harry and Meghan were interviewed on American television by Oprah Winfrey. The broadcast included several errors and cruel allegations about his family. The Duke of Edinburgh was at the time seriously ill and the close family had been told he did not have long to live. A reliable source has told me that Harry has recently been very negative about Camilla, but believes it 'could be part of his therapy process to relive certain things and he may want to blame someone else for his own mistakes. As I understand it his father and stepmother have become hateful in his mind. I've also been told that Meghan has been horrible about her too. As for Prince Charles, the pain he feels about the situation with his younger son must be immense and Camilla is obviously the only person he can really talk to it with.'

Another source added: 'Camilla has been strongly supportive of Prince Charles. What has happened and how [Harry] has behaved has been very upsetting for her. There have been a lot of hurt feelings all round, but like all families you have to embrace it all and hope it will improve.' It is particularly sad as Harry used to be known as the royals' peacemaker and openly defended Camilla when he said before the wedding that 'she's always been very close to me'. An upset, rather shocked Camilla has helped Charles deal with the problems Harry and Meghan have caused.

Jude Kelly, CEO of the WOW foundation, points out how difficult this is for Camilla: 'She is very defenceless because her way of doing things is by being discreet. It is also a matter of dignity. The royals can't retaliate. If you love your children or your stepchildren, and I'm sure that she does, no matter what they do, you can't attack back. There's always the long-term possibility that you will still be able to love each other and come back together again, so you need to be careful that you don't poison the water.'

Fortunately, time has helped improve Camilla's relationship with William, largely thanks to Catherine, who is a peacemaker and wants to strengthen a family rather than tear it apart. Camilla is also a conciliator and doesn't nurse grievances. They both believe that supporting their husbands is a priority. Catherine has a love of the arts, which William doesn't particularly share, and often goes both privately and publicly with Camilla and Prince Charles to see exhibitions of art, crafts and texture. Or she goes with Camilla as a twosome. In February 2022, Catherine joined Charles and Camilla on a visit to the Prince's Foundation in Trinity Buoy Wharf in London's former docklands, which all three enjoyed. In fact, the rift that Harry left seems to have brought William, Catherine, Charles and Camilla closer together. William was not a part of the decision-making process for Camilla to be queen consort when the time comes but is 'supportive' of Camilla and respects the Queen's judgement.

Even Camilla's relationship with Princess Anne keeps improving. Royal expert Robert Hardman says: 'Camilla and Anne see each other at horse racing events, but they don't spend a lot of time in each other's pockets. Anne has her own circle and life, but I'm sure when they meet there is a lot of very animated discussion about horses.'

*

Commonwealth Day has always been a royal highlight, especially for the Queen, who is head of the organisation. Individuals of all ages and backgrounds from the fifty-four countries that make up the Commonwealth of Nations come together. The theme on 14 March 2022 was 'Delivering a Common Future'. This time, however, the Queen was unable to go to Westminster Abbey for the annual service. She had mobility issues, and only a few weeks previously had coronavirus. An alternative entrance that avoided a long walk down the aisle had been found but it was decided that sitting on a chair for over an hour and standing for long periods of time would be too uncomfortable for Her Majesty. She did however release a message: 'In these testing times, it is my hope that you can draw strength and inspiration from what we share, as we work together towards a healthy, sustainable and prosperous future for all.'

She was instead represented by Prince Charles, accompanied by Camilla, and the Duke and Duchess of Cambridge. Outside Westminster Abbey for all to see and in a deliberate show of affection, Catherine leant down to kiss Camilla warmly on her cheek and smiled broadly. William and Camilla also greeted each other with a kiss, a significant public sign that he and Catherine will support Charles and Camilla for both pragmatic and emotional reasons.

As to the future relationship with Harry and Meghan, I was told that there are several options. One is to ignore their comments in the hope that 'interest in what the couple say fades away'. My source said, 'Indeed, it already looks as if they have written themselves out of the script.' Other options suggested were to 'shrug off' any harmful comments Harry might make or 'try to privately negotiate some kind of ceasefire. But that is unlikely to work if Meghan just wants to win.'

An important alternative is to keep America close. My source added, 'The Sussexes are more liked in America than in the UK, which can damage not only Charles and Camilla but the whole monarchy. The American issue has to be dealt with. The Cambridges have to go to the US to show who the real stars are. As will Camilla and the Prince of Wales – either when he is king, or even before.' Prince William and Catherine will go to Boston towards the end of 2022 for the second Earthshot Prize ceremony, when five winners will receive a £1million grant to continue their environmental work. It will be the first time the royal couple have been to the US since 2014.

Although Harry missed the memorial service for his grandfather, partly because he said he wasn't happy with the protection offered to him, just over two weeks later he managed to fit in a quick visit to the Queen, who he hadn't seen for two years. He was on his way to the Invictus Games in the Netherlands – an international sporting competition for injured and sick veterans and service people.

The Queen agreed to see him on condition he visited his father first. Harry concurred but turned up late. Prince Charles and Camilla were representing the Queen at the traditional Royal Maundy Service in St George's Chapel at Windsor Castle and, by the time Harry arrived, father and son only managed about fifteen minutes of conversation. Much too little time to heal hurt feelings. Camilla stayed in the room to listen to what Harry had to say. Afterwards he talked to a US channel about his private meeting with the Queen, saying she was 'in great form' and he'd wanted to 'make sure that's she's protected'. Something that's not possible when you live 5,000 miles away.

Camilla may seem to want to stay in the background but she will not tolerate anyone being rude or aggressive to her husband and the future king. However, her first open response to *The Crown* on Netflix was shrewdly different.

Chapter 24

THE NETFLIX CROWN

It was both subtle and clever of Camilla to invite actor Emerald Fennell to a Clarence House celebration for International Women's Day on 8 March 2022. Fennell played the young Camilla in the Netflix royal drama *The Crown*. (The series is meant to follow the life of Queen Elizabeth II from 1940 to near the present day.) If Fennell felt self-conscious for playing Camilla as callous and unpleasant in the series, one assumes under direction, and thought she'd be able to stay quietly in the background, she got it wrong. Camilla turned the spotlight on her in her speech and joked about her presence. 'For me, it's very reassuring to know that if I should fall off my perch at any moment, my fictional alter ego is here to take over,' she declared. 'So Emerald, be prepared!' The guests roared with laughter, but there could well have been more to it than merely a joke. Using the word 'fictional' was a shrewd way of underlining that the series is fiction and neither fact nor true, as many people appear to believe.

Fennell, who towered over Camilla, looks nothing like her when she was younger, but came well prepared. 'It's particularly nice to meet her today, on Women's Day,' she said, 'because she does so much for so many particularly female-centred charities. So yeah, it's just amazing. I mean, I was nervous I may be thrown in the Tower, but so far, so good.' She later agreed with a reporter who remarked that Camilla was 'a good sport'. 'Absolutely,' she replied. 'She's been in the spotlight for a long time and has always weathered it with a lot of grace and good humour.' Fennell would not be continuing to play Camilla in season five of *The Crown*. The role was scheduled to be taken over by Olivia Williams, who wasn't at the party.

There has been much discussion about how Camilla and other members of the Royal Family have reacted to *The Crown* – whether or not they watched it, were hurt and/or felt insulted. The show's writer Peter Morgan has admitted he fabricated some incidents. For example, Prince Philip was alluded to have had an affair with a ballerina during the second series and, in the third, ignored his mother, Princess Alice, when she came to live at Buckingham Palace in 1967. Neither event ever happened.

Season four was released in November 2020 and plunged viewers into the 1980s love triangle of Princess Diana (Emma Corrin), Prince Charles (Josh O'Connor) and Camilla Parker Bowles. It chronicled the break-up of Charles and Diana's marriage and Diana's struggles with bulimia. Some viewers were enraged over its portrayal of Princess Diana's alleged treatment at the hands of the Royal Family and especially of Charles and Camilla. It also served as a reminder of Camilla's unpopularity, as Charles's mistress, at that time. The public reaction was so angry that it was assumed it was the reason why there was a significant increase in the number of hate comments on the Clarence House Twitter account. The comments section was turned off shortly after the fourth season was aired.

How strange then that it was reported in several newspapers

and magazines that Camilla, with her great sense of humour, was 'quite happy to laugh at the series'. This is not true. An informed insider told me: 'When a certain timeline story is revisited by the press, television or film it causes the duchess a lot of stress and she gets very upset. That is the truth but neither she nor Prince Charles will talk about it. The narrative is that she is the wicked woman, where Diana is presented as the victim and Camilla as evil.' As a result, she was vilified as a 'marriage wrecker'.

Mark Bolland, Prince Charles's former aide, added: 'I think that what was very difficult for her along the way, and must still be difficult for her, are reminders of the bad times in the eighties and nineties. Of course, it comes back from time to time – in books and dramas and documentaries on television. Much of that history is based on untruths at worst or, at best, another version of history.'

Amanda MacManus adds: 'I don't believe Her Royal Highness has ever watched *The Crown*. It's the way she protects herself.' As for the abusive comments, she says: 'You wonder how people can say such things. She rarely talked about it and brushed it to the side. It must have hurt but I think she has got used to it and thinks the people who do it are trolls and possibly look like trolls as well.' Another senior insider said: 'The real truth is that the depiction of herself and the exaggeration of Diana's plight hurt her badly.'

Other royals have largely kept quiet, apart from Prince William, who reportedly told some friends that he was greatly displeased with the depiction of his family, believing that his parents 'are being exploited and presented in a false, simplistic way to make money'.

Diana's brother Lord Spencer appeared on ITV's *Lorraine* in November 2020 to say: 'I think it would help *The Crown* an enormous amount if – at the beginning of each episode – it stated that "This isn't true, but it is based around some real events". Then, everyone would understand it's drama for drama's sake. Obviously, Netflix wants to make a lot of money and that's why people are in the business of making these things.'

It wouldn't have taken much, but the producers refused to highlight onscreen that the episode wasn't factual. As a result, many people who watched it, and particularly younger people, believe that the fictional drama is stating the truth even though historians have pointed out that it is not. It has left allegations that she and Diana were love rivals possibly still hanging over her. It also reignited the public's animosity towards Prince Charles.

They did, however, put up a warning about eating disorders in season four, which gave the wrong impression to some that the content was more fact than fiction.

Prince Harry thought the series was okay as long as it didn't include him. I had gone to talk to him at Kensington Palace in 2017 when I was writing his biography and his first question when he opened the living-room door and shook my hand was: 'Are you watching *The Crown*?' (At the time, the second series was being shown.) 'I am,' said Harry, 'but I wish they'd stopped at the end of the first series. They absolutely must not move on to the younger generation.'

He confirmed he has watched *The Crown* with his wife Meghan Markle 'from time to time' in a 2021 interview with his friend James Corden on *The Late Show* on the American TV network CBS. 'Of course, it's not strictly accurate . . . It gives you a rough idea about what that lifestyle [looks like], what the pressures of putting duty and service above family and everything else – what can come from that.' He added: 'I'm way more comfortable with *The Crown* than I am seeing the stories written about my family or my wife or myself.' The couple had, by this time, signed a multi-year deal with Netflix for making documentaries, docuseries, feature films, scripted shows and children's programming, and were believed to have been offered the mind-blowing amount of £71 million.

Despite *The Crown* being fiction, when it features living people surely more care needs to be taken. One wonders if Netflix hasn't done so because unlike other people who are presented in a terrible light it is unlikely that a senior royal like Camilla will sue for libel. The fourth series presents Camilla immersed in a battle to get Charles back and that she has been having an affair with him throughout the duration of his marriage to Diana. One of the episodes shows Camilla taking a very shy, very young Diana for lunch in a smart restaurant and asking her lots of question that are obviously designed to put her off Charles, showing how little she knows him and how very inexperienced she is. These include the following, all asked with a patronising sneer: 'You know how he loves to be around really old men' and 'Darling, I thought it would be the first thing you noticed.' And when Diana says Charles hadn't called her, the fictional Camilla replies: 'Golly, we speak every day.'

In addition, Prince Philip is seen to warn Charles not to 'fall in love with the Shand girl. She is just a bit of fun.' No wonder the social media platform TikTok launched various anti-Camilla campaigns.

The historian Andrew Roberts is in no doubt: '*The Crown* is vicious republican propaganda. They know they are not going to be sued by a royal for libel or slander even when they are portrayed in a hideous way. King Richard III was not as Shakespeare drew him, but he's been dead for five hundred years. Camilla is still alive, which makes a huge difference.'

'*The Crown* is too horrible for words about her,' adds Esther Rantzen. 'I know she doesn't watch it, but nonetheless it's awful. It's a case of keeping calm and carrying on. The trick is, if you don't read it, you don't watch it, and you don't know they're sticking pins in you, it's amazing how little effect it has.'

A lesser number of people were outraged at how the Royal Family was being portrayed, the invasion into their lives, and how inaccurate it was about both events and personalities. Various anonymous individuals in *The Times* were quoted as saying: 'It is the most cruel and unfair and horrible portrayal of almost all of them.' One said that what *The Crown* did was a 'deliberate attack on the monarchy'. Another called it 'spiteful, it just goes for people's negative points rather than their positive ones. It is unbalanced.' And a third: 'It's like a golden apple that inside is rotten. It is very, very unfair to the Royal Family.'

One Camilla fan told me: 'She is an unfailing public servant, so dignified in her duty and doing very important work. Anyone paying more attention than just watching *The Crown* would happily see her called Queen Camilla.'

Chapter 25

THE DUKE OF EDINBURGH

Camilla's relationship with the Duke of Edinburgh started coldly, but over the years it gradually blossomed as he got to know her better and saw the positive transformation in Prince Charles that she brought about. Despite his initial sharp criticism of her, Camilla never tried to retaliate or complain. Instead, she believed, as she does about most difficulties, that time would heal things. She was right, and in his later years she and Prince Philip enjoyed their improved relationship and shared their many common interests.

The only time Prince Charles was resolute enough to stand up to both his parents was when he told them that removing Mrs Parker Bowles from his life was 'not negotiable'. He had lost her once by marrying Lady Diana Spencer and was not going to let it happen again. The Queen, however, was convinced that if the couple married, countless royal supporters would turn their back on the family and the monarchy would be seriously damaged, an attitude that highlighted her sense of duty and concern for her son's happiness.

As for the Duke of Edinburgh, Charles believed that however hard he tried to please him, his father would believe he had let him down and been a disappointment. At times he felt that Prince Philip wondered whether he, someone who preferred music and poetry to shooting things, was even robust enough to be king.

Nor, for many years, did Prince Philip understand what his son saw in Camilla Parker Bowles compared to his beautiful daughter-in-law Princess Diana. It was a surprisingly chauvinistic attitude for a moderniser like Prince Philip to believe that having a beautiful wife was more important than a stable, warm, witty but less glamorous one. He was, after all, a man who prided himself on being a reformer who had tried to drag the Royal Family into the twentieth century. One of the first things he did as consort in 1953 was to stop the eighteenth-century obligation for Palace servants to powder their hair with flour and starch on state occasions, which he called 'ridiculous and unmanly'.

Prince Philip was the first royal to take advantage of television. In a *Panorama* programme broadcast on 29 May 1961, he became the first member of the Royal Family to give a television interview. He was interviewed by Richard Dimbleby and talked about Commonwealth Technical Training Week, an uncontroversial subject but still a remarkable step forward for the royals. In 1969 he persuaded the Queen to take part in a TV documentary, *Royal Family*, shown on both BBC and ITV, that gave the filmmakers unprecedented access and showed the Queen both at work and off-duty. One memorable scene showed the Duke of Edinburgh cooking sausages on a family barbecue at Balmoral. The Queen quietly refused to let it be shown again after 1977, feeling it was intrusive and that the Royal Family would seem to be too normal, although short clips have been permitted on various occasions. But in retrospect, at a time when the Royal Family was not particularly popular, the documentary gave it a shot in the arm.

Prince Philip also insisted his children went to school rather than be educated by tutors within the Palace, and supported Prince Charles when he said he wanted to go to university. For some years he held the view that Charles and Diana's marriage was salvageable. He felt the couple should manage as best they could, an attitude that reflected his own background as a youth when he was, at times, both penniless and homeless with neither of his parents there to help him.

Between June and December 1992, the duke expressed his feelings about Camilla in several letters he wrote to Princess Diana, of whom he was very fond. Diana's friends, Rosa Monckton, then managing director of Tiffany's in London, and Lucia Flecha de Lima, wife of the Brazilian ambassador, told Gyles Brandreth that they actually read the letters with Diana.

He wrote that Charles 'was silly to risk everything with Camilla', and 'We [he and the Queen] never dreamed he might feel like leaving you for her. I cannot imagine anyone in their right mind leaving you for Camilla. Such a prospect never entered our heads.'

Another frank letter was more down to earth. He asked: 'Can you honestly look into your heart and say that Charles's relationship with Camilla had nothing to do with your behaviour towards him in your marriage?' He also reminded Diana that her husband had made a 'considerable sacrifice cutting ties with Camilla during the early days'. As he was careful not to make her think he was telling her off, he always signed his letters 'with fondest love, pa'. However, after Diana and Charles's divorce was finalised in 1996, Prince Philip's relationship with Diana became strained.

It must have been painful for Camilla to know what her father-in-law thought about her. It also must have hurt that the Queen, who enjoyed Camilla's company when she was still with her notoriously unfaithful first husband, chose to avoid her once she was with Prince Charles. The Parker Bowleses had been regular guests at Sandringham and Balmoral where there were always lively conversations about horses.

The press and the public also lambasted Camilla, but she carried on stoically. It took several years for Prince Philip to realise that Camilla had admirable qualities, some of which were similar to Diana's. For example, she loved talking to people of every age and background, showed compassion with those who were ill and vulnerable, and was particularly warm towards children.

Prince Philip decided to step down from some of his public commitments when he reached the age of ninety in June 2011. He passed BookTrust, the UK's largest children's reading charity, on to Camilla. It was a sign that he recognised her love of literature and their growing friendship and was pleased she became patron in his place. Over the next few years, he gradually withdrew from all his charities.

Although his mind remained alert his body was becoming increasingly frail, and in December 2019 he was taken from the Queen's Sandringham Estate in Norfolk – where close family including Prince Charles and the Duchess of Cornwall would celebrate Christmas – and was admitted once again to the King Edward VII Hospital, London, where he had been treated several times in the previous few years. The public were told he was in hospital for observation and treatment in relation to a pre-existing condition on the advice of his doctor. He was discharged in time for the celebrations.

It was around this time that the relationship between the Duke and Prince Charles improved beyond expectation. Petty differences or even stronger ones ceased to be so important and Prince Philip at long last accepted that although he and his son had a different outlook on life – Prince Philip's was pragmatic while Prince Charles was romantic – they thought alike on many issues. The duke had, for example, championed environmental causes in the 1950s long before they were popular and continued to do so throughout his life. He also toured the world to draw attention to the plight of wildlife endangered by poaching, deforestation and pollution. These causes are equally a priority for Prince Charles, and he has passed the same passions on to his older son and heir Prince William.

Prince Philip found that he and Camilla also had much in common, particularly a love of horticulture and reading. They also shared a self-deprecating sense of humour. More importantly, after she married Charles, he could see her own dedication to duty and how loyal she was to her husband. Prince Philip's number one priority was to always be there for the Queen, and he correctly had come to believe that Camilla felt the same about Charles. He could also see how stable, confident and happy Charles was with the woman he had always loved. It was an enormous relief for him during the last months of his life to know that Camilla understood the huge pressure Charles would be under once he was king.

In 2020, three years after Prince Philip had officially retired, he made a rare but significant public appearance to formally transfer his role as colonel-in-chief of The Rifles to Camilla. He had held the role since 2007, when the new regiment was formed from the amalgamation of the four light infantry and rifle regiments of the Light Division, but his connection to the infantry regiment stretched back to 1953. In his own way, it was a huge thank you to Camilla, and an acknowledgment that he believed the regiment he was so attached to would be in the best possible hands. She, in turn, felt honoured to accept his offer and expressed her gratitude at a Rifles award dinner in November 2021. Sophie, Countess of Wessex, accompanied her. Dressed dramatically in a V-neck floor-length black dress, with a striking necklace of emeralds and diamonds with earrings to match, she had made sure to wear the silver Bugle Horn brooch of The Rifles. She said: 'I know it was a role that he cherished and of which he was immensely proud, and it is one of the greatest honours in my life to have followed him in this illustrious role.'

It is of great credit to Camilla and typical of her nature that she bore Prince Philip no grudge or resentment for his early negative behaviour towards her. A friend who has known Camilla for more than thirty years told me that she was 'a real grown-up. She likes to be positive. She accepts what is difficult and enjoys it when it turns positive.'

The Royal Family and the military have a very special relationship and great respect for each other, which is highlighted on Remembrance Sunday. Camilla has been close to the military all her life and fully understands the importance of her role. Her father and first husband spent time in the military, as have Prince Charles, Prince William and Harry. She visits military bases, presents medals and turns up for parades at Christmas time. When troops are deployed, she sends parcels of goodies and visits those who are wounded. Her key military patronages include: the British Legion, which provides financial, social and emotional support to members and veterans of the British Armed Forces, their families and dependants; the Poppy Factory, which supports veterans with health conditions on their journey into employment; the War Memorials Trust, which protects war memorials across the UK; the Desert Rats Association, which helps keep the history of the Desert Rats alive, and from June 2020 she became vice-patron of ABF, The Soldiers' Charity. This was formed in 1944 to provide a lifetime of support to veterans and their families when they are in need. The Queen has been patron since 1953.

Eighteen months later, in December 2021, she became patron of the British Forces Broadcasting Service, BFBS, which she said via video was 'an honour' and that its work on television and radio raised morale and 'lessened the gap between loved ones'. She went on to add: 'Spanning fifteen time zones, from the deserts of the Middle East to the windswept Falkland Islands, you are a truly worldwide organisation that supports our servicemen and -women wherever they may find themselves.'

She visits military bases, presents medals, is there for parades at Christmas, writes to the regiments, sends them flowers and cards when a baby is born, and gifts when they are deployed. She is known for making people feel comfortable and is good at interacting with young people in the military who might otherwise be unsure of what to say to her. The aim is to make them feel confident they have met a person rather than a representative of the Royal Family. A lot of her intrinsic understanding of the military is a legacy from her father Major Bruce Shand. The military charities also give her a welcome opportunity to speak about her father's service in the 12th Royal Lancers during the Second World War, and that way keep him close to her heart.

She also revealed that her father produced a makeshift news bulletin for his fellow prisoners of war so they could hear voices from home while being held by the Nazis during the Second World War. 'I know a little of the importance of maintaining the connection between serving personnel and their family . . . Officially his role was to be the laundry officer. Unofficially it fell to him and half a dozen others to create and listen to a very basic radio to glean precious news of home and share it with their fellow prisoners.

'Periodic Nazi raids would locate and destroy the carefully built wireless sets, but they were always replaced as quickly as possible – the men could cope with almost anything as long as they were not deprived of some form of contact with home.'

No wonder Major-General Chris Wilson, chairman of the BFBS board of trustees, said: 'The trustees are absolutely delighted Her Royal Highness the Duchess of Cornwall has accepted their invitation to talk on the patronage of BFBS.'

*

At Christmas 2020, because of the coronavirus pandemic, for the first time in more than three decades Prince Philip and the Queen did not go to Sandringham, their usual location for the family to gather, but spent the festive season alone at Windsor Castle. They were regularly visited by Charles and Camilla, and an insider told me that their time together was full of warmth, kindness and emotion. Charles and his father got on particularly well, probably because they both knew that their remaining time together would be short.

Prince Philip was taken to King Edward VII's Hospital on 16 February 2021. He was feeling unwell and was treated for an infection. He also had a variety of tests for a pre-existing heart condition. A Palace source said at the time that the duke had walked into the hospital unaided and that doctors wanted to observe him and give him plenty of rest. The public were also reassured that doctors were acting 'with an abundance of caution'. Rumour had it that he didn't want the inevitable fuss and attention that would have greeted his hundredth birthday on 10 June and joked that it couldn't be done if he wasn't there. Camilla gave an update on her father-in-law's condition while speaking with staff at a vaccination centre in Croydon, south London. She said she had heard he was 'slightly improving', but that his treatment 'hurts at moments'. She added, 'We'll keep our fingers crossed,' before thanking staff for their good wishes.

A few days later Prince Philip summoned Charles to visit him. Charles immediately made the 200-mile round trip from Highgrove to the hospital in central London. The hospital later revealed that they were only allowing visitors in 'exceptional circumstances', but at the time, the prince's visit to his dying father provoked a lot of criticism on social media. One Twitter user said: 'I do hope Prince Philip gets better but why was Prince Charles allowed to visit his father in hospital when families all around the country are not getting to visit their loved ones who are in hospital when it's not Covid-related?' Others, however, asked for people to 'remember their humanity'.

It was significant that the duke would want to see his eldest son and the heir to the throne at this crucial time, regardless of their difficulties in the past. No one else was allowed into the hospital to see him. Prince Charles stayed for about thirty minutes, during which their conversation was described as 'full and frank'. It is believed Prince Harry wasn't mentioned. Instead, Prince Philip advised his son on how to look after the Queen and the family after he had passed away. He is also thought to have told Charles he realised he would not recover and wanted 'to die in his own bed' in Windsor. It must have been an extremely moving time for them both, as the duke showed his desire to hand over to Charles the heavy responsibility of being head of the worthy, dutiful but often dysfunctional Royal Family which, despite its shortcomings, was loved and respected around the world.

Prince Charles was so overcome with emotion that there were tears in his eyes as he was driven away from the hospital. Neither man knew if they would meet again. Charles later said his father felt comforted 'by the fact they had been in touch more regularly than ever in recent months and said all the things that needed to be said'.

After thirteen nights at King Edward VII's Hospital, on 3 March Prince Philip was transferred to St Bartholomew's Hospital, where he had a heart procedure, returning afterwards to the King Edward VII to recuperate. Although the senior royals had been warned that the duke was seriously ill and unlikely to last long, Prince Harry and Meghan chose to go ahead with their tell-all interview on 12 March with the American talk show host Oprah Winfrey, during which they levelled allegations of racism and a lack of mental health support at the Royal Family. The Queen, Prince

Charles and Camilla and Prince William and Catherine were also roundly criticised by the couple, which caused unnecessary extra strain for them all.

Prince Philip was allowed to return to Windsor – and his own bed – on 16 March after his longest-ever stay in hospital. He looked haggard, drawn and very weak as he was driven away, but managed to wave. He was regularly attended there by royal doctors. I was told that when they weren't on the spot he rang them, which he did 'constantly'. Charles and Camilla visited him several times. The author Dame Susan Hill told me: 'The family realised he was very ill and suddenly looking as if he wasn't going to be long with us. During the winter of 2020, when he was quietly at Windsor, he saw a lot of the family and talked to them all. They all became very close in his last year, partly because of lockdown.'

The longest-serving British consort in history, Prince Philip, died peacefully, as he had wished, on 9 April at home in Windsor Castle with the Queen at his bedside. It was just two months before he was due to celebrate his hundredth birthday, and also the sixteenth wedding anniversary of Prince Charles and Camilla. As soon as Charles heard the sad news, he went to Windsor to comfort his mother.

Clarence House chose not to mention Charles and Camilla's wedding anniversary, as they regularly did on that date, as they didn't feel it was appropriate to turn the attention away from Prince Philip. Instead, on their social media accounts they shared a black and white photograph of the duke with the Palace's statement. The Countess of Wessex later told local well-wishers that Prince Philip slipped away peacefully, as if 'somebody took him by the hand and off he went very, very peacefully, and that's all you want for somebody, isn't it?'

The day after the duke's death, an obviously grieving Prince Charles touchingly paid tribute to his 'dear Papa'. Speaking from

Highgrove, he said the Queen and the rest of the Royal Family would 'miss him enormously'. He described his father as a 'very special person' who was much-loved and appreciated and praised him for 'giving the most remarkable devoted service to the Queen, to my family and to the country' for the last seventy years. Dame Susan commented: 'They [the family] miss him and love him as a father, never mind anything else. I think he was a very good father; he was interested in all his children and grandchildren and supported and encouraged them.'

The funeral took place at 3pm on Saturday 17 April in St George's Chapel at Windsor Castle. Despite the government's rule during the pandemic that only thirty people were allowed to attend, they did represent three generations of royals. These included all four children and grandchildren plus their partners. Prince Harry flew in from the United States and quarantined before the funeral while his pregnant wife Meghan stayed in California. Due to William and Harry's estrangement, there was little sign of genuine family unity between the brothers. Although the Royal Family could hide some of their emotions behind their masks, their sad eyes spoke for them.

There can be few formal events more brutal than a socially distanced funeral, and the most anguished sight was the Queen. Dressed all in black, including a black mask, she sat alone in the Quire of Saint George's Chapel. Because of Covid restrictions no one could sit next to her or whisper words of comfort. The millions of viewers who watched the funeral could see a devastated woman who looked more vulnerable and frail than she had ever done before.

The Duchess of Cornwall looked elegant in a black coatdress, statement hat and black and brown patterned face covering. She wore the brooch connected to The Rifles that Prince Philip had passed down to her when she took over the title of colonel-in-chief. It highlighted her respect for her father-in-law's former position and his memory. Camilla and Charles could sit next to each other but had to be socially distanced from other members of the family. At times Camilla gently touched her husband's arm, a comforting and supportive gesture she had used in tense moments when their relationship went public in 2000.

In the wake of Prince Philip's death, mourners left vast amounts of bouquets, drawings and letters of condolence outside the gates of Buckingham Palace, Windsor Castle and in the Royal Parks. Buckingham Palace had previously appealed to the public not to lay flowers, in order to discourage crowds and ensure Covid compliance, but thousands ignored the request, determined to show how much they respected such a remarkable man. All the tributes were subsequently moved to the private gardens at Marlborough House.

Charles and Camilla took their time looking at the carpet of flowers and reading the cards and messages of condolence. Charles pointed out a toy Land Rover to his wife that had been donated and was a miniature version of the one Prince Philip chose to bear his coffin to his funeral. Deeply moved, the royal couple stared at it intensely for quite a while, their eyes full of watery tears.

Prince Philip has, in a way, come into his own after his death. So much was written about him that people who had previously been unaware of him being a man of wide interests and achievements suddenly realised he was a polymath. An aide told me: 'He knew his own mind and was not swayed by pomposity or arrogance. The Duchess of Cornwall was always profoundly interested in him, fascinated by the story of his life and loved talking to him.'

On 24 September 2021, a documentary called *Prince Philip: The Family Remembers* was shown on BBC One. The original idea had been for it to be shown to mark his hundredth birthday, but the royals agreed it could go ahead in a slightly different form to honour his life and the man he was. The only senior royal who didn't take part was the Queen. The absorbing documentary highlighted that 'there was no template' for the husband of the Queen to follow, and the duke had been left to make his own decisions on what role he would adopt as consort both within the Royal Family and as the Queen's partner.

The Duchess of Cornwall admitted in the documentary that she had used Prince Philip's actions to influence her own behaviour and said it would impact her own role as future consort to the monarch. 'It's something I've learnt by watching him,' she said. 'I saw the way he supported the Queen. Not in a flashy sort of way, but just by doing it quietly, you know, following along behind.'

Gyles Brandreth comments: 'In a way she is very similar to him. Like him she is her own person and very funny. Nor is she at all politically correct; instead, she speaks her mind. Every single one of the charities the Duke of Edinburgh was involved in came from inside him, for example the Duke of Edinburgh's Award Scheme. All of which were based on the ethos he got at school. Camilla is the same, and the charities she does are all to do with who she is.' Dame Esther adds: 'One of the odd things is that the amount the royals contribute to the voluntary sectors is very often underestimated. The fact that you have a royal guest at a charity event means you can double, treble or raise ten times the amount of money than you would otherwise.'

Soon after Prince Philip passed away, what once seemed impossible became a reality. Camilla was chosen as one of the four women who would try to help the newly widowed Queen feel less alone. They were called by some as the 'gang of four' or the 'significant four'. Her Majesty is well known for being stoic but the sad, empty look in her eyes was unforgettable, and it was no surprise that she accepted the suggestion of a visiting rota to help raise her spirits.

It was predictable that three of the chosen women were Princess Anne, her only daughter, who is one of the most hard-working royals, her granddaughter-in-law Catherine, Duchess of Cambridge, who is dedicated to her husband, Prince William, has a strong sense of duty and can be trusted to say the right thing at the right time. Plus daughter-in-law Sophie, Countess of Wessex, who is known for quietly getting things done without a fuss. She in particular has taken on more work and spends a lot of time keeping the Queen company. Her daughter, 18-year-old Lady Louise Windsor, is also a favourite and inherited her love of carriage driving from her grandfather, who left her his own carriage.

Bringing Camilla on board – a woman the Queen had refused to see or speak to for years and who had been blamed for breaking up Prince Charles's marriage to Diana, Princess of Wales – was a sign that the Duchess of Cornwall has survived the brickbats, obstacles and insults, and that finally the Queen has admitted to enjoying her company and accepts her for who she is. The aftermath of Prince Philip's passing shifted the dynamics of family life. There may have been some family rivalry, but the priority has been to support the Queen, do anything they can to help her and sustain the monarchy. It has been a time when the royals seem to act more like an ordinary loving family than being concerned about rank.

A thanksgiving service in honour of Prince Philip was held at Westminster Abbey on 29 March 2022, nearly a year after his death. But it was only known a couple of hours before it was due to begin whether the Queen would be able to attend. She had been struggling with her health for a while, had tested positive for Covid the previous month, and her mobility issues meant she found it difficult to walk or stand for long. Once again, her determination won through, and the ceremony became the first major event she attended in 2022. The service was reduced to forty-five minutes for her comfort.

She had been residing in Windsor and was driven down to London with Prince Andrew by her side. A short route through the Abbey, where she and the duke were married, was used and she soon lowered herself into her cushioned chair with her stick at her side. Unlike the funeral in Windsor, she sat close to family members. The Queen, who likes to express herself through her clothes, chose dark green, the colour of The Rifles, as did Princess Anne and other attendees. Camilla was in the same colour too and wore a black hat with a dark green feather. On her coat was the silver Bugle Horn brooch of The Rifles that she had worn at the funeral.

The Abbey was decorated in red, white and blue flowers. There was strict security for the four generations of the family present. It included three heirs to the throne, European royalty, fifty-one members of the late duke's family who travelled across Europe, politicians, staff who had been dedicated to him 'right until the end' and hundreds of representatives of the seven hundred charities he was involved with. It made a total of over one thousand people who came to show their respects. There were also five great-grandchildren, who included Prince George and Princess Charlotte; all of them behaved impeccably. The only family members noticeably absent were Meghan and Harry. Despite the high level of security both inside and outside the Abbey Harry wasn't satisfied that it was safe enough for him and stayed away. His concern led to a legal action against the Home Office.

There were three hymns that the duke had originally chosen to be sung for his funeral but could not be because of the pandemic: 'He Who Would Valiant Be', 'All Creatures of Our God and King' and 'Guide Me O Thou Great Redeemer'. The service was straightforward, as no doubt Prince Philip would have wanted, and extremely moving. The Queen shed a tear as did many who wished to pay homage to the late duke. It marked the end of an extraordinary era and an even more extraordinary man whose passing has left a chasm that will take time to fill. How wonderful it would have been for all the Royal Family if he had lingered long enough to see his beloved wife celebrate her seventy years as monarch, of which he had been a crucial part. He would certainly have enjoyed watching feisty four-year-old Prince Louis show an extraordinary wide range of facial expressions over the four days of celebration, and the Queen taking tea with Paddington Bear. He would have also been modestly gratified to know that he is Camilla's role model, and that on 12 July just before her 75th birthday she said she will follow his motto to 'look up and look out, say less, do more.'

Chapter 26

THE QUEEN'S PLATINUM JUBILEE

The effort that was put into the Platinum Jubilee celebrations in June 2022 to mark the Queen's seventy years on the throne produced something for everyone. This included Trooping the Colour, one of the most renowned military displays in the world, a celebrity singsong, street parties, a somewhat eccentric pageant and a hilarious television sketch of the Queen sharing a cup of tea with Paddington Bear and jokingly revealing that she kept a spare marmalade sandwich in her handbag.

There had been anxiety about the Queen's health and whether she'd be fit enough to attend any of the celebrations. She'd had Covid in February 2022, which she admitted had exhausted her, and she was suffering episodic mobility problems. But on the first day of the celebration on 2 June a smiling and no doubt determined monarch came on to the Buckingham Palace balcony dressed in a pearl-embellished pale-blue coat dress and hat, looking delighted at the tens of thousands of people waving Union Jacks and cheering her as far back along The Mall as you could see.

There were inevitable complaints by pro-republicans that the

£28 million cost was too much when the country was experiencing difficult times, but it was estimated the celebrations would add £1.2 billion to the economy. There was also concern about possible diminished numbers attending the celebrations due to the increase in anti-monarchists, but it soon became clear that the celebrating crowds wanted to show their respect and gratitude for the Queen's life of duty, for what the monarchy stands for and for her family who were supporting her.

Those who couldn't get anywhere near The Mall hung around in tens of thousands over a wide area to absorb the extraordinary upbeat atmosphere that most of us hadn't felt since before the pandemic. On the first day of the four-day event, as I tried to navigate with the help of kind policemen and friendly strangers to get to the media centre close to the Palace, many people said how they hadn't really been out and about since the pandemic began but now believed their inhibitions had lifted and were ready to socialise. I felt just the same. I was also reminded of the mood the London Olympics created in 2012 when you chatted to everyone. It was magical and of course exactly what Her Majesty hoped for.

The Queen's specific wish was that the historic event should be an opportunity for people to come together and that 'happy memories' would be shaped during the four days of festivities. It was a wish that was also close to Camilla's heart, which had been played out in her many engagements and particularly those during the Jubilee: she wanted as many people as possible to come and add a voice to what was happening.

Nonetheless, it felt rather sad that within the Royal Family there were two significant cracks. The disgraced Prince Andrew was banned from everything except the thanksgiving service at St Paul's Cathedral. However, he tested positive for Covid at the last minute and couldn't attend even that. Harry and Meghan had flown over from their home in California the day before the celebrations started. It was the first time they had officially appeared alongside the Royal Family since stepping down as senior royals two years previously. If they expected to be welcomed like the prodigal son and partner, they were in for a shock. The world and the Royal Family have moved on, so much so that the royals have become much closer. Ironically Harry has swapped positions with his stepmother. Camilla bore being treated as an outcast for so long, but is now regarded as irreplaceable and well-embedded within the family. She also has become much more popular. Harry, on the other hand, has become an outsider, much of his own making and has plummeted down the popularity ladder.

The difference between the two individuals is very clear. Camilla has a strong sense of duty, is supportive of Prince Charles, has made him a much happier man, and tries to give a voice to those who haven't one. Harry lectures us from afar on what not to do, like use planes, when he and Meghan flew to and from their home in California in a private jet that creates about ten times as much greenhouse gas per passenger as a commercial flight. He has behaved destructively about his family, become self-focused and has said in a TV interview that the US and not the UK feels like 'home' to him. He'd also been deeply concerned about his own family's safety in the UK, to the extent that the Queen loaned him her personal bulletproof Range Rover. Surprisingly, both he and Meghan wound down the darkened windows to wave at those gathering for the celebrations, a gesture that seriously minimised their safety as anything could have been thrown into the car.

Even if Harry had felt his visit was an opportunity to reconnect with his family, apart from seeing his grandmother, it didn't happen. Instead, careful precautions were taken to prevent him from using his visit for commercial gain. There was also a new difficulty in trusting him to keep personal conversations private, after some of what he had said in recent interviews.

The first event of the four-day celebration was Trooping the Colour. Camilla had pride of place in the first carriage in the procession through The Mall to Horse Guards Parade prior to the beginning of the formal military parade. With her was the Duchess of Cambridge and, for the first time in a carriage, Prince George, Princess Charlotte and Prince Louis. All of them waved, but the children waved hardest, melting thousands of hearts as they moved along. Catherine and Camilla could be seen chatting together and at one point Charlotte leant over and looked through Camilla's handbag, an indication that the two get on well together.

The Prince of Wales was on horseback, supported by Princess Anne and Prince William. He reviewed the troops in Horse Guards Parade and took the salute of the Armed Forces on behalf of his mother, while Harry and Meghan watched from the Major General's Office with minor royals and were photographed playfully shushing some of the Queen's great-grandchildren. How disappointing it must have been for Harry that he wasn't participating in a military parade that he was part of for so long. As non-working royals, he and Meghan were also not allowed to appear on the Buckingham Palace balcony. It must have been hard for him that William and Charles had grown closer and filled the gap he left.

After Trooping the Colour, Prince Charles and William joined the family on the balcony to watch the military fly-past of seventy aircraft including the iconic RAF Red Arrows' nine-strong display team and the historic Battle of Britain memorial flight. From then on, apart from the Queen, four-year-old Louis stole the show. He talked almost non-stop to the amused Queen, showed off a wide range of facial expressions, and dramatically held his hands to his ears to block out some of the noise from the planes overhead. Photographs of him went instantly viral worldwide.

When the fly-past was over and Charles and Camilla were on their way home to Clarence House, they decided to stop for an unannounced walkabout and chat to several people watching the proceedings. Most looked amazed to meet the royal couple and one middle-aged lady jumped up and down with excitement after her chat with Camilla. It was a successful way for them to become more accessible. In a similar vein, the couple appeared as themselves that evening in a special Jubilee episode of the BBC television soap opera *EastEnders* that they filmed in March. They met various actors who stayed in character and appeared astonished to see the royal couple. Not one to miss an opportunity, Camilla talked about a domestic abuse storyline, something that is of deep concern to her, and tied a purple ribbon round a tree in memory of a murdered on-screen female character.

It was announced that the Queen felt tired and was suffering 'discomfort' after the activities on Thursday but would still light the first Jubilee beacon at 9.45 that evening at Windsor Castle. It triggered more than two thousand beacons and bonfires across Britain and the Commonwealth. The Queen 'reluctantly' did not feel well enough to attend the following day's Service of Thanksgiving at St Paul's Cathedral or Saturday's Epsom Derby, both of which she was looking forward to. Princess Anne took her place at the Derby.

Despite not being well, she made time to see Harry, Meghan, Archie and, for the first time since she was born on 4 June 2021, her great-granddaughter Lilibet, who was given the Queen's nickname. Her grandfather George V used it originally and it was subsequently used as a personal endearment by Prince Philip. The Palace refused to discuss the visit, a wise decision perhaps to encourage Harry to also keep the conversation private. An insider, however, said their meeting lasted only fifteen minutes, the atmosphere was formal, aides stayed in the room and the couple's request for their private photographer to take photographs of the two Lilibets together was firmly turned down. It neatly prevented any images from being seen in a Netflix documentary.

The Service of Thanksgiving for the Queen began on Friday morning at 11.30 am. The royal protocol is that the less important royals arrive first with the most senior royals arriving last. Harry and Meghan held hands as they walked up the steps to the cathedral entrance to both boos and cheers from the crowd, sounds which were repeated when the service was over. They were shown to their seats, situated in the middle of the second row alongside other lower-ranking, non-working royals. Harry, who remains sixth in line to the throne, made a gesture as if he should be on the other side of the aisle with his father and brother, but the placement wasn't changed.

The distance meant there was little or no chance for the once very close brothers to connect with each other. Harry wears his heart on his sleeve; he obviously wasn't pleased and looked furious throughout the service. Meghan held her actress's smile. Harry's position may well have felt demeaning, but he had said when interviewed by Oprah Winfrey in March 2021 that he felt 'trapped within the system, like the rest of my family are. My father and my brother, they are trapped'. He added that before his relationship with Meghan he didn't know a way out. He has since found one. His position also prevented any chance of him being photographed with his brother and other senior royals that could be used commercially when he and Meghan returned home.

The Queen's absence had cast a cloud over the service, and Camilla, Charles, Catherine and William, as well as others, looked rather miserable throughout, as if recognising it was the end of an era. Russell Myers, the royal editor of the *Mirror*, detected a 'very frosty atmosphere' in the cathedral. There was a reception following the service at the nearby Guildhall, which most of the other royals attended. Harry and Meghan chose not to.

Saturday 4 June was Lilibet's first birthday, and the Duke and Duchess of Cambridge and the Prince of Wales and Duchess of Cornwall posted birthday messages on Twitter. William and Catherine and the children had apparently been asked to go to Lilibet's party that day, but it had been announced at the beginning of May that William and Catherine would be going to Cardiff Castle as part of the jubilee celebrations. As they took George and Charlotte with them, it wasn't possible for the first cousins to meet each other. It revealed how little each of them knew what the other was doing.

Apart from the Queen, who was unwell, and Harry and Meghan, everyone was back for the Platinum Party at the Palace on Saturday evening. It was a huge success. Tens of thousands of people gathered in The Mall again to listen to a rock concert with every song chosen by Her Majesty. The concert that was shown live on BBC One was held on three interconnected stages erected around the Victoria Memorial in front of Buckingham Palace. Camilla sat between Charles and William in the front row of the royal box.

The family and children enthusiastically waved Union Jacks from side to side in time to the music, and the three heirs to the throne plus wives sang along whenever they could. The artists included Duran Duran, Andrea Bocelli and Diana Ross, who was singing in the UK for the first time in fifteen years. A particular success, especially with George, who seemed to know all the words, was 'Sweet Caroline' sung by Sir Rod Stewart, who was a little croakier than usual but no one seemed to care. The atmosphere turned really electric when night fell, and four hundred drones lit up the sky with a show by SkyMagic that paid a tongue-in-cheek tribute to some of the Queen's hobbies and interests. The visuals included a Corgi after a bone, a copy of the Queen's handbag with love hearts floating upwards, a teapot and soldiers' bearskins.

As soon as the concert finished, William came down the stairs to the stage and spoke passionately about climate change. Charles came next with Camilla by his side. She looked amazing in a floor-length embroidered wool and cashmere black coat with detailing around the neck and swirls of embroidery down to the bottom. It turned out that Charles had been given it during one of his visits to Saudi Arabia and she borrowed it. Her presence by his side was a hugely symbolic gesture silently stating that the future of the monarchy would involve both of them, together.

Charles's speech was a moving address about his absent mother's qualities and abilities: 'Your family now spans four generations. You are our Head of State. And you are also our mother. Your "strength and stay" is much missed this evening, but I am sure he is here in spirit . . . My papa would have enjoyed the show and joined us wholeheartedly in celebrating all you continue to do for your country and your people. Your Majesty, you have been with us in our difficult times. And you bring us together to celebrate moments of pride, joy and happiness.' Tens of thousands cheered and waved their flags when he finished speaking.

Meghan and Harry weren't seen since the service in St Paul's, keeping their promise that they would maintain a low profile. They flew back to the US before the celebrations were over, arriving in California at 6pm on Sunday. The journalist and biographer Tom Bower told MailOnline that the Sussexes had been 'trounced' on their return to the UK. He said: 'I think Palace officials were unusually skilful in managing the Sussexes. Just enough exposure to please the Queen but at the same time so limited to show them that they have been sidelined. Harry's grim expression exposed and confirmed the troubles he now faces. Meghan now faces problems about her status. Netflix are left with a problem: the Sussexes are no longer stars.'

Sunday morning and afternoon on the final day of the celebrations were allocated to The Big Jubilee Lunch. Executive Director Peter Stewart told me 'an estimated 18 million people participated, matched by thousands of events across the Commonwealth and beyond' to celebrate the Queen's amazing landmark by hanging up bunting, waving Union Jacks, sharing food, and most of all getting to know each other. Camilla, who has been patron of The Big Lunch since 2013, hosted her own party for 500 guests, including me, at the Kia Oval cricket ground at Kennington, south London.

A large proportion of her guests belonged to the Royal Voluntary Service, of which Camilla is president, and were invited because they had improved lives in their communities by helping the old and needy during the pandemic. Seventy of them would receive Platinum Champions Awards. Other guests had set up charities. I talked to Courtney Hughes, who launched her Secret Santa 365 when she was twelve and was celebrating its tenth anniversary. It had helped numerous people over the pandemic in different ways, including gathering old laptops for people who didn't have their own, and taking the elderly food when the weather was bad, or they were needy. One of their volunteers willingly waited over four hours to pick up some much-needed insulin for an OAP. The atmosphere made it remarkably easy for strangers to have friendly conversations.

At one stage Charles and Camilla, who was wearing an emerald-green coat dress, raised a glass to toast the Queen, but only took a sip. There was a long day ahead. They both also admired a stunning display, where everything on a brightly coloured felt tablecloth had been knitted, including strawberries, cups of coffee, sliced tomato, several types of delicious cakes and mini sausages, which were so realistic that I saw someone pick one up before quickly realising it wasn't edible and put it back.

Camilla received compliments galore. Jahswill Emmanuel, originally from Nigeria, told me: 'She is doing great things in the community for ethnic minorities.' Another guest, the eminent sculptor Basil Watson from Jamaica, who has designed a permanent national Windrush monument that was unveiled at Waterloo Station on 30 June 2022 by William and Catherine. He is also an ardent royalist. 'I think the Royal Family has done a marvellous job,' he said. 'There is some controversy but then people have different opinions. The Commonwealth is moving but there is always room for leaders and Prince Charles is ready for the job. Camilla stands strong beside him and we expect her to continue to do so.' Another male guest who wanted to be nameless explained this admiration: 'Camilla's story is one of perseverance and has shown the strength of the woman, which is so important. She is an example of women who have felt they have been wrongly judged but are sure they will get there in the end.'

A conjuror entertained the guests along with upbeat music provided by Melodians Steel Orchestra UK from south London and the Shree Muktajeevan Swamibapa Pipe Band from Kingsbury, north London, who were celebrating their own golden jubilee. Charles and Camilla went up and down the long tables chatting to guests, sitting down for longer chats at least once per table. Camilla also cut a massive chocolate Big Jubilee Lunch cake and a smaller lemon one. 'The last time I saw a cake cut was when the Queen used a sword at the G7 gathering [in Cornwall in 2021] but I am sticking to a knife,' she laughed. A vast buffet was awaiting the guests with lots of main-course options. There was also plenty of Lemon Swiss Roll and Amaretti Trifle for pudding, a recipe that had been the chosen dessert for the occasion from five thousand entries.

The royal couple left early to change clothes and be ready for the pageant. It was an amazing, eccentric and imaginative spectacle with street arts, theatre, music, circus, carnival and costume that highlighted the story of the Queen's life, and that of her nation, and underlined her unwavering duty, love of the natural world and dedication to the Commonwealth. The royals turned up in force again, but it was a bit much for Louis who wriggled as he showed off his wide range of expressions, not all of them polite, which was later put down to a 'sugar high'. It gave us an opportunity to see Catherine's skilful mothering. At one point Louis was seen wriggling while speaking to his mother, Charlotte then bent over to speak to her father who in turn spoke to Charles who was so immersed in the music that Camilla had to give him a nudge. By then Louis had walked straight up to his grandfather, climbed on his lap and was happy to be bounced in time with the music. Camilla gave him a huge smile as Louis behaved impeccably. The pageant ended on a suitably contemporary note with Ed Sheeran performing his own song 'Perfect' to a backdrop of video clips showing scenes throughout the Queen's long life.

To the delight of the enormous crowd, the Queen, wearing a grass-green suit, then made a surprise appearance on the Buckingham Palace balcony. The cheering was so uplifting that Her Majesty, who has been well known for not showing her emotions in public, had tears in her eyes. In a statement afterwards, she said she was 'humbled and deeply touched' that so many people had taken part in the celebrations. 'While I may not have attended every event in person, my heart has been with you all, and I remain committed to serving you to the best of my ability, supported by my family. I have been inspired by the kindness, joy and kinship that has been so evident in recent days, and I hope this renewed sense of togetherness will be felt for many years to come.'

The image she wanted to project was crystal clear. The future of the British monarchy would be in the safe hands of the family who shared the balcony with her: her three heirs, Charles, William and George, along with Catherine, Charlotte and Louis – and Camilla. What a long journey she has travelled.

Chapter 27

THE FUTURE

What will happen when Prince Charles becomes King and Camilla is Queen? As with Prince Philip, she will not have any responsibility for the daily red boxes of government papers, which will be Charles's duty to read. She will also not be expected to be involved in the day-to-day operations of the monarchy. That is an area where Charles will take the lead; she will not interfere. What he thinks will be best will most likely be what she will think too. She has a very strong hierarchical sense, which is one of many reasons why their marriage has been such a success. But in her own key areas, like literacy and confronting domestic violence, she will continue to plough her own furrow, with Charles's strong support.

The Queen's passing will be the end of an extraordinary era. She has ruled for longer than any other monarch in British history, is the second-longest reigning monarch in world history and has been a much-loved and respected figure across the globe. The durability of the monarchy has been a fundamental part of British life and there is an understandable fear that the

Queen's death could open the path to a troubled future, partly because according to recent polls Prince Andrew and Prince Harry have presented a negative image to the public, and partly because a majority of 18–24-year-olds want an elected head of state rather than a monarchy.

Fortunately, the monarchy as an institution largely retains general public support, especially among older Britons who not only strongly back the institution in principle but additionally appreciate the forceful commitment Prince Charles has made to public life, especially since he has been with Camilla. She too has developed a profound understanding of the importance of her public role and the opportunity it has given her to help others. The presence of Princes William and George also means the monarchy has been secured for two further generations.

An increasing number of people have stopped thinking Prince Charles is an oddity and now accept instead that he was far ahead of his time over issues like climate change and environmental protection. He was also eating organic food far earlier than most, something Camilla approves of as she is an advocate of healthy and simple eating.

Will Prince Charles be a good king? David Yelland, former editor of the *Sun*, thinks so. 'I have always thought he would make a good king. He's been so far ahead of his time, like with climate change, but most of all he really cares about people in every town and village and also our role in the world. Once he has the job of course he will be a different person. It brings with it a majesty. Partly because of the mail bag and talking to the *Sun*'s readers, I think we have all grown up with the royals. They are part of our life in a way that politicians could never be. Nobody can doubt Charles's commitment to public service, which is quite extraordinary.'

At one time the Royal Family represented the model family and were looked up to. But we didn't really know much about them. In the modern world, the presence of Camilla and Catherine, Duchess of Cambridge, upper middle-class women who have experienced relatively normal lives – for Camilla it lasted over fifty years – will make it easier for the public to relate to them and for them to understand how ordinary people live and the problems they face. Social media has given the royals a direct connection with the public to highlight what is happening in their lives and a place to share photographs. But they are also aware that there can be a negative impact on social media that can be harsh.

The Netflix series *The Crown* has painted a largely false portrait of the Royal Family and Camilla has been the most misrepresented member. It wouldn't be true to say that Prince Charles married her because she was like his mother, but she is a modern version of the Queen in several ways. Camilla doesn't disclose anything about her private life apart from saying she loves her children and grandchildren. More importantly, she is also empathetic to human feelings. She lost her adored brother Mark through an unfortunate accident and her son Tom lost his partner to cancer. Camilla understands sadness, marginalisation and loneliness: she has experienced them all, but she doesn't talk in a way that reveals anything about herself.

Her friend Dame Susan Hill believes one reason Camilla manages all the pressure is because she is down-to-earth. She told me: 'She doesn't pretend to be anything she is not. She might laugh as we all do about not being able to see anything without our specs, or work the remote control, but she is happy to be a grandmother and to wear comfortable shoes and admit that she finds long days of foreign tours exhausting. She is not chasing youth or dressing like a forty-year-old. She's happy in her own skin, which is refreshing, and judging by the reaction the people I've seen her meet, the public appreciate that. They find her genuineness straightforward.'

Camilla and the Queen both come from stable backgrounds with happily married parents. The security has made them strong and taught them how to keep a cool head in moments of danger. They care about helping others. According to the Charity Aid Foundation (CAF), the Queen has been among the world's greatest supporters of charities. She has been an example to us all by creating a culture where supporting charities by giving time or/ and money has become normal. Camilla has built up over one hundred charities that she supports so far, but in a way that gives each more attention and help. Both of them refused to give up on the man they loved.

Like the Queen, Camilla has a natural rapport with horses and dogs and adores racing. They both have a sharp wit, but the Queen is better at mimicking individuals, whereas Camilla is more self-deprecating, running herself down and mocking her age when she is on show and expected to do something practical. It is also a helpful way to protect herself and dodge questions she'd prefer to avoid answering.

In addition to the United Kingdom, the Queen is Head of State of fifteen Commonwealth countries. She is also Head of the Commonwealth itself, a voluntary association of fifty-four independent countries. This adds up to about 150 million people, all of whom she regards as an extended family. Camilla believes hugely in the value of family life. She is at ease talking to people of all ages, from small children to the very elderly. Equally, she can speak effortlessly with people who are destitute, poor or seriously ill. It helps that she is a pragmatist and regularly thinks creatively about how people can help themselves. The concept of family can also link countries and people, rather like The Big Lunch during the Platinum Jubilee celebrations.

With Camilla you don't get the feeling that she chooses what she does to try to boost her image. As was seen during the pandemic, both she and Prince Charles made it a priority to thank the nation, carers, NHS and teachers and to promote the causes they support. She is not a snob and doesn't apologise for who she is or what she likes. She even admitted when she gave an interview about food to her son Tom Parker Bowles, a food writer, that she likes Heinz baked beans and fish and chips wrapped up in paper.

Prince Charles has plans galore but has chosen to be discreet and reveal very little apart from wanting to slim down a modernised monarchy. He thinks it is disrespectful to his aged mother to say what he is going to strip away once she is gone. It will be a heavy burden on Camilla's shoulders to represent the monarchy every hour of the day, but she has been in training for the role, so it won't be a huge surprise. With her inner strength and willpower, she will make it work, not only for herself and her husband, but also by supporting the people. She will stand up for their rights and feelings.

It will inevitably mean that she might have less time to see friends and take part in her favourite interests, not least because Prince Charles is bound to need her to be with him; but giving him support is now in her bloodstream. However apprehensive Charles feels about taking on such a burden, his cast-iron sense of duty and having Camilla by his side will help. Indeed, when the time comes Charles will be more than ready. He and Camilla have increasingly stood in for the Queen since she cut back on her workload in 2016, never complaining and never explaining about their increased workload.

Their moment is almost here.

ACKNOWLEDGEMENTS

The more time I spent researching and writing about the Duchess of Cornwall, the more remarkable she seemed. Like most people, her journey through life had its ups and downs, but few would have experienced the extreme highs and lows that have brought her to where she is today. When they first met, Prince Charles recognised how compatible the two of them were, but the timing wasn't appropriate. Many aspects of her character lay dormant but sprang into life once they were married, and ever since she has given a great deal to the monarchy and the country.

Writing her story has been a privilege and totally absorbing. My plan was to provide a rounded portrait and I am very grateful to her friends, former members of her staff, heads of charities of which she is patron, and the many other individuals who know her well and who generously gave up their time to talk to me. I'd like to thank in particular Clare Balding, Gavin Barker, Professor Vernon Bogdanor, Mark Bolland, Gyles Brandreth, Dame Darcy Bussell, Joy Camm, Lord Carey of Clifton, Dame Judi Dench, Jonathan Douglas, Ruth Ganesh, Catherine Goodman, Robert

Hardman, Ainsley Harriot, Dame Susan Hill, Claire Horton, Suzanne Jacob, Ian Jones, Jude Kelly, Laura Lee, Amanda MacManus, Bruce Oldfield, Dame Esther Rantzen, Craig Revel Horwood, Luke Rittner, Andrew Roberts, Lucia Santa Cruz, Peter Stewart and David Yelland. None of whom asked to be 'off the record'. Others gave me their thoughts but preferred to do so anonymously. I'd also like to thank members of staff at Clarence House, who were very helpful, and in particular the Duchess of Cornwall for letting me join her on engagements.

Simon and Schuster's Ian Marshall, Deputy Publishing Director, Non-Fiction, Kaiya Shang, copy editor Kerri Sharp and my agent Barbara Levy must also be thanked.

Most important of all I want to show my gratitude to my husband, Robert Low, for his endless help and encouragement.

Index

CDC indicates Camilla, Duchess of Cornwall.